The Female Pen

*

By the same Author:

THE PSYCHOLOGY OF GENIUS : STUDIES
IN BROWNING. University of London
Press, 4s. 6d.

WOMEN WRITERS

Their Contribution to
The English Novel
1621 - 1744

BY

B. G. MacCARTHY, M.A., Ph.D.

Third Impression

CORK   UNIVERSITY   PRESS

NEW YORK: WILLIAM SALLOCH

1948

First Impression, September, 1944.

Second Impression, November, 1945.

Third Impression, July, 1946.

Dublin Agents : The Standard (1938), Ltd.,

Pearse Street, Dublin, C.5.

Printed in Eire

By THE KERRYMAN LTD., Tralee.

"But his misfortune was to fall in an obscure world that afforded only a female pen to celebrate his fame."

(Aphra Behn, *Oroonoko,* 1688)

"Nay, even my own sex, which should assert our prerogative against such detractors, are often backward to encourage the female pen."

(Susannah Centlivre, Dedication of *The Platonic Lady,* 1707)

"You know how female writers are looked down upon. The women fear and hate, the men ridicule and dislike them."

(Elizabeth Hamilton, *Letters to a Hindoo Rajah,* 1791)

"Men have had every advantage of us in telling their own story. Education has been theirs in so much higher a degree; the pen has been in their hands."

(Jane Austen, *Persuasion,* 1818)

Patri et Matri
In Memoriam

Foreword

IF Shakespeare had had a sister endowed with literary powers, could she have won to success in that early period? What factors would have impeded her development as a writer? These questions, raised by Virginia Woolf in her penetrating essay, *A Room of One's Own*, seemed to me well worth answering. They were the starting-point of a long journey backwards through the years—a journey which had for its object a consideration of those forces which affected women writers during the sixteenth, seventeenth and eighteenth centuries; and an evaluation of these women's contribution to literature. It soon became apparent that women had mainly contributed towards the development of the novel. Their contribution and the influences which conditioned it have been traced from 1621 until 1817. The present volume represents the first half of the work. It is hoped to publish the second volume in the near future.

It might perhaps have been possible to condense these researches into a single volume, but only by omitting or shortening most of the passages quoted from the writings of these women-novelists. It seemed essential to retain the copious quotations, since they have been taken from books so rare as to be difficult of access to the interested student.

B. G. MACCARTHY.

Contents

Chapter					Page

I—COGENT INFLUENCES 11

II—THE PASTORAL ROMANCE 47
Lady Mary Wroath, Anne Weamys

III—BIOGRAPHY 70
Countess of Pembroke, Duchess of Newcastle,
Mrs. Lucy Hutchinson, Lady Fanshawe

IV—LIVING RESTORATION TRENDS 122
(*a*) Journey to an Imaginary Country
(*b*) Realistic Stories, Tales of English Life, Fables
(*c*) Letters
Duchess of Newcastle

V—MAIN RESTORATION GENRES CONTRASTED 139
(*a*) The Sentimentalised *Novella*
(*b*) The Growth of Realism
Mrs. Aphra Behn

VI—SATIRE—ENGLISH REALISM 189
Mrs. Aphra Behn

VII—FROM 1689 TO 1744 214
(*a*) The Key-Novel
(*b*) The Sentimentalised *Novella*
(*c*) The Novel of Domestic Sentiment and of Manners
(*d*) The Didactic Tale
(*e*) The Picaresque Tale
Mrs. Mary Manley, Mrs. Eliza Haywood, Mrs. Rowe,
Mrs. Barker, Mrs. Penelope Aubin, Mrs. Davys,
Mrs. Elizabeth Boyd, Mrs. Arabella Plantin, Sarah
Fielding

VIII—THE EPISTOLARY FORM PRIOR TO 1740 263
Duchess of Newcastle, Mrs. Aphra Behn, Mrs. Manley,
Mrs. Haywood, Mrs. Rowe

INDEX 287

CHAPTER I

COGENT INFLUENCES.

Women's contribution to literature is no arbitrary or artificial distinction. However much the reformer may welcome, or the conservative lament, the growth of a harmonious sharing of ideals between men and women, that growth has been a hard-fought struggle. It has been an escape from a prison, which, when it did not entirely shut out the greater world, at least enclosed a little world of education meant for women, a literature adapted to the supposed limitations of their intellect, and a course of action prescribed by the other sex. To show how the literary efforts of women developed and justified their claims to free activity is the purpose of this book.

When women at last began to seek after literary expression, it was inevitable that they should attempt to tell a story. There has always been, and there always will remain, deep-rooted in the human heart a desire to hear something told of the world without us and within. From these roots in varying forms and often strangely transmuted grew all education and the arts. For men it was a transition from telling to writing, and for women the transition was no less long, and like their opportunities for literacy, took place far later. Women as listeners influenced the art of story-telling long before they actually shared in it, and naturally the growth of the novel gained in variety and verisimilitude when women were given a place in the subject-matter. The novel is a very improbable development of the Odyssey, but it is an inevitable development of *Daphnis and Chloe*. Beowulf and his firedrake are almost as far from the art of fiction as they are from probability, and such sagas could be of no interest to women It is not the titanic figure, with his death-dealing sword, invincible in his destiny, that a woman loves, in fact or in fiction—or at any rate, not until he has shown himself vulnerable to human emotions. Victorious Perseus, flying through the clouds, does not win a woman's interest until he sees Andromeda and comes down to earth. This descent from free fancy to actuality is, in a word, the evolution of the novel.

Women make their entrance into fiction with the development of the short tale such as the *novella*, which had love-interest as its pivotal point. Marie de France, writing in England in the twelfth century, found in her episodic lays exactly the mould which suited her, and she used it with such ease that she had scope to develop her technique and to create from the oft-told tales of the minstrels works of art which not only endured, but served as an inspiration to later writers. Margaret of Navarre, writing in prose, found the short tale equally suited to her powers, and in her case also, ease in technique allowed her genius to express itself with a power perhaps not surpassed by Bandello or Boccaccio. These women excelled because they were, for the most part, retelling stories they had heard, but most of all because they had for subject-matter themes and events most familiar, if not in their own lives, then certainly in the lives of those about them.

But alas for the women writers! Daphnis and Chloe, neglected on their pastoral slope, were growing up and developing a stultifying artificiality. Their simple idyll was now to be complicated by rival lovers, perfidy, royalty incognito, shipwreck, and chivalrous emprises, into a superfluity of characters endlessly involved in a maze of tedious events. And where Sir Philip Sydney led, what could an ambitious niece do but follow? It could not be expected that Lady Mary Wroath would escape the quagmire of the Pastoral Romance, and in fact, she overpassed its pitfalls with far more success than might have been expected. If women were daring even in attempting to write, it is not to be expected, at that stage, that they would have the extreme audacity to become innovators as well. If only, instead of being satisfied with diligently copying the headline set by men, they could have bridged the great gap between romantic and domestic fiction, then not only would the development of the novel have been hastened by hundreds of years, but women would have been able to exert their talents on exactly the subject-matter which they knew best, and consequently there would have been far more women writers. It is obvious that creative imagination, no matter how individual and how varied its power of synthesis, must have material to synthesise, and this material may be real life, or some artistic reproduction of life, or, as is most usual, both. This does not mean that because women's actual experience of life was limited to only one aspect, therefore they could not exercise creative imagination. Certainly they could have done so, as did, for example, the two gifted women already mentioned, and if we wish to understand why women were not at that time actively creative, we must consider the education at their disposal, and we must remember that an ability to read and write is not education, though it may be a means thereto. Such education as women received was nominal, and creative imagination without education is not productive. One must either admit this fact, or else assert that women in bygone ages lacked the kind of imaginative power which later women most obviously possessed. Any view which claims variation in the mental capacity of women at various epochs is quite untenable. On the other hand, any view which explains the dearth of early women-writers by reference to their limited experience, does not need to be disproved. It simply collapses of itself, because it is illogical in theory, and its invalidity is proved by the evidence of the great women-writers who, despite a human sphere as circumscribed as that of their ancestresses, later achieved fame. We know that the material on which creative imagination may work can be found in daily life no matter how limited in extent. Experience need not be wide for human or literary fulfilment, but it must be deep, and, for literary purposes, it must be artistically realised, and it must be expressed. Depth of experience implies depth of character, but does not connote the power of artistic realisation or artistic expression, and it is precisely in this relation that the question of education arises. Creative imagination transforms experience into a work of art, but it can only give artistic form when it is familiar with such forms, and can manipulate the chosen form with ease. It requires training and familiarity with many aspects of one's art before one masters technique, or develops individuality in technique. Nor can one even say that we achieve a work of art merely by giving artistic form to experience, for the truth is that the artist apprehends experience in a fashion which is partly the result of his mental characteristics, but also the result of his artistic training. Perhaps we may say that art is experience realised in a special way and expressed in a corresponding medium. Emily Brontë's experience of actual human life was unusually limited, and yet she produced not only a work of art, but one of unusual power. If it were possible to analyse her genius, one might suggest that it consisted in intensity of experience, in her case mainly imaginative experience, which she realised in literary terms, and embodied in the artistic form she knew best—the art of fiction. But it is worth noting that not only was Emily Brontë endowed with natural genius, but was, for that period, very well educated and very widely read. Yet despite these advantages, which enabled her to use language in a plastic, even in an intuitive way, *Wuthering Heights* is structurally clumsy, because, of course, a literary education is merely a way by which we recognise and evaluate literary technique, but only by literary experiment can we develop such technique in ourselves. *Wuthering Heights* also shows that imaginative experience is not in itself a sufficing material for realistic fiction, for it is clear that, though Emily Brontë knew hell and heaven, she did not know how farm-hands talk.

In judging the average woman's chance of success in the writing of fiction, it seems, perhaps, a digression to speak of Emily Brontë, whose genius must always entitle her to be judged apart, but we deliberately choose her, because we wish to show that even such genius cannot arrive at technique without an apprenticeship, and that even such genius cannot safely depend on imaginative intuition, cannot dispense with the necessity for everyday experience. Writing of the essential characteristics of a great novelist, Fielding states the necessity for *Genius, Learning, Conversation*, and " *a good heart.*" By *Genius* he means " that power or rather those powers of mind, which are capable of penetrating into all things within our reach and knowledge, and of distinguishing their essential differences." These powers he distinguishes as *Invention* and *Judgment* under the collective name of *Genius*.   By *Invention* Fielding means, not the creative faculty, but quite literally the power of discovery —" a quick and sagacious penetration into the true essence of all the objects of our contemplation.   This, I think, can rarely exist without the concomitancy of judgment; for how we can be said to have discovered the true essence of two things, without discerning their difference, seems to me hard to conceive.   Now this last is the undisputed province of Judgment." [1]

Of the necessity for learning, Fielding finely says: " Nature can only furnish us with capacity . . . or the tools of our profession; learning must fit them for use, must direct them in it, and lastly must contribute part at least of the materials.   A competent knowledge of history and of the belles-lettres is here absolutely necessary; and without this share of knowledge at least, to affect the character of an historian (i.e., a novelist) is as vain as to endeavour at building a house without timber or mortar, or brick or stone.   Homer and Milton, who though they added ornament of numbers to their works, were both historians of our order, were masters of all the learning of their times."

Conversation, by which Fielding meant experience of life, he held to be absolutely indispensable to a novelist: " However exquisitely human nature may have been described by writers, the true practical system can be learnt only in the world." People who write without experience of life are only making a " faint copy of a copy . . . which can have neither the justness nor spirit of an original.   Now this conversation in our historian must be universal, that is with all the ranks and degrees of men, for the knowledge of what is called high life will not instruct him in low, nor, è converso . . . and though it may be thought that the knowledge of either may sufficiently enable him to describe at least that in which he hath been conversant, yet he will even here fall greatly short of perfection: for the follies of either rank do, in reality, illustrate each other."

---

1 Henry Fielding, *Tom Jones* (1749), Preface to Bk. IX.

But Genius, Learning, and Conversation do not dispense a great novelist from the necessity of having a *Good Heart,* by which Fielding means humanity.

Applying Fielding's words to women-novelists, their handicaps at once become only too apparent. Genius and a good heart they might have as natural endowment, but learning and " conversation " were beyond their reach long before and long after Fielding's time. These facts prepare us for the low standard very often observable in the novels written by women, but they do not prepare us for the inexplicable way in which women persisted in proving that they could rise above their limitations. It is not feminism, but the merest common-sense to insist that women's contribution to fiction can only be judged in relation to their opportunities. That this standard of judgment is not sufficiently remembered is, perhaps, because so much that women contributed, by its own merit claims equality with the best attainments of men-novelists, and appears to dispense with the special consideration which is actually its due.

That the writing of fiction becomes clumsy hackwork in the hands of the uneducated is proved in the works of large numbers of the women whom we shall discuss, but we must remember that the art of fiction evolved so slowly and with so many digressions of form and content that there was not, for a long time, any clearly defined standard of what fiction ought to be. This was one reason why women were brave enough to attempt such writing. Women enjoyed stories (particularly love-stories which confirmed their personal view of the focal point of life) and, unlike poetry, unlike essays which called for a cultural mould and commerce in abstractions, a story could be told by anybody who had sufficient gumption to sandwich a middle between a beginning and an end. " To the composition of novels and romances," says Fielding, bitterly, " nothing is necessary but paper, pens, and ink, with the manual capacity of using them." [2]   George Eliot, passing judgment, after several centuries, on the large brood of incapable women-novelists of her day, gives the reason thus: " No educational restrictions can shut women out from the materials of fiction and there is no species of art which is so

[2] *Ibid.*

free from rigid requirements. Like crystalline masses, it may take any form and yet be beautiful, we have only to pour in the right elements—genuine observation, humour, and passion." But pour them into what? George Eliot does not discriminate between the lack of a cultural mould and the lack of the novelist's technique. However, she expresses very well the danger which lay for women in the very looseness of the fictional medium:

> It is precisely this absence of rigid requirements which constitutes the fatal seduction of novel-writing to incompetent women. Ladies who are not wont to be very grossly deceived as to their power of playing on the piano; here certain positive difficulties of execution have to be conquered, and incompetence inevitably breaks down. Every art which has its absolute technique is, to a certain extent, guarded against the intrusions of mere left-handed imbecility. But in novel-writing there are no barriers for incapacity to stumble against, no external criteria to prevent a writer from mistaking foolish facility for mastery.[3]

If this could be said in the middle of the nineteenth century, how much less formulated was the form of the novel, three centuries earlier! And yet one cannot fail to observe that, according as the art of fiction became (as it did) more exigent with advancing years, women continued not only to maintain the required standard, but often to surpass it, and even to contribute to the development of new genres.

It might have been imagined that when Elizabethan fiction developed along the lines of the Pastoral Romance, the picaresque novels, and the guild-tales, that women writers would have retired from the lists, despairing of ever achieving the pseudo-Greek note, the pot-house experience, or the tradesman's touch so necessary respectively to these three types of fiction. Of the three, the Pastoral Romance was the easiest, because though one might not progress with classic grace, one could, at any rate, undulate pleasantly through mazes sufficiently intricate to defy detection. Since pre-Restoration women writers were of the upper-

---

[3] R. Brimley Johnson, *Novelists on Novels* (1928), p. 226 *et seq.* (Extract from George Eliot, 'Silly Novels by Silly Novelists,' *Westminister Review*).

B

classes, it was not likely that they would choose such plebeian realism as the guild-tales for their literary medium, even if they felt competent to portray that aspect of life, and it was not to be imagined that any female pen would then dare to follow, or could successfully follow a rogue, whether Spanish or English, into the unimagined dens of his villainy. The picaro's swashbuckling attitude to women could not be changed unless by reforming the picaro, and a reformed picaro is a contradiction in terms; therefore, with a delicate flutter, the female pens took refuge in gentle valleys, beside murmuring brooks, where shepherd and shepherdess anticipated the poses of Dresden.   Thus Lady Mary Wroath and still later Anne Weamys, both with more success than might be expected in so artificial a type of fiction, and, in the case of the *Urania*, with realism staring out from the courtly inanities like a pair of honest eyes from a mask.

But although the Pastoral novel was moribund with the passing of the Elizabethan age, its mummied form obtruded itself for long upon the attention of the reading public, and its ghostly accents continued to echo in the style of subsequent prose fiction for a century and a half. The persistence of the Pastoral tradition and the delay in the development of realistic fiction is more easily understandable when we recall that people of the sixteenth and seventeenth centuries preferred to find life represented before the footlights than in the pages of a book. Women in Shakespeare's time did not write plays, because the blank-verse form called for a technique in language which they did not possess,[4] but with the Restoration period came a spate of women-dramatists, most notably Aphra Behn, Mrs. Centlivre, Mrs. Manley, Mrs. Pix and Mrs. Trotter. These were highly successful in this new medium for story-telling, mainly because drama had taken a different turn, and instead of tragedies in conception too lofty and in form too difficult for women who lacked learning, now the learned sock was off, and the comfortable buskin which had only to find its way through domestic intrigue, fitted the women beyond any possibility of limping.   Not only

---

[4] Mary Herbert, Countess of Pembroke, rendered into blank verse Robert Garnier's French tragedy of *Antonie*.   For date of publication D.N.B. gives 1592: *Biographia Dramatica* gives 1595.

was the subject-matter more congenial, but the prose dialogue most generally used required only the power of brilliant verbal fencing which would be instinctive in a witty woman. Background and dialogue were rudimentary as yet in the novel, and characterisation was so rare as to be almost non-existent. Still, in a prose story it was necessary to sketch some sort of background, to describe the passage of events and to interpolate conversations, or at least to report them. It was necessary to indicate the passage of time, and in all this there was no very clear precedent for one's procedure. Such freedom was an advantage to the original, but the tendency of the more average person would naturally be to imitate a form which had clear rules for guidance. In drama women found such a form, because, though one could transcend certain of the unities, yet they always remained as a reliable framework of construction. These points, no doubt, served to encourage women, and partly account for the increase in women-writers at this period.

But there was another consideration which, from the beginning of women's literary adventuring had loomed large, and greatly affected their work and their status. This was the condemnatory attitude of the reading public towards women-writers. Masculine condemnation of women's quill-driving was "compounded of many simples" but chiefly of a double fear: fear that women's new occupation might change their attitude towards domestic and social duties, and fear that women's achievements might eclipse those of men. For countless ages women had been given the sort of education which fitted them to become wives and mothers in this world, and saints either here or hereafter. These activities were conducive towards man's happiness, and were no encroachment on the territory he was accustomed to consider as peculiarly his own. But if women were to realise themselves in some separate way, if they, like men, should have an intellectual life, which, of necessity, must be led alone and which, as man knew, was richly self-rewarding, might not women become intolerable from the man's point of view? That is to say, not merely preoccupied with other than domestic details, but no longer looking up to man as the arbiter of her fate. "While thou keepest always looking up at me, and I down at thee, what horrid obliquities of vision may we not contract? " [5]—obliquities not to be quickly cured, capable of distorting all one's impressions, and very painful if readjusted too suddenly.   " I imagine," says the Duchess of Newcastle, " that I shall be censured by my own Sex; and Men will cast a smile of Scorne upon my Book, because they think thereby, Women incroach too much upon their Prerogatives; for they hold Books as their Crowne, and the Sword as their Scepter, by which they rule and governe.   And very like they will say to me, as to the Lady that wrote the Romancy,

> Work, Lady, Work, let writing books alone
> For surely wiser women nere wrote one." [6]

And she continues:

> Spinning with the Fingers is more proper to our Sexe, than studying or writing Poetry, which is spinning with the Braine, but I, having no skill in the art of the first (and if I had, I had no hopes of gaining so much as to make me a garment to keep me from the cold) make me delight in the latter . . . which made me endeavour to Spin a Garment of Memory, to lapp up my Name, that it might grow to after Ages.   I cannot say the web is strong, fine, or evenly spun, for it is a course piece; yet I had rather my Name should go meanly clad, than dye with cold.[7]

Mean indeed was the reputation of women-writers, when they were so fortunate as to have any reputation at all.   The reading public and the general public (those widening circles in the pool of opinion, obedient to the stones cast by the critics) divided women writers into three chief classes, each of which received a different judgment.   First, there were the women-writers, who not only escaped condemnation, but were never even put on trial.   These were the dilettante ladies, the literary dabblers, who wrote polite verse, translated plays and pious treatises, and kept their eyes well averted from the roaring pageant of life. Always they were of the privileged classes.   Often they were the relatives of literary men, and won an amused tolerance or a degree of kindly commendation for their precocity.   In the case

---

5 Robert Bage, *Mount Henneth* (1781).
6 The Duchess of Newcastle, *Poems and Fancies* (1653); an address *'To all Noble and Worthy Ladies.'*
7 *Ibid*, dedication to Sir Charles Cavendish.

of Sir Philip Sydney's sister and niece, they might have written the *Heptameron*, and not the slightest murmur of disapproval would have disturbed the pæans of loving praise which enveloped that illustrious family. Amongst its many virtues was a profound generosity in literary patronage, and so it was that the Countess of Pembroke was accounted a notable success in literature. Yet her works, so lavishly eulogised, consist of a play translated from the French,[8] (never acted, and never even read by the critics who extolled it); a poem whose sole claim to recognition was that Spenser published it with his *Astrophel*; and a metrical version of the Psalms, in which she was helped by her brother and her chaplain. Nash, Spenser, Nicholas Breton, Whincop, Osborn, Langbaine and many others were loud in her praise, and her epitaph was written probably by Ben Jonson.

Let us compare the case of Marie de France, who made so notable a contribution to French literature:

> Tous, à l'exception de Denys Pyramus, qui en a dit peu de chose, ont gardé un profound silence sur cette femme fort supérieure à son siècle par ses lumières, par ses sentiments, et par le courage qu'elle eut de dire la vérité a des oreilles mal disposées ou peu accoutumées a l'entendre.[9]

What is the explanation of this silence? It is, apparently, that Marie belonged to the great company of women-writers who were condemned by their own generation. They were condemned because they were suspected either of looseness or eccentricity. If they were suspect on moral grounds, absence of evidence did not acquit them and the best they could hope for was the grudging Scottish judgment of "Not Proven." The third class, those who were obviously above moral reproach but were still suspect of some abnormality, was labelled "Queer." For whatever cause, it is clear that Marie was attacked, for she says:

> Indeed, wherever there is a man or a woman of great fame, those who are envious of her good work often slander her, and with the intent to lessen her fame, play the part of a wretched

---

[8] Mary Herbert, Countess of Pembroke, *Antonie*. (For date of publication see footnote on page 18).
[9] *Works of Marie de France* (ed. de Roquefort); introductory note.

cowardly dog, a cur that bites folk stealthily. But I will not
leave off for this, even though backbiters and false flatterers
work mischief against me—for to speak ill is their nature.[10]

That the Duchess of Newcastle was considered queer is confirmed by all the criticisms of her own time. Queer she
undoubtedly was, but she had sufficient genius to justify her
eccentricity, a fact recognised by Disraeli. And though she
showed a fine disregard for her critics, male and female, yet she
was very conscious that current opinion was opposed to literary
pursuits for a woman. She appeals endlessly for her right to be
an author. Is it not better for her to occupy her time in writing
than to behave loosely as so many Court ladies do? Is her
occupation really less useful than painting and embroidery, or
" the making of Flowers, Boxes, Baskets with Beads, Shells,
Silke and Strawe?"

> I hope you will spare me [she says to her readers] for the
> Harthe is swept cleane, and a Bason of Water with a cleane
> Towell set by, and the Ashes rak'd up; wherefore let my book
> sleep quietly, and the Watch-light burning clearly . . . and
> let it be still from your noise, that the feminine Cat may not
> Mew, nor the masculine Curs bark nor howle out railings to
> disturb my harmless Booke's rest."

The feminine Cats, however, continued to mew, as they had
done from the beginning of women's literary efforts. Again and
again the women-writers comment on this feminine attack upon
them. " Nay, even my own sex, which should assert our prerogative against such detractors, are often backward to encourage
the female pen." [11] And writing long afterwards (1791) another
woman says: " You know how female writers are looked down
upon. The women fear and hate, the men ridicule and dislike
them."[12]

Still, it must be allowed that, apart from the prejudice and
even the possible envy with which the non-literary woman
regarded her more gifted sisters, there was very often a legitimate

10 *Works of Marie de France* (ed. E. Rickert), 1. The beginning of
Guigemor.
11 Susannah Centlivre: dedication to *The Platonic Lady* (dedicated to
"All the generous encouragers of female ingenuity").
12 Elizabeth Hamilton, *Letters to a Hindoo Rajah*. (1791), ii., 328.

reason for objecting on moral grounds to the women who wrote fiction, and to the kind of fiction which they wrote. Men had created the standard of literary taste, and if women were to write at all they had to compete with men on their own ground. It was not considered improper that men should write loosely for a reading public (or for an audience) composed of women as well as men, nor even that they should write lewdly for women's particular instruction, as for example, did Jacques d'Amiens, whose " *L'Art d'Amors* " was merely one of many such works during the Middle Ages:

> Chez Jacques d'Amiens les femmes ne sont pas considerées que comme des joujoux qui sont là uniquement pour le plaisir des hommes : il ne considère jamais le côté moral des choses; il n'a pas de sens moral.[13]

It seems surprising that women might consume such literary repasts in the privacy of their bowers, but emphatically might not cater for such tastes in others. There is indeed a moral distinction in culpability, but it was not this consideration which inspired the general condemnation of women-writers. It is not for us to determine whether women-writers should have wished or attempted to evangelise the reading public. In any case, they could not possibly have done so. The fact that they entered into literary competition meant that they accepted the code established by the majority of writers in accordance with popular demand. Literary fame and, later, financial success depended on playing the game at least as well as their masculine adversaries, and playing a game involves the acceptance of definite rules and the developing of a particular technique. Women who wrote according to a standard of their own would have had as much hope of success as if they decided to play hockey with a crochet-hook. Playing even in the accepted way, they had to take it for granted that the umpire-critics would always be prejudiced, and that the public would howl them down at every opportunity. They were like a visiting team in hostile country where their every effort would be adjudged offside. If they were ever to win approval, they needed to be not merely as good as, but

[13] Alice A. Hentsch, *De la Littérature Didactique du moyen âge s'adressant spécialement aux femmes* (Cahors, 1903), p. 68 f.

better than their opponents, and the difficulty of this was evident, when one reflects that they were heavily handicapped from the beginning. That they did adapt themselves to the rigours of the contest, that they did score so early in the game was a triumph—unpopular, and not without its price. Wounded reputation was to be expected, and at one period was really deserved, although even then the public put the cart before the horse. The literary women of the Restoration were not loose because they were writers. They were writers because they were loose. They were adventuresses before they adventured into literature. In a word, they were driven by circumstances to drive a quill, and they had the only equipment by which a woman of that time could succeed in letters—a great intellectual vigour and an absence of scruples. It was nothing much to them that, as women-writers, they lost caste. They had lost caste already. Mrs. Behn, Mrs. Centlivre, Mrs. Manley, Mrs. Pix, Mrs. Haywood and the rest of the battered crew, came to the profession of writing with no illusions, almost no education, a wide though ill-balanced experience of life, and an immense vigour of mind and body. They asked, and they got, no quarter, and they stamped their names defiantly into the minds of their contemporaries and into literary history. It is no mean feat at any time to make a living by free-lance writing. In the sixteenth, seventeenth and eighteenth centuries it was incredibly difficult. It was easier to starve than to eat by the sweat of one's brow, as even men-writers, from the days of Nash, Dekker, Fox and Drayton knew to their cost. To be a genius was no guarantee against the gutter or imprisonment for debt. It was necessary to find patrons and to keep them from tiring; to cultivate anyone who might have influence; to ingratiate oneself with editors and booksellers; to flatter the critics; to be hail-fellow-well-met with all sorts of people, in all sorts of places; to be ready to turn one's hand to anything—play-patching, "ghosting," political propaganda, rudimentary newspaper work; to haunt the greenrooms, and "keep in with" the players; to write plays for a small circle of loose-livers at a time when no decent woman would go to a theatre, and even the courtesans went masked. It will be admitted that no conventional woman could do all this, and if a group of unconventional women did it, then we must evaluate the gain entirely from the literary point of view. Nobody can contest the literary contributions of Mrs. Behn, Mrs. Centlivre, Mrs. Haywood, and even of Mrs. Manley. With the exception of Mrs. Centlivre (who excelled exclusively as a dramatist), these women wrote not only plays (which had an indirect but definite influence on the growth of fiction) but notably aided the development of the novel, both by using accepted forms, and by helping to initiate other forms. In their own time (and even now) women-writers of that particular period were strongly censured for their loose writing. One might as well blame an Arctic fox for changing his colour in the winter. He lives by adaptation, and so did they. From amongst the innumerable evidences that a double standard of criticism was exercised on a single standard of writing, we may perhaps mention one example. Aphra Behn, as brilliant as any writer of her generation, was loaded with obloquy for plays which, compared to those of Dryden and Congreve, might almost be considered pure. Dryden, writing to Mrs. Elizabeth Thomas in 1699, expressed his certainty that she would avoid the license which Mrs. Behn allowed herself " of writing loosely, and giving, if I may have leave to say so, scandall to the modesty of her sex. I confess I am the last man who ought in justice to arraign her, who have been too much a libertine in most of my poems; which I should be well contented I had time either to purge, or to see fairly burn'd."[14]

He was, indeed, the last man who should have attacked licentiousness in any writer, and he should have abstained from casting a stone at one of his few direct imitators. " I should be inclined," says Nicol, " to think that it is almost entirely the influence of Dryden which has led this authoress away from the comparatively pure plots to this of most immodest intrigue. ' Mr. Limberham ' could contaminate a whole shoal of writers; and Dryden with his immodesty was showing to the playwrights of his time exactly what the audiences of the time desired."[15] An interesting sidelight on the single standard of popular taste

[14] *Dryden's Works* (ed. Scott and Saintsbury), XVIII, p. 166.
[15] Allardyce Nicol, *Restoration Drama*, 1660-1700 (2nd ed. 1928). p. 211

is given by Sir Walter Scott. He says that an aged lady, a relation of his, " assured him that in the polite society of her youth, in which she held a distinguished place, the plays and novels of Mrs. Aphra Behn were accounted proper reading "; and, " she added, with some humour, it was not until a long interval, when she looked into it at the age of seventy that she was shocked with their indecorum "[16]—shocked, that is, only in retrospect and when influenced by the more correct moral standards of a later age.

This anecdote to the contrary, there is no room for doubt that even in a grosser period the type of women-writers to which we have referred could not avoid ostracism. It is worth considering whether their equivocal position had any effect on their writing, apart from what we have already discussed. There is little question that it had, and there are gains and losses to be computed. It was a gain that declassed and plebeian as they were, they could not shelter behind a coat of arms, or a sermon-ising mediocrity, or a précieux classicism, nor lap themselves about with the facile and soothing adulation of a select coterie. They were in no danger of being praised for powers they did not possess. On the contrary, they had to fight for recognition, and the only compliment they received was that of being treated as responsible writers, able to take and to give blows, and with no privileges at all. The struggle to find and to retain a place for themselves, led them to realise and, so far as they could, to remedy their deficiencies. Sometimes, as in the case of Mrs. Manley, they made the mistake of endeavouring to achieve by slanderous salacity what they could not achieve by literary ability, but this recourse to mere licentiousness for a *tour de force* is rare. The chief women-writers of that period had enough real literary power to have succeeded in a happier age. That they had a wide though unfortunate experience of life meant something on the credit and on the debit side. In losing an idealised view of existence, they found a measure of reality, and they encountered a multiplicity of human types, reacting characteristically to a variety of circumstances—sufficient in number and diversity to enable them to see a pattern in the

16 *Dryden's Works* (ed. Scott and Saintsbury), xviii, 166, footnote.

confusion and a unity in complexity. They could see that
heroes and villains had much in common, and that characterisation deals with material far less easily recognisable than virtues
and vices. It is better to see a courtesan as she really is, than
to imagine a shepherdess as she never really was? One cannot
doubt that for realism in literature it is better to write with one
eye on the object. But an idealised representation of life is not
more unreal than life depicted as entirely without ideals. Realism
must take into account that ideals are actual forces intermingling
with the stuff of events, sometimes shaping and sometimes
merely interpreting them, but in either case by no means to be
discounted. And this is exactly where the Restoration women
writers, following the rules laid down by their stronger brethren
of the pen, lost the authentic touch in interpreting and
expressing human life. But their own experiences made it all
the easier for them to concur in a view of life which mocked at
ethical conventions, and it was natural that they should carry off
their ostracism by laughing loudly at the unco' guid, whose
prudery caused them to miss all the fun. It was easier to go a
step further, and to believe self-justifyingly that all of life was
as they knew it, and that virtue at best was merely a seductive
perfume, an alluring patina; at worst a hypocritical veil for the
subtle. In the writings of these women this added impetus of
experience is often detectable:

> Mrs. Behn, perhaps, as much as any one, condemned loose
> scenes and too warm descriptions; but something must be
> allowed to human frailty. She herself was of an amorous
> complexion; she felt the passions intimately which she
> describes, and this circumstance added to Necessity, might be
> the occasion of her plays being of that cast.[17]

And sometimes added to the impetus of personal experience
is the impetus of personal spite, a desire for vengeance on that
society, which drew its skirts aside. This is one reason why
Mrs. Manley and Mrs. Haywood took to the histoire scandaleuse
like a duck to water. In Mrs. Haywood's case, it was not lack
of ability to do good work in a superior genre of fiction, as is

[17] Theophilus Cibber, *The Lives of the Poets* (1753).

proved in her authorship of *Miss Betsy Thoughtless* and *The History of Jemmy and Jenny Jessamy*. When Defoe [18] and Mrs. Haywood[19] both used the life of the deaf and dumb fortune-teller, Duncan Campbell, as material for fiction, their respective points of view are very evident. Defoe was interested in recounting the wonders of Campbell's powers, and specifically mentions that he omits tales of Mr. Campbell's women consultants, because they were so numerous that, if included, the work would be endless. Mrs. Haywood, however, " was evidently more interested in the phenomena of passion than in the theory of divination,"[20] and she also utilises the opportunity of revealing scandalous secrets, and opening old wounds. In fact, she makes her material serve the purpose of the histoire scandaleuse—an erotic arrow dipped in poison.

The point to be observed is that in the already ill-balanced literature of that period, any added impetus which further disturbed the balance, was artistically inadmissible. Mesure, balance, symmetry—these are in life, and no matter how brilliant, vivid and witty the literature of a period may be, a fault in emphasis is a fault in art, and must lead to the decay of that genre. In this case, the emphasis was on an aspect of life which allowed, after all, very little variety. Few things are less capable of variation, and therefore few things are more monotonous than the representation of vice. The conventions of immorality in drama and fiction are really more stultifying than the conventions of virtue.

But even at worst, such drama and such fiction were alive, and it was easy to see how they might develop when they had outgrown the excesses of youth. In its immature state, however, because it was, perhaps, of more mixed ancestry than the accepted forms of writing, and because it was, at that stage of its evolution, very lacking in art, fiction was regarded as a raggle-

18 *The History of the life and adventures of Mr. Duncan Campbell* (1720). There seems reason to ascribe part authorship to Defoe.
19 *A Spy upon the Conjurer* (1725). Ascribed by Dr. G. B. Wicher to Mrs. Haywood (in *The Life and Romances of Mrs. Eliza Haywood*, Columbia Univ. Press, 1915). Similarly ascribed by Mr. E. A. Baker, *History of the English Novel* (1929), .iii, 178.
20 G. B. Wicher, *The Life and Romances of Mrs. Eliza Haywood* (Columbia Univ. Press, 1915), p. 80.

taggle sort of composition. Sir Philip Sydney claimed that the *Arcadia* was poetry, and later Fielding speaks of *Tom Jones* as " this heroic, historical, prosaic poem." Poetry had a high and ancient tradition, and its female devotees, thus chaperoned by the muses, were regarded with much indulgence.[21] Such a one was Catherine Philips, and though she did not write fiction and therefore does not enter our field of consideration, she serves to show that, by adherence to a classical genre, a mediocre woman could win a literary reputation without sacrificing either her good name or her reputation for good sense. Nothing could be more fantastic than the legend of the Matchless, the Incomparable Orinda. Speaking of the " celebrated scribbling women " of the 17th century, Sir Edmund Gosse says:

Among all these the Matchless Orinda takes the foremost place —not exactly by merit, for Aphra Behn surpassed her in genius, Margaret, Duchess of Newcastle, in versatility, and Catherine Trotter in professional zeal; but by the moral eminence she attained through her elevated public career and which she sealed by her tragical death. When the seventeenth century thought of a poetess, it naturally thought of Orinda; her figure overtopped those of her literary sisters; she was more dignified, more regal, in her attitude to the public than they were, and in fine she presents us with the best type we possess of the woman of letters in the seventeenth century.[22]

Even if " the best " meant simply the most moral, she could claim no prëeminence over Lucy Hutchinson or the Duchess of Newcastle. It is clear that " the best " does not mean the most gifted, versatile or zealous. " The best type " cannot mean the most typical of seventeenth century England, because Orinda is really not even representative, and would have claimed France as her spiritual country.

This incredible précieuse, born of honest, middle-class Cockney parents, is a fine example of what may be achieved when a facile talent is exploited by a pose so convincing that it is even self-hypnotic. Catherine Philips, née Fowler, used her pen as a

21 Of these, in Elizabethan and Jacobean days, there was a fair number, notably Catherine Killigrew, Jane Weston; Mary, Countess of Pembroke, and Anne, Countess of Winchelsea.

22 E. Gosse, *Seventeenth Century Studies* (1885): Essay on 'The Matchless Orinda.'

vaulting-pole into society, and was never so happy as when, by
her imagined poetical genius, she edged her way into a higher
social stratum. She wrote a considerable quantity of artificial
poetry, translated two of Corneille's plays (*Pompée* and *Horace*)
into wooden verse, and carried on an epistolary correspondence
with Sir Charles Cotterel (Poliarchus). These works are the
apparent basis of her literary reputation, and her passport to the
friendship of such men as Cowley and Jeremy Taylor. Her patrons and associates were such people as the Earls of Orrery and
Roscommon, the Countess of Cork, and the Viscountess of Dun-
gannon. When the Countess of Cork caused *Pompey* to be acted,
the Earl of Roscommon spoke the prologue. Orinda was lauded
to the skies, and critics like the sycophantic Langbaine said that
she far surpassed Corneille.[23] Her death left *Horace* unfinished
and it was completed by Sir John Denham and acted at Court by
" Persons of Quality " fourteen years later, the Duke of Monmouth speaking the prologue. What was the secret of that
extraordinary furore which has not withstood the impartial judgment of posterity? It is, simply, that Catherine Philips's
greatest creation was Orinda and she, alas! was subject to
mortality. She was the first sentimental writer in the English
language.[24] She created a cult of sentiment and classicism, and
loved to imagine that she was the leader of a salon which she
called the Society of Friendship. Her house in Wales was a kind
of Hotel de Rambouillet, or rather hers was a peripatetic salon,
following her peregrinations among the houses of her patrons.
Honest English names offended her sensibilities, and her friends
were obliged to masquerade under such titles as Poliarchus,
Palaemon, Lucasia, Valeria. She averred that she read English
books with patience, but French ones with pleasure. She
indulged in an endless series of sentimental friendships with
young women, and was always mortally offended when they
abandoned classicism for marriage. The patient and unassuming
Mr. Philips (alias Antenor) quietly continued to eat roast beef
and Yorkshire pudding, and to live his own life outside the
Society of Friendship. One imagines him smiling in humorous

[23] Langbaine, *An Account of the English Dramatic Poets* (Oxford,
1691), p. 403 f.
[24] See E. Gosse, *Seventeenth Century Studies* (1885), *art. cit.*

resignation on reading his wife's poems, and discovering that she is "dying for a little love."

Writing eight years after Langbaine, Charles Gildon scornfully contradicts his statement that Orinda is a better writer than Aphra Behn, and accuses him of snobbish bias. He says "I must confess I cannot but prefer Mrs. Behn infinitely before her; she seems to be a very cold Writer, while you may find in Aphra both Fire and Easiness, which Mrs. Philips wanted.[25] By 1747 the myth of Orinda, which needed the support of her living personality, had so far faded, that Whincop, under the blunt heading: "C. Philips," records all that remains: "She was commonly called the Matchless Orinda, on account of an Epistolary correspondence carried on between her and Sir Charles Cotterel, under the feign'd names of Orinda and Polyarchus."[26] Then follow, without comment, the names of those plays which surpassed Corneille.

The case of Catherine Philips illustrates the fact that a woman of mediocre mind and a veneer of education could, by adherence to an accepted genre of writing, not only secure powerful patrons, and an immediate success, but also an immunity from that criticism which ever pursued the women who wrote fiction, and which persisted even in the days of Jane Austen and the Brontës. "Orinda" was a *nom de panache*, but "Ellis Bell" was a guilty expedient, and it is strange to reflect that though, with the lapse of centuries, the novel increasingly proved its claim to be recognised as a particular form of art, and the world became increasingly familiar with the ability of women-novelists, yet the old stigma remained, and drove even genius to conceal itself under a pseudonym.

But there was a kind of literary composition, other than poetry, which even in the sixteenth and seventeenth centuries was considered legitimate for female pens. This was the biography or autobiography, and it is interesting to note in how far it shaped towards fiction in the hands of those women who employed it. Anne Clifford, Countess of Pembroke, the Duchess of Newcastle, Mrs. Lucy Hutchinson, and Lady

[25] Gildon's Langbaine, *The Lives of the Poets* (1699), pp. 110-111.
[26] T. Whincop, *Scanderbeg* (appendix).

Fanshawe wrote their biographies, the first so as to clarify her daughter's claims in a legal dispute; the Duchess and Lucy Hutchinson, as it were, *en passant*, their particular interest being centred in writing their husbands' biographies. Lady Fanshawe more evenly develops her own life-story with that of her husband.

Biography had for women the advantage of giving them a chance to write on a subject they really knew, but the necessity for authenticity which was the object, and to them the justification of their compositions, crippled their imaginative powers. Their very familiarity with the people and the events in these works made it difficult for them to realise the necessity for describing them fully for other people. Thus, with the exception of Lady Fanshawe (the most vivid and detailed of the female biographers), they do not essay descriptions of domestic events, nor attempt to sketch in, however roughly, the backgrounds they knew so well. One does not often find in the biographical writings of Anne Clifford, the Duchess of Newcastle, or Lucy Hutchinson a realistic and full presentation of such events as are described, though frequently one is conscious of emotion flowing, with awakened memory, into their narratives. Still, they do not recreate happenings by the illumination of subsequent experience. They do not show much perspective. There is no dramatic irony. There is an entire lack of humour, due, no doubt, to the fact that when these women wrote they were worn out by many griefs. Their unrelieved seriousness must also be ascribed to an excessive anxiety. They are determined to present their husbands, their families and themselves in the best possible light, and it is hard to smile with one's teeth clenched. With all four women there is a definite effort to achieve character-portraits, and not much notion of how to proceed. For the most part, they simply enumerate the ineffable virtues and bodily characteristics of those whom they wish to describe. Apart from the self-consciousness and difficulty in perspective which are obvious disadvantages in recording one's own life or that of a near relation, these women were also confronted with another serious handicap, namely, the necessity of showing the development of their family fortunes in relation to a complicated background of political events. Anne Clifford simply presumes such knowledge, as well she might, since she wrote only for her daughter. Lucy Hutchinson and the Duchess, forced to deal with the maze of the Civil War, and aware of their inability to do so, depend on others for their account of political and military events, the Duchess with her usual frankness, and Lucy Hutchinson without acknowledging her sources. As is only to be expected, both fail to control this extremely complicated mass of material, and they are very much at a loss as to how best it might be introduced into their narratives. The result is clumsy, and no wonder, seeing that the genre of the historical novel, shadowed faintly forth in their compositions, was yet almost a century and a half from its full evolution. When, about fifty-five years later, Defoe published, in 1722, the *Journal of the Plague Year* and *Colonel Jacques*, we see that despite the power and realism which characterised his works, he also failed to manage the historical background which his circumstantial method of composition forced him to introduce. Actually he should have experienced less difficulty in mastering his historical material, since, as his aim was really fiction, he had naturally no hesitation in juggling with historical data. In the *Journal of the Plague Year* this lack of technique is clearly evident. "Large parts of the book are cast into statistical form: they read more like a Blue Book than anything else."[27] This goes to show that even the freedom of fiction in the hands of a genius could not yet give ease in the interweaving of historical and personal material, and gives us moreover a true idea of what might reasonably be expected from the Duchess and Lucy Hutchinson. Lady Fanshawe makes no attempt to sketch in a comprehensive background of the Civil War—a wise abstention on the whole, although it often leaves the causes of the great Fanshawe Odyssey too obscure. Whatever the short-comings of these biographers, it was a step in the right direction that they were endeavouring to tell a story which was part of their lives, and much of which came within their personal experience; but it is amusing to reflect that while these women, pen in hand, endeavoured to marshal troops, to take castles, to summon and dismiss Parliaments and to discuss treaties, Mr. Pepys was

27 E. A. Baker, *History of the English Novel* (1927), iii. 201f.

C

committing to an undreamed immortality the colour (and price) of his wife's dresses; the furnishings of their house; the sort of dinner one might expect on washing-day; the servant problem; the latest play; his outings with his wife, their friends, their quarrels, their reconciliations—in fact all the fabric of daily life, the fabric of domestic fiction, which had never yet been attempted by any writer, man or woman.

Mrs. Manley's efforts at disguised autobiography came later than the *Life of William Cavendish* and the *Memoirs*, and went much nearer to direct fiction. In the new *Atalantis* she had introduced in a spasmodic and vagrant way some account of herself under the name of Delia, and this idea evidently developed in her mind, and claimed fuller expression in *Rivella*. The fact that *Rivella* is a biography in the form of a key-novel gave Mrs. Manley a great advantage over her more forthright predecessors. The thin cloaking of reality in the key-novel gave just the necessary amount of freedom for the exercise of imagination and individuality. When Mrs. Manley wrote *Rivella* she stood outside her life and contemplated its happenings in the light of after-knowledge, and this detachment, this escape from the hair-splitting responsibility of authenticity, from the dogmatism of the everlasting " I," was exactly what was needed for the development of biography into fiction. The close analogy between Defoe's *Roxana* and *Rivella* shows how two genres, originally separate, eventually became telescoped, and for opposite and corresponding reasons. Defoe veiled his fictions under the appearance of fact; Mrs. Manley veiled her facts under the appearance of fiction. The point to be made is briefly this: that though women-writers were more successful in fiction than in any other type of writing, because their bent and their abilities alike indicated that medium of expression, yet convention decreed that, if they must write at all, then they ought to limit them-selves to authenticated compositions; if they must feign, then it must be the sort of feigned writing called poetry. If a woman had written the life of Mrs. Manley, thoroughly authenticating every fact, suitably deploring her immoral adventures and drawing elevated lessons from every lapse from grace, she really might have managed to escape severe popular censure; at any rate, she would have a much better chance of doing so than if she enlivened her subject by giving it, as Mrs. Manley did, the form of a novel.

Nevertheless, and despite the passing of the Restoration school of female desperadoes, women continued to write fiction. What else could they do, if they were to write at all? In the words of Mary Davys:

> The Pedant despises the most elaborate Undertaking, unless it appears in the World with Greek and Latin Motto's; a Man that would please him, must pore an Age over Musty Authors, till his brains are as worm-eaten as the books he reads . . . I have neither Inclination nor Learning enough to hope for his favour, so lay him aside.
>
> The next I can never hope to please, is the Dogmatical Puppy, who like a Hedgehog is wrapt up in his own Opinions . . . I leave him therefore . . . I confess the Royal Exchange, South-sea with a P-x, Exchange Alley, and all trade in general, are so foreign to my understanding that I leave 'em where I found 'em and cast an oblique glance at the Philosopher, who I take be a good clever fellow in his way. But I am again forced to betray my ignorance. I know so little of him that I leave him to his, *No Pleasure, No Pain;* and a thousand other Chimera's while I face about to the Man of Gallantry. Love is a very common topick, but 'tis withal a very copious one; and wou'd the Poets, Printers, and Booksellers but speak the truth of it, they wou'd own themselves more obliged to that one subject for their Bread, than all the rest put together. 'Tis there I fix.[28]

Mary Davys, a clergyman's widow, was typical of a new kind of woman-writer—the respectable woman who, forced for some reason to support herself, could find no other way of doing so save by writing or keeping a school. Sometimes, like Harriet and Sophia Lee, women did both, and even then found it difficult to exist on their earnings. One of these writing-women gives a description of herself which might easily be taken to designate her kind: "Resident not very far from the market-place, immersed in business and in debt; sometimes madly hoping to gain a competency; sometimes justly fearing dungeons and distress."[29] They appear to be overwhelmed by doubts as to

---

[28] Mary Davys, *The Reformed Coquet* (1724), p. 2 f.
[29] Mrs. Mary Latter, *The Miscellaneous Works in Prose and Verse* (1759), Introd.

the legitimacy of fiction, and of a female authorship. If they have any real impulse to write, any real conviction of ability, or any real literary ambition, they hasten to disclaim them so that they may propitiate their public:

> As I never was ambitious of the Name of Author, nor even design'd to indulge my inclinations in writing any Thing of this Nature, more than for my own Amusement. I have printed this Manuscript (which otherwise I never had done) with a View to settling my self in a Way of Trade; that may enable me to master those Exigencies of Fortune, which my long illness had for some time past reduc'd me to suffer: That I may be capable of providing for my now ancient, indulgent Mother; whom Age, and the charge of many Children hath render'd incapable of providing for herself; As I shall directly sell Paper, Pens, Ink, Wax, Wafers, Black Lead Pencils, Pocket Books, Almanacks, Plays, Pamphlets and all manner of stationary goods. I must humbly beg the Favour of my honourable Subscribers (who are not already engag'd) to be so very good as to be my Customers. .
> E. Boyd.
> March 2, 1732.
>
> N.B.—Be Pleas'd to send to me in George-Court, in Prince's Street near Leicester-Fields, the First House on the Right Hand.[30]

There were legions of such women, a few with real ability, most of them without; all protesting, expostulating, explaining, defending their having dared to write. Not all, however, were as humble as Mrs. Boyd: Mary Davys says in justification of her writing: " Let them [her critics] consider that a woman left to her own endeavours for Twenty-seven Years together, may well be allowed to catch at any opportunity for that Bread, which they that condemn her would very probably deny to give her."[31]

But, fortunately for the quality of women's literary work, it was not merely external necessity which continued to drive women to authorship. There was sometimes an inner compulsion of genius which neither ignorance nor convention could stifle; and it is useful to recall in this connection that women of the eighteenth and early nineteenth centuries still received no

30 Advertisement in front of E. Boyd's *The Female Page* (1737).
31 Mary Davys, *Collected Works* (1725), Preface to Vol. 1.

education worthy of the name. This was true even of those women who came of cultured families, and this lack of education was to a great extent deliberate, so that we may say without exaggeration that the ignorance of woman in those days was an effect of the prevailing convention. " It was not the fashion for young ladies to be literary; a woman who wrote or read much was thought to be a HALF-MAN!"[32] To be a half-man was an infinite disaster, because it was the business of every young lady to catch a husband, and what man would wish to marry a blue-stockinged hermaphrodite? It was the business of women to be all that men admired, and they naturally did not admire a counterpart of themselves. No, the ladies, God bless them, must be lovely, gracious, gay, arch, inconsequent, diffident in weighty matters, sure only of their own beauty, bent only on pleasing, the dear, delightful fairies! " I consider woman," says Addison, " as a beautiful, romantic animal that may be adorned with furs and feathers, ores and silks. The lynx shall cast its skin at her feet to make her a tippet; the peacock, parrot and swan shall pay contributions to her muff: the sea shall be searched for shells and the rocks for gems; and every part of Nature furnish out its share towards the embellishment of a creature that is the most consummate work of it." But since woman was not a study in still life, some rules were necessary, lest she might forget her role of charming vacuity. They were glibly supplied by Hannah More:

> *The animated silence of sparkling intelligence* with an occasional modest question which indicated at once rational curiosity and becoming diffidence is in many cases as large a share of the conversation as it is decorous for feminine delicacy to take.

This being the case it does not surprise us that Fanny Burney was so badly educated that at eight years old she did not know the alphabet; nor does it appear at all unnatural that Frances Sheridan's father disapproved of women being taught to read, and was vigorously opposed to their being taught to write. But the child who at eight years did not know the alphabet was

---

[32] *Catherine Hamilton, Women Writers and their Ways* (1893), ii, 'Harriet Martineau.'

scribbling stories, odes, plays and songs two years later, in hieroglyphics which only she herself could read; and the child who was forbidden to read or write secretly prevailed on her brother to teach her, which, recognising her intelligence, he did, thus saving from illiteracy the author of *Miss Sydney Bidulph*, the mother of one of our finest dramatists.   At fifteen, Fanny Burney became overwhelmed with a sense of guilt at her passion for writing, and thought it her duty to subdue it, so, taking advantage of her parents' absence from home, she made a bonfire of all she had written.   This holocaust included *The History of Caroline Evelyn*—a tale which she found it impossible to forget, and which later she was again to commit to paper, under the title of *Evelina*.   After her decision not to go on writing she commenced to keep a diary which she dedicated "TO NOBODY."   "To whom must I dedicate my private opinions, my wonderful, surprising and interesting adventures? To whom dare I reveal my private opinions of my nearest relations?   My secret thoughts of my dearest friends?   My own hopes, fears, reflections, and dislikes?—Nobody."   But she could not stifle her impulse towards literary expression, and like Jane Austen, she wrote on scraps of paper, alone when she could escape her vigilant family, in the common living room when escape was impossible—making a pretence of occupying herself with her needle.   Ah! those deceptive needles of the female scribblers!   How zealously they flashed, what ground they seemed to cover, and how curiously little they achieved!   Jane Austen knew that trick too—Jane, that frightful warning to young ladies of her day of the price one paid for secretly plying the pen.   Miss Mitford's mother describes her as "the prettiest, silliest, most affected, husband-hunting butterfly she ever remembers,"[33] and the next thing we hear is that "she has stiffened into the most perpendicular, precise, taciturn piece of

---

[33] *Life of Mary Russell Mitford* (ed. Rev. A. G. L'Estrange, 1870), i., 305. J. E. Austen-Leigh flatly contradicts "this strange misrepresentation of my aunt's manners" (see last pages of *Memoir of Jane Austen,* Oxford. 1926).   Nevertheless, although Mrs. Mitford evidently could not have gained her opinion through intercourse with the Austen family, she could have gained it by hearsay, which is not, after all, a bad guide to the more obvious aspects of behaviour. Jane Austen's letters show that she took a lively interest in finery and balls.

'single blessedness' that ever existed . . . no more regarded in
society than a poker or a firescreen."[34]   As for the motherless
Brontës, they missed, alas, the training that young ladies ought
to receive, and really behaved in the most unsuitable way.
Wolfing books and scribbling among the gravestones could lead
only to such unnatural works as *Wuthering Heights* and *Jane
Eyre*. For such women not even a moulting parrot would cast
a single feather.

Harriet Martineau, perhaps, was less to be blamed, for the
poor thing was really very ugly.   She never received but one
civil speech about her looks, which accounts, no doubt, for
the fact that she always looked glum.   As she showed every
sign of being a superfluous woman, it was perhaps just as
well that she took to her pen.   She also, however, had to
pay tribute with her needle.   " She was at the work table
regularly after breakfast, making her clothes or the shirts of the
household, or engaged on fancy work.   She studied almost by
stealth, meeting her brother James at seven in the morning to
read Latin with him or translating Tacitus, that she might
compress her thoughts."[35]   When she became deaf and penniless,
she had to earn her living.   No doubt it was because she was
so plain that she wrote didactic tales on various aspects of
political economy, but possibly, however, she may have been
influenced by the fact that the Reform Bill was pending and
that cholera had begun to rage.   Harriet Martineau published by
subscription, and she got reasonably generous terms, in view of
the fact that she was quite destitute, and deaf, and only a woman:
five hundred copies were to be taken before her book came out,
and if one thousand copies were not sold in the first fortnight,
the publication would be stopped.   She accepted the proposition
and took the prospectus into town, then stunned by the certainty
of failure, and half-starving, she walked the four and a half miles
back to her lodgings.   "On the road, not far from Shoreditch,
she became too giddy to stand without support.   She leaned
over some dirty pailings, pretending to look at a cabbage-bed,

[34] Quoted by Virginia Woolf, *The Common Reader* (1925), 'Jane
Austen.'

[35] Catherine Hamilton, *Women Writers and their ways,* (1893), ii,
'Harriet Martineau.'

but saying to herself with closed eyes ' my book will do yet.' She wrote her preface that evening, and finished it as the Brewery clock struck two. At four o'clock she went to bed and cried herself to sleep, but at 8.30 she was up again, preparing and sending out her circulars. Thin, yellow and coughing with every breath she returned to Norwich."[36] She was self-sufficient and self-assertive. Her stories were dry and heavy; she was obviously a woman at whose feet no self-respecting lynx would cast his skin.

And what of George Eliot, sprung from the tradesman class, who, when the women of cultured families had had little hope of education, still could not repress her ambition for learning, and could not stifle in her mind the impulse to clothe in fiction a whole philosophy of life? We watch her acquiring knowledge, withdrawing into a world of her own fashioning, experimenting in literary form, doggedly driving upwards out of the stultifying mediocrity of her surroundings, until she becomes the assistant editor of a highly intellectual London review; the friend of Spencer; the author of novels which led Lord Acton to say that she was greater than Dante, and Herbert Spencer to exempt her works, as if they were not fiction, when he banned all novels from the London Library. She was guilty, however, of an unforgivable lack—she had no charm: " In fiction where so much of personality is revealed, the absence of charm is a great lack, and her critics who have been, of course, mostly of the opposite sex, have resented, half consciously perhaps, her deficiency in a quality which is held to be supremely desirable in a woman. George Eliot was not charming; she was not strongly feminine."[37] She was at the same time condemned for being an errant woman, and for being too masculine, for being depressingly equine and for being, in the words of George Meredith, " a mercurial little showman." And yet she wrote at least one immortal novel, this strange dark soul, whose gloom was rent by the lightnings of genius—this butt for youthful derision—a woman whom neither furs, nor ores, nor gems, nor silks, nor tippets could adorn.

[36] *Ibid.*
[37] *Ibid,* 'George Eliot.'

Whether women novelists wrote from genuine inspiration or from mere financial necessity, certain it is that they did not do so to win fame. Novels were a more likely source of notoriety than of fame even in Jane Austen's time. Writing at the end of the eighteenth century Fanny Burney had to say: " In the republic of letters there is no member of such inferior rank, or who is so much disdained by his brethren of the quill, as the humble novelist." [38] And Robert Bage, in proof that even the didactic school of novelists were not exempted from popular censure, says: "Novels are now pretty generally considered as the lowest of the human productions." [39]

Writing in 1798, Jane Austen, in her defence of the novelist's art, shows how contemptuously it was regarded even by the novelists themselves:

> I will not adopt that ungenerous and impolitic custom, so common with novel writers, of degrading, by their contemptuous censure, the very performances to the number of which they are themselves adding: joining with their greatest enemies in bestowing the harshest epithets on such works, and scarcely even permitting them to be read by their own heroine, who, if she accidentally take up a novel, is sure to turn over its insipid pages with disgust. Alas! if the heroine of one novel be not patronised by another, from whom can she expect protection and regard. I cannot approve of it. Let us leave it to the Reviewers to abuse such effusions of fancy in threadbare strains of the trash with which the press now groans. Let us not desert one another; we are an injured body. Although our productions have afforded more extensive and unaffected pleasure than those of any literary corporation in the world, no species of composition has been so much decried. From pride, ignorance, or fashion, our foes are almost as many as our readers; and while the abilities of the nine-hundredth abridger of the History of England, or of the man who collects and publishes in a volume some dozen lines of Milton, Pope, and Prior, with a paper from the Spectator, and a chapter from Sterne, are eulogised by a thousand pens, there seems almost a general wish of decrying the capacity and undervaluing the labour of the novelist, and of slighting the performances which have only genius, wit, and taste to recommend them. "I am no novel reader; I seldom look into novels; do not imagine that I often read novels; it is really very well for a novel." Such is the

---

[38] Fanny Burney, *Evelina* (1778), Preface.
[39] Robert Bage, *Hermsprong* (1796).

common cant. "And what are you reading, Miss ——?" "Oh!
it is only a novel!" replies the young lady; while she lays down
her book with affected indifference, or momentary shame. "It is
only Cecilia, or Camilla, or Belinda"; or in short only some
work in which the greatest powers of the mind are displayed, in
which the most thorough knowledge of human nature, the happiest delineation of its varieties, the liveliest effusions of wit
and humour, are conveyed to the world in the best chosen
language.[40]

One of the most striking proofs of the attitude which a sensible
and discreet person might take towards seeing his name on the
title page of a novel lies in the fact that Sir Walter Scott at first
published under a pseudonym. If a man shied away from such
publicity, a woman had an added reason for doing so, since
her defiance of conventionality would be so much greater than
his. Thus it is that the student of women's works of fiction
needs a pretty wit in resolving the mysteries which they have
woven about their authorship. Even literary success did not
always lure them into declaring their identity as we see, for
example, in the case of Jane Austen. Her novels were published
anonymously after they had mouldered in a drawer for years.
Pride and Prejudice, completed in 1797, was published in 1813;
Sense and Sensibility, completed in 1798, was published in 1811.
Northanger Abbey was sold to a publisher in Bath for £10 in
1803. He did not venture to print it, and was glad to take back
his money and return the manuscript to one of her brothers a
few years later, not realising until the bargain was complete that
the writer was also the author of four popular novels. Though
the authorship of the novels was an open secret to Jane Austen's
friends during her lifetime, it was not made public until after
her death, and while she lived she remained in obscurity. It
has been said that Fanny Burney "forced the superior sex to
acknowledge a woman's wit and grant her the right, never before
admitted, to think for herself and express her own opinions,
without loss of respectability or caste." [41]   If such had been
the case, Jane Austen and her works would not so long have
remained unknown; and there are not wanting many other
examples to prove that the prejudice against women-novelists

---

40 Jane Austen, *Northanger Abbey*, Ch. 5.
41 Brimley Johnson, *Novelists on Novels* (1928), page xxvi f.

persisted after Jane Austen's day. Fanny Burney, in addition to a small group of women-writers, was so fortunate as to win the praise and encouragement of Dr. Johnson, and it would have needed a stout heart indeed to have attacked the protégées of so doughty a champion of morality and learning.

But, with the coming of Jane Austen, a new note appears in the attitude of women-novelists. Criticism and indifference had until then driven them to expostulate, to cringe, or to defy, in accordance with their particular temperaments or circumstances. Jane Austen does neither. Her only apologia was a defence, not of women-novelists, but of the art of fiction, and she showed that neither fear nor opportunism could deflect her from her particular métier. She was fully aware of the artistic value of her work, and equally conscious of her limitations. Not even the patronage of a Prince Regent could persuade her to relinquish the right of keeping her own literary conscience. This is a milestone in the story of women-novelists, and though, there being only one Jane Austen, many women after her were to wheedle or to flout their public, the miracle had been accomplished, the miracle of a woman-novelist who was not conscious of inferiority, and whose work was not influenced in any way by what Fielding inimitably calls " a little reptile of a critic." [42]

Looking back over the long years since 1621, during which women persisted in writing fiction, we see, rising above the flood of mediocrity, certain names which connote something of value, which mark some definite contribution to the development of English fiction. In fact, so consistently did women keep step with the advance in novel-writing that to trace their progress is to trace the progress of the novel itself. To trace women's contribution to fiction is somewhat like tracing the contribution of a common soldier in a great campaign. It looks, at first, as if no one should ever hear of this undistinguished fighter—of his tireless energy, endurance and good humour, of his dogged refusal to go under without giving a good account of himself. It seems as if, granted these qualities, his natural limitations and an invidious convention would keep him in the ranks. But nothing in life is surer than that real ability coupled with ambition must

[42] Henry Fielding, *Tom Jones* (1749), Introd. to Bk. IV.

find its own level, and as the common soldier, indispensable even in his normal sphere, often by a stroke of genius so natural that it appears merely an impulse, saves the situation and turns the tide, so also women-writers not only shared all the dust and heat, but often by a culmination of originality and technique initiated a new genre of fiction.   There is no kind of novel which they did not attempt, and there are few kinds which they did not enrich. The pastoral novel, the novella, the picaresque, the satire, the novel of authenticated realism, the novel of sensibility, of manners, of domesticity, of social purpose, the Gothic novel, the Oriental novel, the epistolary novel, in all these genres they were active, many of them they helped to initiate, and in some of them they showed genius.

What is literary initiation?   It is easier to show what it is not.   It is not to give birth to an entirely new type of fiction which leaps fully armed like Pallas Athene from the head of Jupiter.   Literary initiation is the result of a slow development of certain literary tendencies which, almost unconsciously, come into being, and which await the mind which will recognise their value, and which by experiment will unify them and give them a recognised place among mature literary genres.   This Mrs. Radcliffe did for the Gothic novel, exerting an immense influence on the writers of the Romantic Revival; this Fanny Burney and Jane Austen did for the domestic novel and the novel of manners, revolutionising completely the conception of realism in fiction; this Charlotte Lennox did for the Anti-Romantic satire; this Mary Manley did for the epistolary novel; this Mary Shelley did for the pseudo-scientific tale of wonder; this George Eliot did for the philosophic novel; this Charlotte Brontë did for the subjective novel—the novel which shows life chiefly as it is reflected in an isolated soul.   Emily Brontë did far more than all this in her novel which, without ancestors or progeny, by one superb explosion of genius defies criticism and classification.

And it is not only in strength and patience, marching side by side with the men-writers who disowned them, nor in leadership to which they did not aspire, but to which their inspirations carried them, that women contributed to the English Novel.

They contributed to it also by giving to it a new conception of women. This they could not do for a long time, impeded by the Heroic tradition in accordance with which men and women writers alike purveyed to an apparently satisfied public women-characters who bore not the slightest likeness to reality. Not indeed that these heroic beauties, without passions or any characteristic of humanity, were more fantastic than the heroes whom they spurred on to terrific feats of devotion and valour. Both the authors and their public knew these fictional characters to be as completely outside nature as their background was outside geography. They were not aiming at reality, but at heroism which, fortunately for human comfort, does not much invade every-day life. Still, if the disguised princes subscribed to an amazing code of life, it was chiefly the incognito princesses who formulated it, and it does not surprise us to see, as time progressed, that these heroines, under the strain of such lofty sentiments, tended to an extreme delicacy of mind and body. No doubt another contributory cause of the lack of stamina in these ladies was that throughout an entire novel, running into many folio volumes, they never ate or drank. The men are almost as ethereal. Sir George Bellmour, romancing after the style of such knights so as to win the interests of Arabella, The Female Quixote, describes the hardships he endured for the love of his fair mistress (Polly Acorn, the milkmaid). His sufferings include ten months of melancholy sojourning in a forest:

> " Give me leave," said Sir Charles [the voice of common sense], " Give me leave to ask, If you eat in all this Time."
> "Alas! Sir," replied Sir George, "Sighs and Tears were all my Sustenance."[43]

By the time Charlotte Lennox wrote her burlesque, the heroic tradition was dead, but the era of sensibility was an established fact. That is to say, women in fiction now ate and drank, rode in coaches and went to balls like ordinary mortals; but whereas before they had wandered elegantly through an unreal world, now their surroundings were real, and the unreal world was within their breasts. If it had not been put there by Richardson, it had certainly been confirmed and licensed by him, and

[43] Charlotte Lennox, *The Female Quixote* (1752), ii, 98.

never surely did a more absurd fable delude the public, than that fable of Richardson's marvellous insight into the female heart. But so great was Richardson's vogue with his woman readers that, had it been possible for them to abjure nature, and regulate their cardiac activities according to the Richardsonian scheme, they would have done so. Alas! this was beyond even feminine adaptability. It must have been with mingled feelings of regret and relief that they found in the pages of Fanny Burney and Jane Austen just such women as themselves, women whose beauty, wit and wisdom were subject to decay; whose virtue was not infallible; who could suffer without histrionics, and who could love without illusion. True this had all been clothed in language a very long time before by the writer of the *Portuguese Letters*, but whether or not that authorship is to be ascribed to the nun of Beja, certain it is that English fiction had to await the coming of Emily Brontë to hear the authentic accents of love and grief.

And so at last we find women writing with confidence, for men and women alike, in a way both knew to be true, in language which they could mould to the technique of their art; and supported by a tradition of literary achievement which was so necessary for the free exercise of the female pen. Courage and self-respect are the necessary ballast of any fine endeavour. George Eliot, who withers with her scorn the silly and pretentious school of women-novelists, quietly turns away from them to show that women's achievement in fiction is so firmly established that it cannot be degraded by the fatuous female scribblers:

" Happily we are not dependent on argument to prove that Fiction is a department of literature in which women can, after their kind, fully equal men. A cluster of great names, both living and dead, rush to our memories in evidence that women can produce novels not only fine, but among the very finest; novels too that have a precious speciality lying quite apart from masculine aptitudes and experience " [44]—no mean record this, as we shall realise when we consider more fully their contributions.

[44] R. Brimley Johnson, *Novelists on Novels* (1928), p. 236 *et seq.* (Extracts from George Eliot 'Silly Novels by Silly Novelists, *Westminster Review*).

CHAPTER II

THE PASTORAL ROMANCE

"And when in Sydney's death, Wit ebbed in men,
It hath its spring-tide in a Female pen."
(Vaughan, *A Continuation of Sir Philip Sydney's Arcadia*.)

In 1621, in the person of Lady Mary Wroath, woman made her first contribution to English prose fiction. Having barely mentioned the name of the first English woman-novelist, we must at once retrogress after the manner of a writer who introduces his heroine only to leave her standing while he laboriously sketches in the background. But truly it would quite impossible to judge the work of Lady Mary Wroath without at first considering briefly the state of Elizabethan and Jacobean prose fiction of which her novel was an integral part.

The main point to be observed in regard to the prose fiction of the Elizabethan age is that on the whole it did not recognise itself as a separate literary medium. Narrative had undergone many changes in aim and in form, since the days of the old epics which had for their object the recital of certain events. This uncomplicated aim led to a direct form, to a treatment which Heine rightly called a classic treatment.[1] This treatment was classic because the form of that which was portrayed was identical with the idea of the portrayer. The wanderings of Ulysses, for example, represented merely the wanderings of a

[1] See *The Prose Writings of Heinrich Heine* (1887), 'Religion and Philosophy in Germany,' p. 163 ff.

man who was the son of Laertes and the husband of Penelope. There was no wider meaning, no esoteric significance, and for this reason there was complete harmony between the idea and the form. Classic art aimed only at representing the finite, and it succeeded by direct means. But this simplicity of aim and medium did not last. Man began to be troubled by subjective views of life. He realised that direct descriptions would not express what he now wished to say, and he attempted to convey his thoughts by parabolic means. This new treatment of the subject-matter was romantic; that is to say that the form did not reveal the idea through identity, but suggested what was beyond literal expression. To attain their effects the narrators changed and adapted the material of their tales, thus departing from the classic ideal of authenticity. But the fictional nature of these tales appeared to them a sign of decadence; deliberate fiction appeared too much of a pretence, and so we find, for long ages, a persistent effort to give authenticity to feigned stories.

From the epic to the cycles of romance, from classicism to romanticism, was the natural transition. It was held by some that romanticism was merely the decadence of classic art. But this would be to arraign also the realm of poetry, and particularly of lyric poetry. Romanticism grew from taking thought, from finding in life a depth of meaning below the surface. Romanticism either endeavoured to suggest such meaning through the agency of language, or else attempted to escape this subjective reality by taking refuge in literary compositions as far as possible unlike the world around them. This was the starting-point and material witness of their mental state. The ideal of the ancients was the man of action, and they feared for the man of action who might lose his manliness and become thought-sick. It is to be observed that with the Greeks romanticism did not arise until a period of national deterioration had set in. With the humiliation of Athens, the destruction of the Macedonian monarchy and of Asiatic Greece, political liberty was lost, and the main activities of the Greek people were rendered henceforth impossible. Disillusionment led to scepticism in religious and other forms of thought. Prose fiction grew from the decadence of poetry at this time. It was far from being an introspective kind of writing. On the contrary, it was merely an objective record of imaginary events which never had been, and which never could take place in the mortal world. This unreal, this romantic fiction was of different kinds; the short story, the imaginary journey to incredible countries, the romance of adventures, and the love intrigue; the Milesian tale—a particular type of amatory short-story—and the Pastoral romance. These tales were a refuge from the life which pressed too sorely upon men: and to escape more fully from reality, writers not only depicted unreal events, but projected them against a background which had no identifiable locus. The *Golden Ass* of Apuleius, the first romance of antiquity, was to have a strange and varied posterity, but, though the symbolic presentation of truth or beauty was often obscured, the escapist characteristic always remained, frequently with dire effect.

In common with every other literary movement the Romance of Chivalry had established itself abroad before reaching England. *Amadis de Gaul*, published in 1508, was available in manuscript and in oral recitative since about the year 1300. The Pastoral Romance, a sub-development of the Romance of Chivalry, had its originator in Longus, who was to pastoral prose fiction what Theocritus had been to pastoral poetry, but the fine simplicity of *Daphnis and Chloe* did not survive, and the pastoral novel really began its sophisticated course in the *Arcadia* of Sannazzaro. This work was surpassed in interest by Montemayor's *Diana Enamorada*, which was translated into English in 1583. Sydney's *Arcadia* was a fusion of the main characteristics of the Amadis cycle of chivalric romance, and of the pastoral romance.

Sydney was not aware that in his *Arcadia* he was adhering to a moribund form. The astonishing fact is that the Pastoral Romance which had first arisen in a decadent period was received in England with great enthusiasm at a period of re-birth. There were several reasons for this anomaly. In the first place, English prose fiction was in a very undeveloped state. It was too young to know its own nature or its bent, and not only so, but it was suffering from under-nourishment. Men's attention and abilities were focussed on the drama and on poetry. These Siamese

D

twins, considered really as one, were carefully nurtured and exhibited with pride, while fiction, that disowned foundling, pined in the cellar. The coming of the Pastoral Romance, with its pseudo-poetic style, made it possible for the poets to redeem the rickety outcast from inferior darkness, and to give it a place in the family circle. Under the protection of the poetic tradition, the Pastoral Romance, though always sickly, persisted in living for a long time. It was, for example, primarily because Sydney was a poet that he wrote the *Arcadia*. He maintained always the fallacious contention that all imaginative creation was poetry. This obsession which he shared with the established, conservative, literary forces of his period serves to show all the more clearly that the slow and painful transition from prose to poetry had not yet become an established fact in English story-telling.

In 1400, Chaucer had written an excellent story in verse. Although it owed much to Boccaccio, *Troilus and Cresseyde* showed at one stroke a remarkable power of construction and characterisation, and much subtlety in narrative device. But at least two hundred years elapsed before English fiction profited by this example, simply because it was impeded by the transition from verse to prose. Prose had an obvious advantage in story-telling. It was more economical than verse, and it could represent life more closely and more fully. Furthermore, the invention of printing gave to prose works a certainty of remembrance which until then had been possible only in verse. The trend towards prose was thus greatly hastened. But as verse had taken time to perfect itself as a medium for story-telling, so prose had now to be forged into a fit instrument for the writer of prose fiction. It had to become clear, ample, vivid, flexible and yet strong, capable of expressing the entire gamut of human experience. And while prose was thus evolving, the writers of prose fiction were endeavouring to clothe their stories in a kind of prose not yet suited to the purpose. The Elizabethan novel at its best was a living entity, with endless possibilities of thought and action, but unable yet to speak or act freely. Not only was the medium of expression lacking in resilience, but the very method of telling a story was as yet only glimpsed. The lesson of Chaucer's technique in story-telling was lost to succeeding prose writers, because they were confused by the change in medium, and seemed unable to apply to prose tales the methods which Chaucer had employed in verse-form.

This transition period gave to the prose story-teller a choice between two schools of writing, radically different in every respect. On the side of the privileged class, and springing from the poetic tradition, there was the Heroic Romance and the Pastoral Romance (the elements of which were often fused, as in the *Arcadia*); there was also, as a sub-classification, the sort of romance initiated and typified by Lyly's *Euphues* which for a long time had a great success, and which, strangled in an impossible style, contained portents of future developments in fiction. On the popular side, and chiefly of prose origin, there were the short, pithy, unpretentious stories which found their best expression in the form of the Italian *novelle,* and which were available in the collections of Painter, Whetstone, Fenton, and others; there were the moral tales, closely allied to the *novelle* and typified in the *Gesta Romanorum*[2]; there was popular satire which Langland's verse had established long before and which was now developed vigorously by such men as Nash and Greene; there were the stories of low life, such as the gest books, the picaresque tales, the cony-catching pamphlets; there were semi-fictitious and real biographies; there were Deloney's guild tales; and there was much letter-writing to imaginary people (an activity which later became a very important development in form). This popular school presented the realistic trend in fiction, which, because it had its roots in actual life, became increasingly alive, and held its ground through succeeding centuries to develop triumphantly into the modern novel.

Between the extreme right wing and the extreme left wing in fiction there was the simple prose romance of the burgher class, which later became the chap-book of the seventeenth and eighteenth centuries, as for example, *Guy of Warwick* and *Huon of Bordeaux.* These last were offshoots of the mediaeval cycles of romance which had found new life in homely soil, and which

2 Published by Wynkyn de Worde, 1577.

lived, therefore, when the larger cycles had passed from the memory of the people.

The popular school had its origin in folk-tales which had always existed orally side by side with the elaborate stories of the privileged classes. Its prose tradition and its unambitious aim saved it from an involved form. In fact, in identity of form and idea it might almost be called classic. It was direct, simple and all the more vital because it did not dissipate its energies in devious symbolism or elaborate intricacies. It was spontaneous, but often crude. The romantic kind of writing had its origin in poetry, but it had also found copious expression in prose. In the use of this prose medium it was, however, hampered by the conviction that its mission was poetic, and it therefore expended its energies on a mistaken object. It contained a diffused beauty and a deliberate melodiousness which were not evident in the people's tales, but it was cumbrous, artificial and in no way a representation of life. Indeed it intentionally aimed at portrayal of a world unconnected with reality. It is clear that the modern novel could not develop from such a school of fiction, because such writing could not become real. And it is equally clear that the novel could develop from the popular school of fiction, because the realistic writing of the ordinary people *could* become aesthetic and *could* find artistic devices to suit its purposes. The reality on which the novel must feed, if it were to grow, was the main virtue of this popular fiction, and time would enable it to achieve artistic form. When Sydney wrote, the Pastoral Romance was dying. To save it there would have been needed a transfusion of common blood, rich and varied food, great draughts of wine, fresh air and sunshine, and a complete change of scene. An inbred parent-stock, and a thin and rarefied existence had produced anaemia not more pernicious, however, than its posthumous influence. But it was not to die yet awhile. Unnatural fungus that it was, it was to draw new life from Sydney's death. When Sydney died at Zutphen, he established a tradition for romantic heroism which prolonged the life of the heroic romance, and which perpetuated its repute. It would have been well for subsequent fiction if Sydney had not been as noble in character as in lineage.

To be young, gifted, and heroic, to love with passionate austerity, and coin one's heart into lyrics; to die with an immortal sentence on one's lips—this is to create a legend, and the dazzling legend of Sydney blinded even the critical to the grave defects of the *Arcadia*.

Published in 1590, the *Arcadia* had an immense success. By 1600, there had been four editions. There were fourteen editions during the seventeenth century. In 1725 a three-volume edition appeared, and was reprinted in Dublin in 1739. From that time until 1907, only abridgements were printed. In 1725 appeared Mrs. Stanley's modernised version, with which Richardson was doubtless familiar, and from which he took the name of his heroine Pamela.

The *Arcadia* attracted a great number of imitators, who wished either to continue the story or to use it as a model for similar themes. In 1606, John Day wrote *The Ile of Guls*: "A little string or rivulet drawn from the full stream of the Right Worthy gentleman, Sir Philip Sydney's well knowne *Archadea*." Shirley dramatised many episodes in his *Pastoral called the Arcadia* (1640). Shakespeare may have embodied in the scenes between Gloster and his son, in *King Lear*, the story of the dispossessed king of Paphlagonia. Mr. C. Crawford has found traces of the *Arcadia* in *The Duchess of Malfi* and other plays by Webster. Francis Quarles, author of the *Emblemes*, made the story of Argalus and Parthenia the subject of a long poem (1622). Many writers linked their works to the fame of Sir Philip Sydney by mentioning his name on their title-pages, and one writer in particular found in her near relationship to this idolised man the courage to emerge into the world of letters under the protection of his glory.

In 1621, years after the first appearance of the *Arcadia*, Lady Mary Wroath published her stout folio, the *Urania*. This attempt at Pastoral Romance has for the most part been buried in oblivion. Very occasionally some searcher among the minutiae of literature brushes aside the dust of ages, and glances inside her book. The elaborate frontispiece does certainly justify Mr. E. A. Baker's remark that Lady Mary made great play with her pedigree on the title-page. The title runs:

The
Countesse
of Montgomeries
URANIA
Written by the right honourable the Lady
MARY WROATH
Daughter to the right Noble Robert
Earle of Leiçester
And niece to the ever famous and renowned
Sr. Phillips Sydney, Knight.   And to
The Most exelet Lady Mary Countesse of
Pembroke late deceased.

Lady Mary Wroath grew up within a charmed circle, in an
atmosphere of social and literary impeccability.   Sir Philip
Sydney was not only a true poet himself, but an extremely
generous literary patron.   The centre of all that was best in
Elizabethan poetry, and with his house and purse ever open to
needy writers, it was only natural that he should have been
beloved, and that he and his family should have been liberally
praised by the best poets of the day.   Sydney himself was
indeed worthy of the encomiums lavished upon him as a poet
and as a man, but, as we have already shown, the Countess of
Pembroke merely shone in a reflected glory which her literary
talents did not deserve.   It is not surprising that Lady Mary
Wroath should trust that the spell would hold in her case also.
Yet she did not determine to write until she was driven to it as
a last expedient.

The eldest daughter of Robert Sydney, first Earl of Leicester,
she married Sir Robert Wroath in 1604, at the age of eighteen.
She was often at court after her marriage, and King James
frequently visited her husband's estate at Durrants.   She was
a liberal and sympathetic patroness of literature, and as such was
honoured by many of the chief poets of the age.   It is recorded
that on Twelfth Night, 1604-5, she acted at Whitehall in Ben
Jonson's *Masque of Blackness*.   Jonson dedicated to her his play

The Alchemist (1610), as well as a sonnet and two epigrams. Chapman addressed to her a sonnet which was prefixed to his translation of Homer's *Iliad* (1614). George Wither and William Gamage offered similar tributes to " the most famous and hero- ike Lady Mary Wroath." But these pleasant circumstances came to an end with the death of her husband in 1614. She was left with an infant son, an income of £1,200 a year, and an estate swamped in debt. Nor had death ceased to ravage her happiness. Two years later her son died, and then her father. This last blow led to the complete wreck of her financial affairs, because, ignoring the trustees whom her father had appointed to administer her small possessions, she insisted on managing them herself. She soon proved her inability to do so, and her financial embarrassment became so serious that, in 1623, she was forced to petition the King for protection from her creditors for the space of one year. Prior to that date, however, she had determined on authorship as a solution of her difficulties.

The Countess of Montgomeries Urania was modelled on the *Arcadia*. As this literary venture was a financial speculation, it was to be expected that Lady Mary Wroath would adhere to the form which had already been received with acclamation, and which, to judge by sedulous imitators, was in the main stream of literary development. No doubt, she also hoped that a descendant of Sydney, using the pastoral medium, would strike home to the hearts of the reading public. It is quite possible, too, that she believed that she might be an inheritor of poetic gifts, and the fact that she was a woman would not deter her, in view of her aunt's reputation as a writer. Prolonged adulation is apt to destroy the critical faculty, and Lady Mary was not likely to judge aright either her aunt's talents or her own.

The *Urania* is an exceedingly complicated pastoral romance, after the Sydneian pattern. The scene is laid partly in the island of Pantaleria, governed by the Lord Pantalerius who, because of a grievance, is self-exiled from his own country. The heroine is Urania, apparently a shepherdess, but really a princess, daughter of the King of Naples. The hero is also of noble blood, Parselius, Prince of Morea. Minor characters linked to the main plot are Amphilanthus, brother of Urania, and

heir to the throne of Naples; and Leonius, the younger brother.
There are various subplots very slenderly connected with the
main plot. The story of the king of Albania and his children
is dull and digressive. There are other inset stories which are
equally digressive, but so far from dull that we must make
particular mention of them, when the main plot of *Urania* has
been outlined.

The beginning of *Urania* is a good example of the style in
which the book is written:

> When the Spring began to appear like the welcome messenger
> of Summer, one Sweet (and in that more sweet) morning, after
> Aurora had called all careful eyes to attend the day, forth came
> the faire shepherdesse URANIA (faire indeed; yet that farre too
> meane a title for her, who for beautie deserved the highest stile
> could be given by best knowing Judgements). Into the Meade
> she came, where usually she drave her flocks to feede, whose
> leaping and wantonesse showed they were proud of such a
> guide. But she, whose sad thoughts led her to another Manner
> of spending her time, made her soon leave them and follow
> her late begun custom: which was (while they delighted them-
> selves) to sit under some shade, bewailing her misfortune;
> while they fed to feed upon her owne sorrow and teares, which
> at this time she began again to summon, sitting down under
> the shade of a well-spread Beech; the ground (then blest) and
> the tree with full and fined leaved branches growing proud to
> beare and shadow such perfection. But she, regarding
> nothing in comparison of her woe, thus proceeded in her grief:
> Alas, Urania, said she, (the true servant of misfortune) of
> any misery that can befal a woman, is not this the most and
> greatest which thou are falne into? Can there be any neare
> the unhappinesse of being ignorant, and that in the highest kind,
> not being certain of my owne estate or birth? Why was I not
> still continued in the beleefe I was, as I appeare, a Shepherdes,
> and Daughter to a Shepherd?[3]

Other shepherds and shepherdesses having come into the
plain, the unhappy Urania endeavours to avoid them. She
climbs a hill and comes to a cave, the first of these subterranean
recesses mentioned in the story, but unfortunately not the last.
A jaundiced reader might be forgiven for thinking of the *Urania*
as a succession of caves, all full of royal personages, bemused

---

[3] Lady Mary Wroath, *Urania* (1621), .i., I.

and forewandered, who sit about endlessly narrating their misfortunes. On entering this, the first cave of the series, Urania
penetrates to an inner chamber, and discovers a sonnet (newly
written) lying on a stone table. A more remarkable discovery,
however, is a young man, lying on a bed of boughs, raving with
love and anguish of Limena. The Sydneian sentence is rather
an involved medium for delirium, and we learn, only after much
circumlocution, that this miserable wight is Persissus, nephew of
the King of Sicilie. He recounts the story of Limena whom he
believes murdered, and Urania very sensibly suggests that she
may not be dead. If not, let him find her. If so, let him
avenge her. Having thanked her in a speech of some thousand
words, Persissus leaves the cave to follow her advice, and Urania
drives home her flock.

Next day, Urania encounters a wolf, which is slain by two
beautiful youths, who are seeking food for their aged father.
Urania gives them for their food a lamb to which she has been
confiding her troubles a few minutes before. They all repair
to a sea-cave which shelters the aged father of Urania's rescuers.
Having bewailed their respective fates in the loftiest language,
they exchange mutual compliments, and Urania bids farewell to
the old man (who is, in fact, the exiled King of Albania)
and to his sons. She has not proceeded far when she meets still
another beautiful youth: Parselius, Prince of Morea. He has
left that country with his great friend and kinsman, Amphilanthus (heir to the Kingdom of Naples), with the object of finding
the lost sister of Amphilanthus, who was stolen when an infant.
It has been revealed to her father by divination that she is still
living. (The reader immediately smells a rat, but alas! it
takes hundreds of pages, a wilderness of misunderstandings and
oceans of tears before it becomes perceptible to Urania.)
Arrived in Sicily, Amphilanthus and Parselius go in different
directions in their search, arranging to meet a year later at the
court of the King of Naples. Parselius, while talking to Urania,
sees in her a resemblance to Leonius, a younger brother of
Amphilanthus, and he suspects her identity. He accompanies
her to the cave where the King of Albania and his wolf-slaying
sons have taken up quarters. Parselius engages to restore him

to his rights, and the aged man dies of joy.   Unfortunately, his sons are less susceptible to strong emotion.   Parselius then goes to see Persissus (the distraught adorer of Limena) and Urania goes home, in love with Parselius.

It would serve no good purpose to continue to outline so complicated, repetitive and extravagant a plot.   The scene shifts in kaleidoscopic fashion, and we find ourselves now in Pantaleria, now in Morea, now in Constantinople, Rhodes, Delos, Negropont, Pamphilia or Mytilene.   But in fact the scene is always Arcadia, and the blue-blooded shepherds and shepherdesses remain ever faithful to the heroic-pastoral code.   After many wanderings, exploits, and sufferings which serve merely to discover their enduring constancy, all the lovers are united, all the kings reinstated, and all the mysteries are resolved.

Since we have shown that Lady Mary devotedly copied the romantic characteristics of Sydney's novel, it is only just to show that like him she sometimes gives us beautiful little passages which are quite free from exaggeration.   She has been describing a disputatious, angry man who has deafened the company with his talk, and she says:

> When he was gone, the Roome was like a calme after a storme, or as after foule weather the Aire is silent, and sweete; so all being quiet, they pleased themselves as Birds in the Spring with their own tunes.

It has been maintained by such critics as have thought it worth while to mention Lady Mary Wroath, that the *Urania* is only a slavish imitation of the *Arcadia*, and that in her novel Lady Mary Wroath " copies and outdoes Sydney's utmost extravagances, both in the story and in the mode of telling it." [4] Certainly the *Urania* is " tedious . . . awkward and long-winded," [5] but is it really more so than the *Arcadia*?   One sometimes suspects the *Arcadia* of being so sacrosanct that it is not judged on its own merits even now.   Horace Walpole had the courage to judge the *Arcadia* apart from the aura of its author.   It was a critical honesty never displayed before and

4 E. A. Baker, *History of the English Novel* (1929), iii, 88.
5 D.N.B.

seldom since in this connection. Who will say that it is not wearying to plough through the *Arcadia,* or how many do so conscientiously, even in the cause of literary research? Indeed, it is so sacred that it is not often approached. The claims of the most learned commentators are not based on the intrinsic worth of the *Arcadia*—a question which they pass over almost in silence—but are entirely concentrated on its position in the development of English fiction, and on its influence on succeeding generations. Its position is said to emphasise the period of poetic invention which came between the period of traditional writing, and the development of realism. This is true, but it is perhaps more cogent to note that the *Arcadia* copied a mode of fiction which was passing, if not already past, and that, in consequence, the *Arcadia* is simply a digression in the development of the English novel. Its direct imitators were therefore splashing about in a backwater, while the main river and its tributaries flowed on surely to the open sea. As for the influence of the *Arcadia,* it is entirely to be deplored, and its occasional poetic beauties do not compensate for the fact that for long centuries English fiction was cursed with this heritage of artificial sentimentality. Certainly the French Heroic Romance was a most powerful influence in perpetuating this sort of writing in England, but it could not have had such a ready reception if Sydney had not already prepared the English mind for these extravagances, and established the Heroic Romance by force of his own personal and literary prestige.

The *Urania* sedulously copied, and possibly exaggerated, all the defects of the *Arcadia,* and if it could claim nothing individual it would simply not be worth mentioning. But this work of Lady Mary Wroath's does contain an individual feature of great interest and significance from the standpoint of fictional development; that is, the introduction of minor stories in subject and manner of the type of the *novelle.* These sub-plots are attached by very slender filaments to the main theme of the *Urania* and they are not ambitious in quality, but they give to the *Urania* the significance of uniting the realistic and the romantic genres. In a word, the *Urania* is not merely, like the *Arcadia,* representative of a decadent and retrogressive kind of fiction. It is also symptomatic of the way in which realism was developing in its own genre and was henceforth to obtrude itself in alien territory.

The best of these stories is that of Limena and Persissus. It is simple, direct, vivid. When the characters speak, they do so without circumlocutions. Limena is the daughter of a duke, who before departing for the wars in support of his king, bestows her in marriage on " a great Lord in the Country," named Philargus. This he does to ensure her safety and protection, but he does not take into account that Limena and a noble youth called Persissus are deeply in love with each other. Persissus, indeed, does not know that Limena loves him until he visits her some time after her marriage, in the home she shares with her husband and her father. They see each other frequently though innocently, but the husband is suspicious. " That night," says Persissus, " I saw her, but spake not to her, so curiously her husband watched us, yet could he not keepe our eies, but by them we did deliver our soules." The next day Philargus in his jealousy takes her away with him from their home; "And so went all worth with this odd man to have her delicacy like a Diamond in a rotten box." Persissus, however, takes the opportunity of seeing her on his way to camp, and she tells him of her husband's jealousy. Persissus had observed her paleness.

Desirous to know the cause, I remain'd almost impatient not venturing to speak to her before her husband for hurting her; but he going out of the roome, after we had supped, either to cover the flames which were ready to break out in huge fires of his mistrust, or to have the company fitter for him, affecting still to be chiefe: his absence, however, gave me opportunitie to demand the reason of her strangeness; she sigh'd to hear me call it so : and with tears told me the reason, concluding; and thus do you see my Lord (said she) the torments I suffer for our love; yet do you more torture me with doubting me, who have no happiness left me, but the knowledge of my faith to you, all afflictions being welcome to me, which for your sake I suffer. Between rage and paine, I remain'd amazed, till she, taking me by the hand, brought me more wofully to myselfe with these words. And yet am I brought to a greater mischiefe; with that fixing her weeping eyes upon mine . . . I must my Lord (said she) entreat you to refraine this place since none can tell what danger may proceed from mad, and unbridled jealousie; refraine your sight? Command me then to die (said I) have I deserved to be thus punished? Shall this brutishness undoe my blessings? Yet this place I will, since you will have it so, hoping you will find some means to let me know Philargus house is not in all places. That I will doe, or die (said she).

Persissus departs the next day. He gets news from Limena that her husband intends to murder her. Persissus gives the following description of the interview between husband and wife:

After my departure from his house to the Citie, and so to the Campe, the Jealous wretch finding my Ladie retired into a Cabinet she had where she used to passe away some part of her unpleasant life; coming in, he shut the dore, drawing his sword, and looking with as much fury, as jealous spite could with rage demonstrate, his breath short, his sword he held in his hand, his eyes sparkling as thick and fast as an unperfectly kindled fire with much blowing gives to the Blower, his tongue stammering with rage bringing forth these words; thou hast wrong'd me, vild creature : I say thou hast wrong'd me; she who was compounded of virtue and her spirit, seeing his wild and distracted countenance guest the worst, wherefore mildly she gave this answere : Philargus, saide she, I know in mine owne heart I have not wrong'd you, and God knows I have not wrong'd myself.

There was no dialogue in the *Arcadia*. There is breathless dialogue here. There is dramatic urgency in the abrupt sentences, in the emphatic repetition, in the suspense which awaits violence. The simple dignity of the wife's reply makes the husband's fury seem all the more savage. This is how the scene might be described orally, by one who was actually present, and its spontaneous rightness, its realism is in complete contrast with the flowery Arcadian style. Space does not permit further quotation, so we must content ourselves with recounting briefly the remainder of the story. The husband is not depicted as a complete villain. We are shown love struggling in him before finally, through jealousy, it turns to hatred. He gives his wife two days in which to decide whether to lure Persissus to death or to die herself. She chooses to die, and Philargus takes her into a nearby wood. There he intends to murder her, but having inflicted some minor wounds, changes his mind. He takes her with him then into a distant retreat, and continues daily to torture her until she is rescued by a passing knight, who engages Philargus in combat and slays him. At that moment Persissus chances to pass that way. Philargus gives his blessing to the lovers before expiring, and they live happily ever after.

Limena's account of her sufferings is not in as realistic a style as Persissus's narrative, but although the end of the tale is rather romantic in language, it is quite just to say that this minor story is in substance and manner reminiscent of the *novelle*. Other stories worthy of mention in the same connection are that of Belizia which is good but brief, and the story of Bellamira which is also illustrative of the same trend.

It is not for a moment suggested that Lady Mary Wroath deliberately aimed at realism in those parts of the *Urania* which we have described. On the contrary, we know that she did everything in her power to imitate the style of the *Arcadia*. But apparently there were times when the strain of the Arcadian prose proved too great, and Lady Mary took a short respite to draw breath, before returning to her precarious and exhausting performance. It has been excellently said that " Sidney in the ' Arcadia ' is like the coryphée in some elaborate ballet, swimming indefatigably through the mazes of an intricate dance." [6] Lady Mary's weaker muscles craved relief from the exquisite agony of unnatural posturing, and in the intervals she became her real self. Perhaps, also, she was more at home in some of her tales, simply because she was drawing on events within her experience.

One cannot at this late date assert that Lady Mary's realistic little stories were those founded on the amorous adventures of some of her contemporaries. It is not possible now to identify the details of age-old scandals, but we know that the book had, to some extent, a satiric intention and that it set Jacobean society by the ears. On December 15th Lady Mary wrote to Buckingham, assuring him that she had never intended her book to offend anyone, and stating that she had stopped its sale.[7] On March 9th, 1623, Chamberlain wrote to his friend Carleton, enclosing " certain bitter verses of the Lord Denny upon the Lady Mary Wroath, for that in her book of *Urania* she doth palpably and grossly play upon him and his late daughter, the Lady Mary Hay, besides many others she makes bold with: and, they say,

6 E. A. Baker, *History of the English* Novel (1929), iii, 88.
7 Hist. MSS. Comm. 2nd Rep., p. 60.

takes great liberty, or rather license to traduce whom she pleases, and thinks she dances in a net." Chamberlain adds that he has seen the answer by Lady Mary to these verses of Lord Denny, but that he did not consider it worth the writing out.[8] These proofs make it clear that Lady Mary's declaration of innocence was disingenuous, and it is a sobering thought that the first woman-novelist in English literature could not refrain from that kind of veiled slander which later developed into the histoire scandaleuse. There was a vast moral and social gap between a Lady Mary and a Mrs. Manley. Why did Sir Philip Sydney's niece stoop to besmirch a family record of nobility which so recently had been a national glory? Perhaps she had observed that, though the dead Sydney moved the hearts of men " more than with a trumpet," those same hearts were quite impervious to the misfortunes of his nearest descendant. Perhaps she realised that though the Countess of Pembroke was revered for literary feats which were either puerile or supposititious, the Lady Mary Wroath could expect no indulgence from the literary world of which she was no longer the patron. It was precisely because she anticipated cold criticism that she larded her title-page with the names of those who had died at the zenith of fame, before they could commit the social solecism of becoming poor. The satiric intention in the *Urania* was not without antique precedent, for the Eclogues of Baptista Mantuanus satirised allegorically in pastoral dialogues the social and moral vices of fifteenth century Italy. No doubt, in attacking her contemporaries, she aimed at making her book more saleable. Veiled slander, however, is not a passport to fame, however productive it may be of immediate notoriety. Even if the *Urania* were as good a book as John Barclay's *Argenis* which appeared in the same year, it would have had less permanent success, and less influence, because while political or social satire is sufficiently wide in aim to save it from an appearance of spite, personal satire always creates a revolution of feeling in its own time, and falls into oblivion when the earth lies heavily alike on the slanderer and the slandered.

---

8 *Court and Times of James I,* ii, 298; Cal. State Papers. Dom. 1619-23. p. 356; Hist. MSS. Comm. 3rd Rep., p. 179. Hatfield. Mss.

It is unnecessary to comment on the fact that Lady Mary copied, in the Urania, the practice of introducing verse into the romance.   This custom, to which Sydney adhered in the *Arcadia*, was of Italian origin, and was certainly no advantage to prose fiction.   Most of Lady Mary's poetry is facile and superficial.   In dismissing it, however, one may mention some verses which combine sincerity and grace: chiefly " Love, what art thou?" "Come, merry Spring, delight us," and "Who can blame me if I love?"   She used the sonnet with little depth, but with great mastery of form.   The perfect Italian form of sonnet 4 is worthy of note.

It is a paradox that Lady Mary Wroath's best claim to remembrance lies in her accidental realism.   Two other women wrote Arcadian novels.   In 1651, Anne Weamys published *A continuation of Sir Philip Sydney's Arcadia*, which had its second edition in 1690.   When she wrote it a king had been beheaded, and England had been convulsed in political revolution and civil war; when it was republished, a King had returned, bringing with him a new era in national and literary history—a curious proof, if proof were needed, of the divorce between the Pastoral and the real, of the difficulty of killing a romantic school of writing, and of its escapist nature.   Between the two editions of the *Continuation* appeared Mlle. de la Roche Guilhem's *Almanzor and Almanzaida.   A Novel written by Sir Philip Sidney, And found since his Death amongst his Papers.* This work merits no particular attention, but it will not be out of place to comment on the novel of Anne Weamys.

The full title of this novel defined the particular subject-matter of the narrative:

> *A CONTINUATION of Sir Philip Sydney's Arcadia wherein is handled the Loves of Amphialus and Helena Queen of Corinth, Prince Plangus and Erona*
> *With the Historie of the Loves of Old Claius and Young Strephon to Urania*
> *Written by a young Gentlewoman*
> *Mtis A.W.*

Thomas Heath, the bookseller, woos the " ingenius Reader " in an introductory letter. He begs him not to marvel that heroic

Sydney's renowned fancy should be pursued to a close by a feminine pen. Here is " Sir Philip's fantasie incarnate: both Pamela's Majestie and Philoclea's Humilitie exprest to the life in the person and style of this Virago. In brief, no other than the lively Ghost of Sidney, by a happie transmigration, speaks through the organs of this inspired Minerva."

It is to be feared that the lively ghost of Sydney would not endorse Heath's volatile words. In fact, if it were possible for lively ghosts to tear their hair, then indeed Sir Philip's locks would fall thick as autumnal leaves. Granted that a continuation always lacks cohesion with the original work, at least it should aim at artistic unity, and it should have for its object the same aesthetic principles. Sydney was guided by the principle that all imaginative invention was poetry, and to this end he evolved a prose style which was intended to be poetic, and which in its billowing, emotional prolixity was in itself a figure of the romantic complications which it expressed. But, though Anne Weamys continues the adventures of some of Sydney's characters, she does not do so in Sydneian prose. Lady Mary Wroath imitated Sir Philip Sydney's style with more or less success, and occasionally lapsed into everyday language. Anne Weamys never lapses into everyday language, and never attempts Sydneian prose. She never attempts it—not because she could not. Her writing has a consistent style of its own which shows her ability to govern language. She tells her story in a pastoral manner, but she avoids the swaying garrulity of Sydney's style, and expresses herself in a style which, though certainly romantic, is clear, straightforward and economical. Let us for a moment ignore the story which has really nothing to do with our contention, and support our argument by comparing certain characteristic manners of writing. Here is Sir Philip Sydney's description of the love of Pyrocles for Philoclea:

> Pyrocles, who had that for a law unto him, not to leave Philoclea in anything unsatisfied, although he still remained in his former purpose, and knew that time would grow short for it, yet hearing no noise, the shepherds being as then run to Basilius, with settled and humble countenance, as a man that should have spoken of a thing that did not concern himself, bearing even in his eyes sufficient shows that it was nothing but

E

Philoclea's danger which did anything burden his heart, far stronger than fortune, having with vehement embracing of her got yet some fruit of his delayed end, he thus answered the wise innocency of Philoclea: "Lady, most worthy not only of life, but to be the very life of all things; the more notable demonstrations you make of love so far beyond my desert, with which it pleaseth you to overcome fortune, in making me happy: the more am I, even in course of humanity, to leave that love's force which I neither can nor will leave, bound to seek requital's witness that I am not ungrateful to do which, the infiniteness of your goodness being such as I cannot reach unto it, yet doing all I can and paying my life which is all I have, though it be far, without measure, short of your desert, yet shall I not die in debt to my own duty.[9]

" Faire Mistress " (says Nicholas Breton, once in the service of Sir Philip Sydney, and on Sydney's death devoted to the service of the Duchess of Pembroke):

Faire Mistresse, to court you with eloquence were as ill as to grieve you with fond tales: let it therefore please you rather to believe what I write, than to note how I speake . . . I could commend you above the skies, compare you with the Sun, or set you among the Stars, figure you with the Phoenix, imagine you a goddesse, but I will leave such weak praising fictions, and think you only yourself, whose vertuous beauty, and whose honourable discretion in the care of a little kindnesse is able to command the love of the wise, and the labours of the honest.[10]

Anne Weamys gives the following description of the love-sick Plangus:

In this sweet place, he sat himself down, with an intention to rest his wearied limbs under a branched tree, whilest his servants refreshed themselves and baited their horses, but no ease could be harboured in his disquieted heart, his eys being no sooner closed, but that he saw Erona burning in their unmerciful fire: at which sight he staringly opened them, and determined with himself, that since sleep would procure no comfort to him, other than Tragical scenes, he would never enjoy any contentment before he had settled Erona in her throne in safetie.[11]

9 Sir Philip Sydney, *Arcadia* (ed. Baker, 1907), Bk. IV, p. 545.
10 The Works in Verse and Prose of Nicholas Breton (ed. Grosart, 1879): 'Letter of Love to a Gentlewoman' (No. 19)
11 Anne Weamys, *The Continuation of Sir Philip Sydney's Arcadia* (1651), pp. 10, 11.

One observes that Anne Weamys' style is neither as flowery as Sydney's, nor as direct as Breton's. If, however, we compared her with Breton alone, her pastoral romantics would seem emphasised. She thus describes a summer morning:

> At last he entered the pleasant country of *Arcadia,* which was adorned with stately woods : no cries were heard there but the lambs, and they in sport too sounded their voices to make their playfellow lambs answer them again in imitation of the like. And the abundance of shadie trees that were there, were beautiful with the sweet melodie of birds.

But Breton exclaims, in his *Merry Dialogue*:

> Oh, to see in a faire morning, or a Sunnie evening the lambes and Rabbits at bace, the birds billing, the fishes playing, and the flowers budding. Who would not leave the drinking in an Ale-house, the wrangling in a dicing house, the lying in a market, and the cheating in a fayre; and think that the brightness of a faire day doth put down all the beauties of the world.[12]

This world of Breton's is the real world, and he wrote in the springtime of realism, when the sap was running free in the youthful stock and showing its energy in proliferation. Anne Weamys' style was very far from this, but it was far also from the style of Sydney. She could steady herself to write with dignified incisiveness such passages as the following:

> It is Justice to bring murderers to their deserved punishments. And because you Prince Plangus testifie yourself to be such an affectionate friend to my dear children, shew yourself one in their revenge; you I will entrust to be the General of my Armie; prove as valiant now as you have ever done; let all your aim be at Plexirtus; and, if possible, convey him hither alive, that he may die a publick spectacle of shame and terror before all the People.[13]

As for the plot of the *Continuation,* it is complicated, but well constructed. It is a noticeable fact that, in a period of literary long-windedness, and in a medium which has always connoted

[12] *The Words in Verse and Prose of Nicholas Breton,* (ed. Grosart, 1879) : 'A Merry Dialogue,' originally published in 1603.
[13] Anne Weamys, *The Continuation* (1651), p. 288.

prolixity, Anne Weamys tells her involved story without a single digression, and without a single ambiguity.   No doubt there are parts which are too synoptic, and which might have pleased more if they had been elaborated, but this is the fault of her very good quality of verbal economy.   Anne Weamys subscribes to the Pastoral convention, but she keeps one eye on real life.   Her heroes and heroines (and there are about ten of them) show energy and commonsense in achieving their purposes, and never evince the slightest inclination to confide their troubles to lambs. They pursue a life which contains love and adventure—too much love and too much adventure to be realistic, but also too much realism to be truly pastoral.   Anne Weamys' book is at the parting of the ways.   Mopsa, in the *Continuation* is presented with humour.   Her fairy-tale of the King's daughter is really funny, and is told with all the deviousness and love of proverb one would expect in such a narrative.

To conclude, the works of Lady Mary Wroath and of Anne Weamys are of value, because of their position in regard to the romantic and the realistic schools.   The social position of these writers made it inevitable that they should choose the aristocratic medium.   Had a woman of a lower social stratum wished to write a novel, she would, no doubt, have gravitated towards the realistic fiction of her class, but in point of fact no such woman could have written a book at that period, because she would have lacked the necessary education.   Women of the upper classes, in Elizabethan and Jacobean times, had such " education " as permitted them to read romances.   They had no education in the real sense of the word.   Naturally, the books they read were those written for their own social class, and very often dedicated actually to their sex, for in that period well-bred women assumed an important position as readers of fiction.   Such works, for example, as Lyly's *Euphues* were dedicated to feminine readers. If a female were actually entreated to read such works, then a female, greatly daring, might write one—if she could.   But to begin one's career in fiction with no choice but the Pastoral medium might well have daunted the stoutest feminine spirit. Lady Elizabeth Carew, for example, wrote a play,[14] but the

14 *Mariamne, or the Fair Maid of Jewry.*

drama, with its acts, and scenes, gave, as it were, a neat form into which one might pour one's ideas, and this form was far shorter, and required less of a sustained effort. The construction of the pastoral novel, and the exigencies of the style were such feats for these first women-novelists, that one can only liken it to a child who achieves an entrechat before he has learnt to stand. Both women are best in their more realistic vein—so that however small their contribution it was in accordance with the vital trend in fiction. " Be eloquent in plainness " said Nicholas Breton, " You must not speak in the clouds to them that are acquainted with the moon." [15]   We shall see in the following chapter whether other women writers were able to comply with this injunction.

[15] *The Works in Verse and Prose of Nicholas Breton* (ed. Grosart, 1879) : 'A Post with a Packet of Mad Letters,' No 19.

CHAPTER III

BIOGRAPHY.

"There is nothing I dread more than Death, I do not mean the Strokes of Death, nor the pains, but the oblivion in Death."

"Tears are apt to flow especially from moist brains. But deep sorrow hath dry eyes, silent tongues and aching hearts."

(Both from the *Sociable Letters* of the Duchess of Newcastle.)

From the Arcadian shepherdesses to the representation of real women in fiction was a great transition, and it was long before this gap was bridged. In the meantime, however, we are not without testimony as to the manner in which women of flesh and blood acquitted themselves in the environment in which it was their fate to live. We may listen to their voices endeavouring to relate how they fared in the complicated adventure of life. Such records remain in biographical form.

In the second half of the seventeenth century, four women wrote biographies. They were: the Countess of Montgomery, the Duchess of Newcastle, Mrs. Lucy Hutchinson and Lady Fanshawe. Their narratives are simply the written testimony of actual fact, but nevertheless they are significant in the development of prose fiction.

The biography is a form of writing which is analogous to fiction and which became a recognised fictional form. It requires sound construction and the sustained power of telling a story. In structure, therefore, its kinship with the novel is obvious. In

treatment, both genres require imagination, with this fundamental difference that the biographer may not invent or adapt
his material as the novelist does. But in the biography, as in
the novel, the imagination is exercised by the need for selectivity,
artistic emphasis and vivid presentation. These characteristics
give the biography a quality not easily distinguished from fiction
of the simple narrative form. This parallelism is extremely
important, as it paved the way for the pseudo-biographies which
from very early times had been presented as truthful narratives.
Such literary imposition arose from the necessity of disarming
the suspicions with which the reading public regarded fiction.
Readers continued to be haunted by the old classical tradition of
authenticity, and they enjoyed their feigned stories with a freer
conscience if they were assured that these stories were veracious
accounts of actual happenings. The biography was a type of
prose narrative which originally was its own guarantee of truth,
so it was natural that writers of fiction, who wished to give
plausibility to their narratives, should take advantage of this self-
authenticating form. The biographical form was indeed so much
used as a passport to credulity that it became difficult to distinguish a true narrative from mere fiction. Now, it is clear that
to have an appearance of authenticity, a narrative should record
credible events, and should depict them in a convincing manner,
that is to say, in a realistic manner. Thus, this pseudo-authentic
kind of writing was a powerful agent in the development of
realistic fiction. Finally, as we have already remarked, the real
and the invented telescoped, and facts presented as fiction seemed
ultimately to belong to the same genre as fiction which was
circumstantially vouched for as fact. Realistic fiction was served
by pseudo-authentic biography, which, in turn, was modelled
on real biography. We cannot therefore adequately review the
work of women in prose fiction without examining their earlier
efforts as biographers. It should be remembered that biographies
written by women, after prose fiction had established its right
to independence, have a separate existence, and therefore do not
come within our scope. The most immature biography, at this
elementary stage of fiction, is of more significance than the most
perfect biography at the period when biography and prose fiction

had established themselves as distinct genres of writing—the reason being that women who tried to tell a story of real events were in the main stream of realistic story-telling, whether or not their stories were true.

Because of their sex, it was daring of Lady Mary Wroath and Anne Weamys to write, but they had employed a form which was considered to be poetry, and which, furthermore, was sanctified by its greatest exponent in England. Had they attempted a *Jack of Newberie* or some other form of democratic fiction, it would have been considered an outrage. The four women whose writings we are about to consider also chose a safe medium, because, although biography cannot naturally be considered as poetry, neither is it a feigned tale. Not indeed that the Duchess of Newcastle would have given a fig for such conventions, if she had chosen to write a romance, but actually she had the most complete scorn for " romanceys ", which she stigmatises as the adulterous offspring of History and Poetry—a significant remark. To Lucy Hutchinson, as a rigid Puritan, romances were anathema. Whatever were the views of Lady Fanshawe, her wanderings gave no leisure for writing. The Countess of Montgomery's life was not of a kind to give her much faith in romance, and, in addition, hers was the sort of mind which prefers facts not softened by illusion.

Anne Clifford, fourth Countess of Montgomery, was more redoubtable as a woman than as a writer. In fact, she never aimed at a literary production, and her biography is little more than a summary of the main events of her life. Probably she undertook it to verify for the benefit of her children her claim to the Clifford possessions in the North of England, which had been the object of litigation for thirty-eight years of her life. There are touches in the narrative, however, which show that it was to her something more satisfying than a mere deposition of facts that might be useful to her legal heirs. The manuscript in the first person, as written by the Countess, has never been published. It was copied by Henry Fisher, 1737, and this copy is available in the British Museum. *The Proceedings of the Archaeological Institute at York*, edited by Hailstone in 1846, contains a third-person version of the autobiography. This account was taken from a small quarto volume containing an abstract of the great volumes of records which were " collected by the care and painfull industry of Margaret Russell, Countess Dowager of Cumberland, out of the various offices and courts of this Kingdom, to prove the right title which her only childe, the Lady Anne Clifford, now Countess of Pembroke, had to the inheritance of her ancestors." The original first-person account is naturally more vivid and more authentic, and has, therefore, been used by the present writer. It is part of a manuscript entitled: *A summary of the Lives of the Veteriponts, Cliffords and Earls of Cumberland, And of the Ladye Anne, Countess Dowager of Pembroke, Dorsett, And Montgomery, and Daughter and Heir to George Clifford Earl of Cumberland, in whom ye name of the said Cliffords determined! Copied from ye original manuscript ye 29th of December 1737 by Henry Fisher.* Then follows the heading: *A summary of the Records, and a True memorial of the life of me the Lady Anne Clifford.* Her titles are fully appended.

Anne Clifford began to write her autobiography when she was sixty-three years old. Twenty-four years later the narrative was broken off by her death, but it was practically complete then, enumerating all the main events of her life from the moment of her birth. Enumerating but not describing—that is the main characteristic of Anne Clifford's writing—for nothing which she records is as astounding as her omissions. This woman lived under six reigns—Elizabeth, James I, Charles I, the Commonwealth, Charles II, and James II, and yet she contrives to say nothing at all about the great fluctuations in government, in religion, in social life, and in literature which constituted the background of her life. She has nothing to say of Elizabeth's court, nothing to say of Jacobean times or of the Mayflower's sailing; nothing to say of Cromwell, or of the beheading of Charles. She makes two references to the Civil War—one being that, as it were " very hot ", it was necessary for her to change her residence; the other, a remark that her estates in the north were for a time rendered profitless by these disturbances. She does not profess herself an adherent of either party. Of the extraordinary event of the Restoration, of the surprising marriage of James II, and of the insecurity of his rule she has still nothing to say. She never refers to a single literary work, out of all the poems, plays, romances, polemics, and multiform writings which deluged England during her life-time, and many of which she certainly read. She is silent as to the changing social customs which she saw arise and decline within her span. Only once does she designate a friend, and an enemy. Certainly it is true that she dictated her narrative to a secretary, and that it would therefore be necessary for her to keep her own counsel as to private matters, but there are many omissions and reticences which discretion did not require, and one is at a loss to explain them. Perhaps she believed that commentary should not be included in a biography. Perhaps she was so busied in performing all that she deemed necessary before death snatched her away, that she saw little value in recording her thoughts. She was a practical woman, and when she wrote she was already old.

What was she doing for the eighty-seven years of her life? She was involved in a tedious law-suit. Her mother died. She had two worthless husbands and seven children. She gained possession of her estates, and restored them. But this is merely the framework of a life, within which the mind and character would demonstrate themselves. Not from her utterances, but from her reticences are her mind and character revealed, and it needs the external testimony of her contemporaries to fill in the outline of her personality: " She had a clear soul shining through a vivid body ",[1] said Dr. Rainbow, who preached her funeral sermon. " She knew well how to discourse of all things, from predestination to slea-silk."[2] testified Dr. Donne. " Her house was a school for the young, and a retreat for the aged; an asylum for the persecuted, a college for the learned, and a pattern for all."[3] It is characteristic that this woman who never refers to Spenser, had a monument erected to him in Westminster Abbey. Neither did she mention the poet Daniel, her tutor, nor the verses he dedicated to her in her youth, but the

1 *Funeral Sermon of the Countess of Pembroke,* preached by Edward Rainbow, Bishop of Carlisle, 1677.
2 *Ibid,* p. 38.
3 Dr. Whitaker, in his *History of Craven.*

memorial to him in Beckington Church is the material testimony of her affection.

Anne Clifford was of a strong and undemonstrative character, not imaginative, quite free from sentimentality, but capable of deep feeling. She was inflexibly tenacious of her rights, meticulously observant of the rights of others; frugal in her own way of living, extremely generous to her friends and dependants. Her benevolence and her sense of justice rose above her sense of injury, as is well seen in the fact that she even educated and portioned the illegitimate children of her first husband. She never was, however, a sweet, suffering saint, but was strongly combative of any infringement of her proper prerogatives. However dubious the authenticity of the letter she is supposed to have sent to Sir Joseph Williamson, in style and sentiment it is very characteristic. Williamson, then secretary of state to Charles II, had written to the Countess, naming a candidate for her pocket borough of Appleby. The following answer is ascribed to her:

> I have been bullied by an usurper, I have been neglected by a Court, but I will not be dictated to by a subject. Your man sha'n't stand.—Anne Dorset, Pembroke and Montgomery.

Anne Clifford was born at Skipton Castle on the 30th January, 1590. The woman of sixty-three looks back over the years, and thus describes the childish self she remembers:

> I was very happy in my first Constitution both in mind and body, both for internal and external endowments, for never was there child more equally resembling both father and mother yn my self, ye color of mine Eyes were black like my father, & ye form and aspect of ym was quick & lively like my Mothers, the hair of my head was brown & very thick, & so long yt it reached to the calf of my legs, when I stood upright, with a peak of hair on my forehead, & a Dimple in my Chin, like my father full Cheeks & round face like my Mother, & an exquisite shape of body resembling my father, but now time & age hath long since ended all those beauties, which are to be compared to the grass of the field. Isaiah 40.6.7.8. 1 Pet. 1.24. for now when I caused those memorables to be written I have passed the 63d year of my Age. And tho I say it, the perfection of my Mind, were much above those of my body; I had a strong and copious memory, a sound Judgment and a discerning Spirit,

and so much of a strong imagination in me, as that many times even my Dreams & apprehensions before hand have proved to be true.

Her father died when Anne was about 16 years old, and by his will all his castles, lands and honours were left to his brother, Francis, who succeeded him in the earldom, and to Francis' male heirs, but all these possessions were to revert to Anne if the male heirs failed. Anne chose as legal guardian her mother who at once began " to sue out a Livery in the Court of Wards for my right to all my fathers lands by way of prevention to hinder . . . . the livery which my Uncle of Cumberland intended to sue out in my name, without either my consent or my mother's ". Thus the great law-suit began its tortuous course.

Anne Clifford was married in 1609 to Richard Sackville, afterwards second Earl of Dorset. By him she had three sons, all of whom died young, and two daughters: Margaret, who married the subsequent Earl of Thanet, and Isobel, who married the third Earl of Northampton.

In 1616, Anne's mother died, about six weeks after Anne had visited her for the last time:

And the 2nd of that April 1616, I took my last leave of my Dear & blessed Mother with Many tears & much sorrow to us both. Some quarter of a mile from Brougham Castle in ye open Air after which time she and I never saw one another.

Of all the afflictions which beset Anne Clifford this was the heaviest, and again and again she recurs to this focal point of pain. In fact, in no other point was she very vulnerable, as she later explains.

After she had been married for fifteen years, her husband died. Her life with him had made her averse to marrying again, and this disinclination was confirmed by an attack of small-pox, which destroyed her good looks. She did marry, however, in 1630, and it seems probable that she was influenced in this decision by her feeling that a powerful connection would strengthen her legal claims: " This 2nd Marriage of Mine was wonderfully brought to pass by ye providence of God, for the crossing and disappointage, ye envy, Malice, & Sinister practices of my Enemies." This husband was Philip Herbert, Earl of Pembroke and Montgomery, Lord Chamberlain of the King's Household, and Knight of the Garter. He was the son of Mary Herbert, second Countess of Pembroke, the nephew to Sir Philip Sydney, and the first cousin of Lady Mary Wroath.

To the third Countess of Montgomery Lady Mary had dedicated the *Urania*, but Anne Clifford stood in no danger of dedications from the Sydney family. In disposition she was quite unpoetic, although she exerted a pastoral care over all her belongings. Philip Herbert, however, vied with her in business acumen, and it was not long before he brought pressure to bear on his wife so that she should force her younger daughter Isobel to marry one of his younger sons. This was but the starting point of their differences, and after four and a half years, Anne lived apart, having left the Court at Whitehall on 18th December, 1634, " by reason of some discontents." This discreet explanation was no doubt worded thus so as to keep her secret from the secretary who wrote at her dictation. The true explanation appears in a letter to her uncle, Edward, Earl of Bedford,[4] in which she entreats him to obtain her husband's consent that she may go to London to transact some business. She says: " I dare not venther to come upe witheoutt his leve, lest he shoulld take that occasion to turne mee out of this howse, as he did outt of Whitehall, and then I shall not know wher to put my hede."

In 1647, Isabella married James Compton, Earl of Northampton, " but I was not yr present at ye Marriage for many reasons "—obviously to avoid further friction with her husband, or because he compelled her to absent herself. She had succeeded to all the disputed property on the death of her first cousin without male issue in 1643, and so was in a position to defy her husband if she had so wished, but she did not intend to expose her matrimonial troubles by openly ignoring her husband's wishes. That she was on friendly terms with Isobel is clear, since on June 3rd, 1649, she went to visit her at Islington prior to travelling north to enter into her possessions. Before going to Islington she took leave of her husband " in his

[4] *The Harleian Collection.* Letter dated January 14, 1638.

lodging in ye Cockpit "—a last farewell, actually, since he died
seven months later. She was at Appleby when the news reached
her, and she did not return to London for the funeral. She had
never been a hypocrite.

She did not remember either of her husbands with bitterness,
and speaks of that part of her life with justice and restraint.
She had never submitted to a husband in the management of
her own personal affairs. She might have been a happier woman
if she had been weaker, but suffering is invariably the price
of strength.

> I must confess [she says] with inexpressible thankfulness that
> tho' through the goodness of Almighty God, & the mercies of
> my Saviour Christ Jesus Redeemer of the World, I was born
> a happy Creature in Mind, body & fortune, & that those 2
> lords of mine to whom I was afterwards by the Divine Provi-
> dence marryed, were in their Several Kinds worthy Noblemen
> as any then were in this Kingdom, yet was it my misfortune
> to have Contradictions and Crosses with them both, with my
> first Lord, about the desire he had to make me sell my Rights
> in ye lands of my Antient inheritance for Mony, which I never
> did, nor never would Consent unto, insomuch as this matter
> was the cause of a long Contention betwixt us, as also for
> his profuseness in consuming his estate & some other extra-
> vagancies of his; and with my 2nd Lord, because my Youngest
> Daughter, the lady Isabella Sackvill, would not be brought to
> marry one of his younger sons, and that I would not relinquish
> my Interest I had in 5000 pounds, being part of her portion,
> out of my lands in Craven, nor did there want diverse malicious
> illwillers to blow & forment the Coals of Dissention betwixt
> us, so as in both their lifetimes, the Marble Pillars of Knowle
> in Kent, & Wilton in Wiltshire were to me oftentimes but the
> gay arbour of Anguish, insomuch as a wise man yt Knew the
> insides of my fortune, would often say that I lived in both
> these My Lords great familys as the River of Roan or Rodamus
> runs through the lake of Geneva, without Mingling any part
> of its Streams with that lake, for I gave myself wholly to
> retiredness as much as I could in both those great families, &
> made good books and virtuous thoughts my Companions, which
> can never discern affliction, nor be daunted when it unjustly
> happens, and by a happy Genius I overcame all those troubles
> . . . . the prayers of my blessed Mother helping me therein.

Anne Clifford was fifty-three years when she gained her
estates; six years later she entered into the north, and the joy
that attended her gives vivid life to the narrative. This happiness

is expressed mainly in computing how long it has been since she last saw these childhood scenes. She stays from July to August 7th at Skipton Castle where she was born, and most of which had since been destroyed by order of Parliament as it was used as a Cavalier stronghold during the Civil Wars. She says: " I was never till now in any part of ye castle, since I was 9 or 10 weeks." From there she visited the old Tower at Barden for the first time. On August 8, 1649, she goes to stay at Appleby Castle:

> I came into Appleby Castle, ye most antient Seat of my Inheritance & lay in my own Chamber there, where I used formerly to lye wth my Dear Mor. & there I continued to lye till about ye 13th of Feb. following, this 8th of Augt. being the 1st time yt I came into ye sd Appleby Castle ever since I went out of it wth My Dr. Mor. ye 8th day of October in 1607.

There had been an interval of forty-two years. Time has no power over a loving heart, but love ever seeks some defence against oblivion. So it was that Anne Clifford erected a memorial pillar at the very place on the road between Appleby and Penrith where she and her mother had their last parting.

That Christmas of 1649 she held at Appleby, as she had done the previous year at Skipton. Through many storms she had won to peace, and there was fulfilment in her old age which her youth was denied. She had endured much, and the litigious struggle was at the root of all her great contentions. In maintaining her rights, she adhered to her mother's parting counsel, and so achieved a double fidelity. Now:

> From Many Noble progenitors I hold Transmitted lands, Castles & Honours which they swayed of old . . . And in this settled abode of Mine, in these 3 antient houses of mine inheritance, Appleby Castle & Brougham Castle in Westmoreland, and Skipton Castle . . . in Craven, I do more and more fall in love with ye Contentments & Innocent pleasures of a Country life, wch humor of mind, I do wish wth all my heart . . . may be confirmed on my posterity, yt are to succeed me in those places, for a wise body ought to make their own home ye place of self fruition, & ye comfortablest pt of their life.

Her happiness lasted twenty-seven years, and she died at the age of eighty-seven, having worn out all her troubles by sheer longevity.

A biography which merely chronicles events is not a good biography. It is the infrequent glimpses of Anne Clifford's mind which render her manuscript worth reading, and it is strange to notice that, despite her complete discretion, her strong personality impresses itself upon her measured words. The three motifs in the narrative represent the three main forces which went to the moulding of her life: religion, love for her mother, and determination to succeed to the Clifford possessions. Her particularity in regard even to unimportant dates, her reminiscent discoveries of odd coincidences as to time and place, and her continual repetition of facts show the senescent mind. She died before the manuscript was completed, and she does not appear to have made any effort to revise it. Hence many facts which might have been incorporated in the narrative hang raggedly about its fringe.

Her secretary writes the final page, in which he describes very simply her last few days of life. The closing words stress that ancestral note which was most fitting to the death of such a woman.

> After she had endured all her pains with a most Christian fortitude, always answering those that asked her how she did, with I thank you, I am very well, which were her last words directed to mortals, she with much cheerfulness in her own chamber in Brougham Castle in Westmoreland wherein her noble father and her blessed mother died, yielded up her precious soul into ye hands of her Merciful Redeemer.

In the brilliant days of the Restoration, when Anne Clifford was finding such deep happiness in Cumberland, an extraordinary woman might very occasionally be seen in London. Her rare visits were one of the sights of the town, and never failed to arouse the vociferous delight of the populace, the tittering amusement of the fashionable, and the puzzled disgust of conventional citizens. The Count of Grammont thought he saw one evening:

> As I was getting out of my chair, I was stopped by the devil of a phantom in masquerade . . . It is worth while to see her dress; for she must have at least sixty ells of gauze and silver

tissue about her, not to mention a sort of pyramid upon her
head, adorned with a hundred thousand baubles.

"I bet," said the king, "that it is the Duchess of Newcastle."[5]

Pepys really saw her one April day, and records the event with
all the gusto of a child describing a circus:

> Met my Lady Newcastle going with her coaches and footmen
> all in velvet; herself (whom I never saw before), as I have
> heard her often described, for all the town talk is now-a-days
> of her extravagances, with her velvet cap, her hair about her
> ears, many black patches . . . about her mouth, naked-necked,
> without anything about it, and a black just-au-corps. She
> seemed to me a very comely woman; but I hope to see more
> of her on May-day.[6]

He saw her again on May 30th, as she went to attend the
Royal Society, and this time, the novelty having staled, he did
not like her at all, and feared she might make the Royal Society
ridiculous, " as her dress was so antick and her deportment so
ordinary."[7] Evelyn, received with great kindness at the Newcastle house at Clerkenwell, stresses, although with pleasure,
" the extraordinary fanciful habit, garb, and discourse of the
Duchess."[8] Such was the universal judgment of her contemporaries on Margaret Cavendish, Duchess of Newcastle—
commonly called " Mad Madge."

Who could depict with a mere pen's point this dear, delightful,
opinionated, child-like, fantastic genius? One may draw a
rhombus to represent a diamond, and sketch in some radiating
lines to suggest the effulgence of light, the depth, the colours,
the fluctuating radiance. But such a sketch would only be a
crude diagram, unless the mind which knows the quality of the
precious stone evokes from memory its dazzling light. The
Duchess of Newcastle was a diamond of the first water, partly
obscured by its original covering of clay, uncut save for a facet
or two which sent out a fitful and ill-balanced brilliance. Her
genius was so productive and so various, her ideas so original
and so ill-regulated, her vision so exalted, her ignorance so pro-

5 *Memoirs of the Count of Grammont,* p. 134.
6 Pepys' Diary, April 26, 1667.
7 *Ibid,* May 30, 1667.
8 Evelyn's Diary, April 18, 1667.

F

found, her style alternately so preposterous and so perfect, that one despairs of ever reducing to the cold canons of criticism the inspired confusion of her works.

Of the many women whose intellectual powers were rendered ineffectual by a want of education, the Duchess of Newcastle is an outstanding example. Like other well-bred women, she had had her tutors, who were paid to give a semblance of schooling, but who were not even supposed to exact the discipline of study. A young lady could read, write and cipher, she could chatter a foreign language, dance, and play the virginals, embroider and make bead bags. In the name of common sense what more could any one expect? Let her carry her "education" as she would a handkerchief—in case she should need it. It were unnecessary, and indeed rather ill-bred to make great play with either or flourish them about. But Margaret Newcastle was haunted by a dual hunger—for knowledge and for fame. She wanted to know " whether it be possible to make men and other Animal creatures that naturally have no wings, flie as birds do? " " Whether the Optick Perception is made in the Eye or Brain, or in both? " " Whether there could be self-knowledge without Perception? " " Whether snails have a row of small teeth orderly placed in the gums "? Such knowledge was not forthcoming, and the undisciplined and voracious mind raced on to other fields of enquiry. There was not time enough in eternity to know all she wished to know, or to write all she felt impelled to write. She writes so fast that she cannot stay to form the letters properly. She never revises. She fills twelve folio volumes, and the more she writes the more her readers tap their foreheads significantly, and rock with laughter. She knows, but she does not care. If writing is a disease, then countless great men have been at death's door. "All I desire is fame," she says; and again: " I have an Opinion, which troubles me like a conscience, that 'tis a part of Honour to aspire to Fame." [9]

> As for Learning, that I am not versed in it, no body, I hope, will blame me for it, since it is sufficiently known, that our Sex is not bred up to it, as being not suffer'd to be instructed in

[9] The Duchess of Newcastle, *Poems and Fancies* (1653); 'Epistle to Mistris Toppe.'

Schools and Universities; I will not say, but many of our Sex may have as much Wit, and be capable of Learning as well as Men; but since they want Instructions, it is not possible they should attain to it; for Learning is Artificial, but Wit is Natural. [10]

Writing over two centuries later, Sir Egerton Brydges says:

That the Duchess was deficient in a cultivated judgment; that her knowledge was more multifarious than exact; and that her powers of fancy and sentiment were more active than her powers of reasoning, I will admit; but that her productions mingled as they are with great absurdities, are wanting either in talent, or in virtue, or even in genius, I cannot concede. [11]

Disraeli supports the same view:

Her labours have been ridiculed by some wits, but had her studies been regulated she would have displayed no ordinary genius . . . Her verses have been imitated even by Milton. [12]

And finally in the following criticism we find the same judgment more fully expressed:

There are [in the writings of the Duchess] the indisputable evidences of a genius as highborn in the realms of intellect as its possessor was in the ranks of society: a genius strong-winged and swift, fertile and comprehensive, but ruined by deficient culture, by literary dissipation and the absence of two powers without which thoughts are only stray morsels of strength, I mean Concatenation and the Sense of Proportion. She thought without system, and set down everything she thought. Her fancy turning round like a kaleidoscope changed its patterns and lines with the most whimsical variety and rapidity. Nevertheless, I believe, had the mind of this woman been disciplined and exercised by early culture and study, it would have stood out remarkable among the feminine intellects of our history. [13]

[10] The Duchess of Newcastle, *Observations on Experimental Philosophy* (1666): 'Reader's Preface.'

[11] *A True Relation of the Birth, Breeding and Life of Margaret Newcastle, Duchess of Newcastle* (ed. Lowers, 1872). Critical Preface by Sir. E. Bridges, p. 255 f.

[12] Isaac Disraeli, *Curiosities of Literature* (1849), i, 365.

[13] *The Cavalier and his Lady* (ed. Jenkins, 1872): Introductory essay, p. 8 f.

Happily, however, two of the Duchess of Newcastle's works are free from those fixed ideas and exaggerated fancies which distort her other writings. These are the two biographical works which we are about to consider. In them, the turgid current of her thought flows clearly and surely to the end she had in view.

In 1656,[14] appeared *Natures Pictures drawn by Fancie's Pencil* . . . which contained, as the eleventh and last book *The True Relation of My Birth, Breeding and Life*. It preserves, as all autobiographies should, the quintessence of the writer's individuality.

Anne Clifford had presented a chain of events with few comments. Margaret Newcastle presents thoughts in which events are caught like flies in amber. She does not lose her way in the tangled happenings of her career, because external events never constituted her life. Life to her was thought. Well might she say: " I have made a world of my own." [15] Out of the press and hurry of the years she gathered something timeless— a conception of values which took its nature from her own personality. She might have been embittered by her misfortunes, intoxicated by her powers of endurance, made querulous by her poverty, or disillusioned by that spiritual weariness which always follows the triumph of a political cause. But she had an inner existence against which the tide of external events beat in vain. She does not particularise her backgrounds, and yet she gives sufficient to convey a feeling of vivid intimacy. The depth of her judgments, the unpretentious sincerity of her story and the steady undercurrent of emotion which carries it onward give this biography an unforgettable pathos and beauty.

In 1667, the Duchess published *The Life of the Thrice noble, high and puissant Prince, William Cavendish, Duke . . . of Newcastle*, a book " both good and rare " for which, says Lamb, " no binding is too good: no casket is rich enough, no casing sufficiently durable, to honour and keep safe such a jewel." [16] Since husband and wife shared the same fortunes, it is best

14 Some copies appeared in 1655.
15 Prefatory letter to *The* . . . *Blazing World* (1666).
16 Charles Lamb, *Last Essays of Elia*: 'Detached thoughts on Books and Reading.'

to consider these biographies together, thus avoiding a wearisome repetition of background.

Margaret Lucas was the youngest daughter of Sir Thomas Lucas of St. John's, Colchester, a gentleman of sound reputation and estate, who died when she was still an infant. She and her brothers and sisters were reared by their mother with great affection and care. It was a very happy home at St. John's, in those days, before the storm of the Civil War bore furiously down upon the Lucas family, scattering and slaying. Eight children played there of whom any mother might justly be proud, they were all so spirited and so good. They must have made a very pleasant picture, they were so properly proportioned, and so " well-featured ", with their " clear complexions, brown haires, but some lighter than others, sound teeth, sweet breath, plain speeches and tunable voices." Lady Lucas was the kind of mother every fortunate child remembers: lovely, loving and brave.

> My mother was of an heroick spirit, in suffering patiently where there is no remedy, or to be industrious where she thought she could help : she was of a grave behaviour, and had such a majestic grandeur, as it were continually hung about her, that it would strike a kind of an awe to the beholders, and command respect from the rudest of civilised people, [17] I mean not such barberous people as plundered her, and used her cruelly, for they would have pulled God out of heaven, had they had the power, as they did royaltie out of his throne : also her beauty was beyond the ruin of time, for she had a well-favoured

[17] Not from Mr. T. Longueville, who in his bad-tempered book (*The First Duke and Duchess of Newcastle-on-Tyne*, 1910) shows an active dislike towards the subjects of his research. He considers it extremely cogent to mention that Lady Lucas's great-grandfather had been town-clerk in Colchester, and that the eldest son of Sir Thomas and Lady Lucas was born before the marriage of his parents. "For this trifling confusion of dates," says Mr. Longueville, "the excellent Lady Lucas endeavoured to atone by the prudishness upon which she insisted in her children" (p. 174. f.) Mr. Longueville considers it highly amusing that the Duchess of Newcastle omitted to record this part of her mother's life. This is merely one example of the regrettable attitude which this most ungenerous biographer brings to his task. In speaking of Margaret Newcastle's estimate of the Duke's first wife, Mr. Longueville says "The Duchess is condescending enough to say that 'his first wife was a very kind, loving and virtuous Lady,' which, in most cases, might be taken to mean about the worst that one lady could politely say of another" (p. 11). The spirit of this work renders it valueless as an honest biography, and we need not refer to it again.

loveliness in her face, a pleasing sweetness in her countenance, and a well-tempered complexion, as neither too red nor too pale, even to her dying hour, although in years, and by her dying, one might think death was enamoured with her, for he embraced her in a sleep, and so gently, as if he were afraid to hurt her. [18]

Margaret Newcastle gives a delightful account of the young Lucases. She describes their clannishness, their mutual affection, their mother's careful training, their education, their amusements and much more.

As for tutors, although we had for all sorts of vertues, as singing, dancing, playing on musick, reading, writing, working, and the like, yet we were not kept strictly thereto, they were rather for formality than benefit, as my mother cared not so much for our dancing and fidling, singing and prating of sev- erall languages, as that we should be bred virtuously, modestly, civilly, honourably, and on honest principles. [19]

Even when they were growing up they were little inclined to go outside the family circle for companionship. There were enough of them to make a merry party when in winter the river froze and they skimmed over the ice, their laughter ringing in the frosty air; or when they went to London to visit a play- house and to see the thronging life of the busy streets. In the fine weather there were expeditions to Hyde Park, or Spring Garden, and there were long summer days upon the water, " when they would have music and sup in barges." When it was not high-holiday, the boys had still such pastimes as fencing, riding and shooting; the girls had country walks, embroidery, the making of simples, and all the pleasant arts of housewifery. But there was one of the Lucas family who did not take part in these diversions. She was too shy, too withdrawn, and too self-absorbed. She took her pleasure in reading or scribbling. Whether the trees were afoam with blossom, or the trout leaped in the weir, or the snow fell hissing an invitation to merriment, Margaret Lucas's pen scrabbled over the paper, in mad pursuit of the ideas which ever sped faster than hand could follow. She

18 *The True Relation of My Birth, Breeding and Life* (Everyman ed.) p. 196.
19 *Ibid*, p. 190.

set down what she could catch in hasty, frantic hieroglyphics which took their erratic course among huge mountains of blots. Where are now the sixteen books which this ambitious child felt impelled to write—those curious effusions which were such a mixture of " sense and no sense, knowledge and ignorance " ? She tells us herself that they were not worth reading. At any rate, they vanished as surely as her youth.

The young Lucases were very tolerant of their youngest sister's shyness. One would not say that they understood her (except perhaps her sister Pye, whom she loved " with a super-natural affection "), but they were good natured, and sheltered her from the necessity of those social contacts which caused her such awkward misery. Picture, then, their amazement when this bashful Margaret suddenly declared that she wished to go to Court. She had heard that the Queen, Henrietta Maria, had now fewer maids of honour than formerly, and either a sense of loyalty to the Stuart cause, or an impulse to conquer her anti-social habits led her to volunteer for this service. With much difficulty she obtained the consent of her mother and family, who feared lest her excessive timidity and inexperience might make her miserable among so many strangers. Still, they let her go, and miserable she was for two years. She lacked the power to adapt herself to Court life, and was soon the laughing-stock of the women, whom she could not understand, and of the men, whom she avoided. They could make nothing of this fantastic maid of honour who was so awkward and so naïve.

In 1645, the Queen moved to Paris, and Margaret Lucas was one of those who accompanied her. In Paris she met the Duke of Newcastle, then a widower of fifty-three. He was just the sort of man to appeal to a young girl's hero-worship—good-looking, kindly, whimsical, cultivated, a Royalist refugee who had lost almost everything in the King's cause. She says:

> My Lord the Marquis of Newcastle did approve those bashful fears which many condemned, and would choose such a wife as he might bring to his own humours, and not such an one as was wedded to self-conceit, or one that had been tempered to the humours of another; for which he wooed me for his wife; and though I did dread marriage, and shunned men's companies as much as I could, yet I could not, nor had not the power to

refuse him, by reason my affections were fixed on him, and he was the only person I ever was in love with; neither was I ashamed to own it, but gloried therein. For it was not amorous love, I never was infected therewith, it is a disease, or a passion, or both, I only know by relation, not by experience; neither could title, wealth, power, or person entice me to love. But my love was honest and honourable, being placed on merit, which affection joyed at the fame of his worth, pleased with delight in his wit, proud of the respects he used to me, and triumphing in the affections he profest for me, which affections he hath confirmed to me by a deed of time, sealed by constancy, and assigned by an unalterable decree of his promise; which makes me happy in despight of Fortune's frowns. [20]

They were married in Sir Richard Browne's Chapel at Paris, in 1645, Margaret being at that time twenty years of age.

Then began the extraordinary career of the exiled Newcastles. Not the least thing they had in common was their poverty, for as the Duchess says, both the family to which she allied herself and the family from which she sprang were both ruined in the Civil War. It was very fortunate that she and her hus-band shared a magnificent indifference to worldly possessions and a child-like ignorance of money matters. If either had been of an anxious disposition, it would have been a very unhappy marriage. As it was, they were ideally suited, and displayed what one might call a reckless common-sense in ignoring the impecuniosity for which they had no cure. Their creditors, however, were not likely to be convinced by such logic, and though very long-suffering, did not by any means share the facile optimism of these Micawbers. In Paris, a short time after the marriage, the Duke found himself at bay. His creditors, no doubt disgusted at the levity with which he added a wife to his other liabilities, refused absolutely to trust him any longer:

My Lord, being always a great master of his passions, was—at least showed himself—not in any manner troubled at it, but in a pleasant humour told me that I must of necessity pawn my clothes to make so much money as would procure a dinner. I answered that my clothes would be but of small value, and therefore desired my waiting-maid to pawn some small toys which I had formerly given her, which she willingly did. The same day in the afternoon, my Lord spake himself to his

20 *Ibid*, p. 195. f.

creditors, and both by his civil deportment and persuasive arguments, obtained so much that they did not only trust him for more necessaries but lent him money besides to redeem those toys that were pawned. [21]

About two years afterwards, when the Duke had again prevailed upon his creditors, the first thing he did was to move out of lodgings into a house which he rented and furnished on credit,

and withal, resolving for his own recreation and divertisement, in his banished condition, to exercise the art of manage . . . bought a Barbary horse for that purpose, which cost him 200 pistoles, and, soon after, another Barbary horse from the Lord Crofts, for which he was to pay him £100 when he returned to England.[22]

Some time later, the Queen-mother being security for their debts in Paris, the Newcastles followed their Prince to Rotterdam, lived there for six months at a great charge, keeping an open house and a noble table for all comers. Thence, having spent £3,000 of borrowed money, they retired to live quietly at Reubens' house, which they rented from his widow. The two Barbary horses died, but though the Duke

wanted present means to repair these his losses, yet he endeavoured and obtained so much credit at last that he was able to buy two others, and by degrees as many as amounted in all to the number of 8. In which he took so much delight and pleasure, that though he was then in distress for money, yet he would sooner have tried all other ways, than parted with any of them; for I have heard him say that good horses are so rare, as not to be valued for money.[23]

The Duke acted in accordance with this principle, foiling alike the would-be purchasers of his horses and his desperate creditors. The Duchess, so far from being enraged at his irresponsible behaviour, was happy to think that he could squeeze even this much pleasure from life. Finally, however, the situation became so serious that the Duchess and her brother-in-law, Charles Cavendish, returned to England to effect a composition

[21] *The Life of William Cavendish* (Everyman ed.) p. 64.
[22] *Ibid*, p. 65.
[23] *Ibid*, p. 71.

for the sequestered family estates. They were in such dire straits that they had not even enough money to carry them to London, and Sir Charles had to pawn his watch in Southwark to pay for their night's lodgings. Even here they were pursued by the frantic entreaties of her Micawber husband whose Augean stable of debt was none the less fearful for that it contained eight prancing Barbary steeds. By heroic efforts they scraped together £200, which they sent him.

> But in the meantime, before the said money could come to his hands, My Lord had been forced to send for all his creditors, and declared to them his great wants and necessities; where his speech was so effectual and made such an impression in them, that they all had a deep sense of My Lord's misfortunes; and instead of urging the payment of his debts, promised him, that he should not want anything in whatsoever they were able to assist him; which they also very nobly and civilly performed.[24]

This indeed was a very strong proof of the Duke's persuasiveness and amiability.

After eighteen months in England, Margaret heard that the Duke was ailing and returned to Antwerp. His brother remained behind and died soon afterwards. There is no doubt that the Newcastle family was greatly to be pitied, their estates not only being seized and sold, but many of their houses deliberately pulled down. They lost in all about £10,000. The Lucas family also paid dearly for their loyalty, and Margaret had many deaths to lament. Her eldest sister died first, then her mother, then her two brothers, one of them being executed during the war. If poverty did not matter greatly to the Duchess of Newcastle, she had enough of other sorrows to break the strongest heart. Her only joy was in her husband, and her loyalty to him during their bitter years of exile makes a story in which the epical and the humorous are inextricably entwined. She loves to show that there was grandeur in the Duke's life abroad. She relates incidents to prove that their house was visited by all the people of quality who came to Antwerp, even by the entire court of Don John of Austria. Every civility shown to her husband, every compliment, every kind word from the

24 *Ibid*, p. 77.

King is treasured by this loving woman, " onely to declare My Lord's happiness in his miseries."

At last the Restoration, so long and so vainly awaited, becomes a fact. The Duke is invited to come to England in one of his Majesty's ships, but begs leave to hire a vessel for himself and his company. He crosses to England in " an old rotten frigate that was lost the next voyage after . . . . At last, being come so far that he was able to discern the smoke of London, which he had not seen in a long time, he merrily was pleased to desire one that was near him, to jog and awake him out of his dream, for surely said he, I have been sixteen years asleep, and am not thoroughly awake yet." [25]

Alas for the Duchess! That indomitable woman was left behind as a pawn for her husband's debts. Nothing daunted, she busied herself in her writings, and quietly awaited her release. Soon she had the joy of returning to her own country, when she and the Duke retired to their ruined estate, and devoted the rest of their lives to each other and to their particular pursuits. The Duchess died thirteen years later at the age of forty nine. Her husband survived her by three years, and was buried with her in Westminster Abbey. Their tomb, on which lie two life-size images in white marble, bears the following epitaph:

> Here lies the loyal Duke of Newcastle and his Duchess, his second wife, by whom he had no issue. Her name was Margaret Lucas, youngest sister to the Lord Lucas of Colchester, a noble family, for all the brothers were valiant, and all the sisters virtuous. This Duchess was a wise, witty and learned Lady, which her many books do well testify: She was a most virtuous and loving and careful wife, and was with her Lord all the time of his banishment and miseries; and when they came home never parted from him in his solitary retirements.

The biography of the Duke of Newcastle ran into three editions even within the life-time of the subject. The first edition, in 1667, was followed in 1668 by a Latin version,[26] translated by Walter Charlton, subsequently well known as

25 *Ibid*, p. 86. f.
26 *De Vita et Rebus gestis G. ducis Novo-Castrensis commentarii* (Fol. Londini : 1668).

President of the College of Physicians. The third edition was in quarto, published in 1675. There was a reprint of the first edition in 1872, and various other editions and extracts have been published since then. *The True Relation* is generally appended.

There have been diverse opinions as to these biographical works of the Duchess. Pepys was very forthright in his condemnation. On March 18th, 1667, he writes: " Staid at home reading the ridiculous History of my Lord Newcastle, wrote by his wife; which shows her to be a mad, conceited, ridiculous woman, and he an asse to suffer her to write what she writes to him and of him. So to bed my eyes being very bad."

His myopia, however, was nothing to that of Horace Walpole, who fulminates against the Newcastles " with less taste and justice than are commonly to be found in his censures, and with more than his usual spleen." [27]   Disraeli dismisses as mere levity Walpole's criticism which in brief is as follows:

> Of all the riders of [Pegasus] perhaps there have not been a more fantastic couple than his Grace and his faithful Duchess, who was never off her pillion. One of the noble Historian's finest portraits is of the Duke: The Duchess has left another; more diffuse indeed but not less entertaining. It is equally amusing to hear her sometimes compare her Lord to Julius Caesar, and often to acquaint you with such anecdotes as in what sort of coach he went to Amsterdam.

Having jeered at the Duchess's claims to genius and at her peculiarities, he ends thus:

> What a picture of foolish nobility was this stately poetic couple, retired to their own little domain, and intoxicating one another with circumstantial flattery on what was of consequence to no mortal but themselves. [28]

And what a picture of finicking celibacy was Walpole himself, retired into his little pseudo-Gothic stronghold at Strawberry Hill, surrounded by an arid collection of artistic curiosities, and

[27] Edmund Lodge, *Portraits of Illustrious Personages of Great Britain* (1835), viii, 8 f.
[28] Horace Walpole, *A Catalogue of the Royal and Noble Authors of England* (2nd ed., 1759), ii, 12ff.

drawing his life-breath from the sterile eulogies of his select coterie! Whereas the Newcastles left a memory of faithful love, this doyen left a miasma of malicious preciosity. Before he sneered at Margaret Newcastle's literary absurdities, he should have wiped the bloody drop from Alfonso's nose.[29] Before he stigmatised a childless woman as a " fertile pedant," he should have considered for a moment his own barren existence.

Happily, however, there have been few such critics. The general consensus of opinion has always emphasised the profound value of *The True Relation* and the *Life of William Cavendish*. To the worth of the latter biography, Firth has finely testified:

> The special interest of the book lies in the picture of the exiled Royalist, cheerfully sacrificing everything for the King's cause, struggling with his debts, talking over his creditors, never losing confidence in the ultimate triumph of the right, and on his return, setting to work uncomplainingly to restore his ruined estate. It lies . . . in the portrait drawn of a great English nobleman of the seventeenth century; his manners and his habits, his domestic policy, and his alliances with neighbouring potentates, all are recorded and set down with the loving fidelity of a Boswell. [30]

The Duchess of Newcastle was not the only woman biographer in the north of England. While she was writing *The Life of William Cavendish*, or more probably after it had been written, another woman was committing to paper the memoirs of her husband. This was Lucy Hutchinson, widow of Colonel Hutchinson of Owthorpe, whose family had for generations been near neighbours of the Newcastles in Nottinghamshire. The Hutchinsons belonged to an old and respected family, and were on amiable terms with the Newcastles, but the two families differed entirely in political and religious outlook. They took opposing sides in the Civil War, and consequently their fortunes soared and fell for opposite reasons. The Battle of Marston

---

[29] 'The Castle of Otranto' (*Works of Horace Walpole,* 1798), ii, 76 f.
[30] *Life of William Cavendish* (ed. Firth, 1886), Preface.

Moor ushered in for each family a widely different era—for the Newcastles exile, poverty, and sorrow; for the Hutchinsons success and security. The Duke of Newcastle lost all but life for the cause of Charles I; Colonel Hutchinson was one of the regicides. Nevertheless, the Duke did all he could to protect Colonel Hutchinson and his family when the Restoration demanded vengeance on its enemies. These facts are cogent to the problem presented by Lucy Hutchinson's biographical works.

Lucy Hutchinson's writings remained unpublished for well over one hundred years after they had been written. During this interval, they remained in the careful possession of the Hutchinson family. Thomas Hutchinson, who held the family estates at the end of the eighteenth century, had refused to permit publication of these works, but when his nephew, the Rev. Julius Hutchinson, succeeded to a part of the property, he showed himself of a different mind. He found in the library of Hatfield Woodhall (the Hertfordshire house) the following manuscripts:

(1) The Life of Colonel Hutchinson.
(2) A book without a title in which Lucy Hutchinson recorded certain events, and which she used when she came to write her husband's Life.
(3) A fragmentary account of Lucy Hutchinson's own life.
(4) Two books dealing exclusively with religious subjects.

Of these manuscripts, numbers 1 and 3 were published by the Rev. Julius, in 1806, under the title of *The Memoirs of Colonel Hutchinson*; number 4 was published by him in 1817, under the title of *Principles of the Christian Religion*; number 2 is in the British Museum (Add. Mss. 25, 901), but only a fragment of it, as part was lost or destroyed.

Before we give any detailed account of *The Memoirs of Colonel Hutchinson*, it would be well to discuss the interesting contention of Mr. A. H. Upham in regard to the spontaneity of this work.[31] Mr. Upham considers it very probable that Lucy Hutchinson modelled the fragmentary account of her own life on the Duchess's *True Relation of my Birth, Breeding and Life*, and planned *The*

31 A. P. Upham, 'Lucy Hutchinson and the Duchess of Newcastle,' Anglia, xxxvi (1912).

Memoirs of Colonel Hutchinson on *The Life of William Cavendish*. Mr. Upham's argument has as its starting point the similarities to be found in these works, and he reinforces his view by pointing out striking parallels in the fortunes of these two women.

External1y, there were many coincidences in the circumstances of the Duchess and Lucy Hutchinson. Both sprang from families which were staunchly Royalist in the Civil War, although Lucy Hutchinson subsequently adhered to her husband's Roundhead principles: each had lost a brother fighting on the Royalist side; both had married widowers; both had made heroic exertions, Lucy Hutchinson to save her husband's life, and the Duchess to save her husband's possessions; both lived in neighbouring estates in Nottinghamshire, and ordered their lives upon similar lines, the Duchess a voluntary exile from the corruption of the Court, Lucy Hutchinson forced to go into seclusion which, however, well suited her Puritan mode of life; both had such educational possibilities as the age offered, and were given to unregulated reading, and no study; both had a bent towards writing. There had never been any enmity between their families, even when party feeling was at its highest. On the contrary, the Duke had several times tried to protect the Hutchinsons. All these points, taken in conjunction with the fact that each woman wrote her own life and that of her husband, and that there are similarities to be observed in these works, lead one to suspect that one woman imitated the other. The Duchess had been writing all her life, and was to the fullest degree original. She was already an established literary figure when her *True Relation* and her husband's *Life* appeared, and these works were written before Mrs. Hutchinson began hers, so there is no doubt at all that, if there was imitation, Mrs. Hutchinson was the culprit.[32]

Now the work which Mrs. Hutchinson most obviously and clearly modelled on that of the Duchess is the fragmentary account of her own life. Upham has collated parallel passages in proof of Lucy Hutchinson's indebtedness, and to the present

[32] Upham presents all these arguments in the article already mentioned.

writer, at any rate, he has proved this point quite conclusively.[33] Lucy Hutchinson's autobiography is, like all her manuscripts, undated, and all one can really say is that it must have been written sometime after the Duchess's *True Relation of my Birth, Breeding and Life* which appeared in 1656 (some copies in 1655).[34]

In regard to *The Memoirs of Colonel Hutchinson,* the question of imitation is more troubled. Convincing internal evidence need not be expected, as the lives of Colonel Hutchinson and the Duke differed widely in incident, and the only parallels which could have been made were those which might appear in the portrait presented of each man and his pursuits. These parallels are actually to be found in the *Memoirs,* and can be classified under such headings as personal appearance, recreation, self-control, foresight, humility, etc.[35] Moreover, the *Memoirs* are in plan similar to the *Life of William Cavendish.* The Duchess divided her biography and her husband thus:

(1) His birth, breeding and his share in the Civil War
(2) The story of his exile
} Strictly biographic.

(3) Description of his person, disposition and habits.
(4) Notable sayings of the Duke.
} A character study.

(5) (Appended) *The True Relation of my Birth, Breeding and Life.*

The Memoirs of Colonel Hutchinson follow in general the same plan, although the parts are not set out in the same order:

(1) The Life of Lucy Hutchinson, written by herself (a fragment).
(2) To my children (Mrs. Hutchinson to her children concerning their father).
} A character study.

[33] The reader is referred to A. P. Upham's treatment of this point in the article already indicated. He deals with the matter in a way which is too long to quote and which cannot be improved.

[34] Upham suggests that Lucy Hutchinson's autobiography was written three years after the Duchess's *Life of William Cavendish,* i.e. about 1670. There is no reason to accept this date.

[35] Upham has done this very effectively.

(3) The Life of Colonel } Strictly
Hutchinson. biographic.

Now, the greatest complication in this entire question is the impossibility of assigning a definite date to any of Mrs. Hutchinson's manuscripts. The most we can say as to the date of the *Memoirs* is that they were written at some time between the death of the Colonel in 1664, and the release of certain of his fellow-prisoners on July 7, 1671.[36] Since Mrs. Hutchinson appears to have been influenced by *The Life of William Cavendish* which was published in 1667, it would be reasonable to suppose that she wrote, or at any rate completed *The Memoirs* after that date. Her biography, however, contains a passage which seems to suggest that she began *The Memoirs* very soon after her husband's death. She says:

> But I that am under a command not to grieve at the common rate of desolate women, while I am studying which way to moderate my woe . . . can for the present find out none more just to your dear father nor consolatory to myself than the preservation of his Memory.[37]

The passage is ambiguous, and the interpretation of it as an immediate expression of grief is based on the idea that sorrow is lessened by time. So it is, but not in every case, and besides, a widow writing the life of her husband may not have been inclined to admit time's softening qualities. Indeed, the narrative flowing from her pen may have revived all her first grief, and the foregoing passage may have been written in that frame of mind, although years afterwards. The Rev. Julius Hutchinson did accept the *Memoirs* as "a simple unstudied utterance," the immediate expression of the widow's first unmoderated woe, but in this acceptance he entirely overlooked the significance of manuscript number 2, and of other facts to be mentioned later.

[36] When Colonel Hutchinson was arrested, Capt. Wright and Lieut. Franck were arrested also, and brought to Newark "where," says Mrs. Hutchinson in the *Memoirs,* "they are yet prisoners, and to this day, know not why" (p. 345). Mr. Baily, in his *Annals of Nottinghamshire,* pointed out that, as Capt. Wright was arraigned before Judge Hale at the King's Bench, on July 7, 1671, and then discharged for want of evidence, the *Memoirs* could not have been written after that date.
[37] *The Memoirs of Colonel Hutchinson* (revised ed. Firth, 1906), p. 17.

G

Manuscript number 2 was not a diary of events in the Colonel's life. If it had been, the events would have been dated. Actually, spaces were left for dates which were to be filled in later. It is, then, an account of events, written a considerable time after they had occurred, and written for a specific purpose. Surely that purpose obviously was the deliberate marshalling of facts, preparatory to writing the *Memoirs*. Manuscript number 2 was a rough sketch of these political happenings which Mrs. Hutchinson knew she must accurately reconstruct as the background of her husband's life. Manuscript number 2 disproves the theory of the " simple unstudied utterance." But it does not disprove the theory that the *Memoirs* may have been begun soon after Colonel Hutchinson's death, that is, at some time before *The Life of William Cavendish* appeared in 1667.

Accepting the evidence that the *Memoirs* were modelled on *The Life of William Cavendish*, we must adhere to either of two alternative views:

(a) That the *Memoirs* were not begun, or not completed until after 1667, when Mrs. Hutchinson would have the opportunity of studying the published *Life of William Cavendish*.

(b) That the *Memoirs* were begun soon after Colonel Hutchinson's death in 1664, and that Mrs. Hutchinson had access to *The Life of William Cavendish* which existed in manuscript as early as 1665.

Upham makes out a case in support of both theories, but his case for view (b) is not at all convincing. Taking the similarities in the circumstances of the Duchess and Lucy Hutchinson, and the fact that they were neighbours, he builds up an intimacy between the two women, makes it appear that they exchanged visits, and that the Duchess showed her unpublished manuscript to Lucy Hutchinson. Apart from the slender nature of these arguments which rest upon pure surmise, they are untenable because they were highly improbable. Similarity of external circumstances does not connote or induce similarity of outlook, and the world is full of people in whom similarity of circumstances does not awaken the slightest mutual sympathy. Furthermore, though the Duchess and Lucy Hutchinson shared an aversion to society, and were characterised by high ethical principles, the difference between the Duchess and Lucy Hutchinson is the difference between rectitude and righteousness. The Duchess disliked the Puritan sisterhood, as many of her letters show. She considered them extremely boring and presumptuous. Again, as to the intimacy between these women, it should be remembered that they became neighbours only after the Restoration. Prior to that time, the Duchess lived abroad except for one hurried visit to England. This gave no opportunity for deep roots of friendship to grow. In fact, although Lucy Hutchinson in the *Memoirs* highly praises the Duke of Newcastle for his kindness to her husband, she makes one remark which surely she would have omitted, had she been truly a friend of the Newcastles. She says that no man in the North of England was a greater prince

> till a foolish ambition of glorious slavery carried him to court where he ran himself much into debt to purchase neglects of the King and Queen and the scorn of the proud courtiers.

This sort of gibe would certainly have prevented Lucy Hutchinson from showing *her* manuscript to the Duchess, whatever the Duchess might have shown to her. And really, nothing is more utterly improbable than that the Duchess showed her manuscript to Lucy Hutchinson, even if they had been sister spirits. The dearest of friends show a distinct reserve as to their unpublished manuscripts. Literary emulation is a deterrent, not a spur, to such exchanges. Since the theory that Lucy Hutchinson began the *Memoirs* soon after 1664, and before 1667, involves the belief that she had access to the unpublished manuscript of *The Life of William Cavendish,* we must abandon it. It is far more probable that she knew the Duchess was engaged on the Life of her husband, determined to do likewise, wrote manuscript number 2 as a necessary first sketch of background, studied *The Life of William Cavendish* when it appeared in 1667, modelled the *Memoirs* on this fair pattern, and completed them in due time.

Upham finds not only a marked similarity of plan and detail, but also a close resemblance in the literary style of these two women. With this criticism it is not easy to agree. One can really see no similarity in the style of the Duchess and of Lucy Hutchinson, except such general traits as characterised the prose of the period.   Within these limits, there is a vast difference in the styles of Mrs Hutchinson and of the Duchess.   That of Mrs Hutchinson is clear, smooth-flowing, firm and uninspired; that of the Duchess is vivid, turgid, choked with metaphor, impeded by a plethora of ideas, startling with sudden patches of sheer beauty.   One is the style of an intelligent and systematic mind; the other is the style of an erratic genius.

Lucy Hutchinson was born about the year 1620.   She was the daughter of Sir Allen Apsley, Lieutenant of the Tower of London, by his third wife, Lucy St. John.   Her parents, considering her beautiful and unusually intelligent, spared no pains with her education.   She had at one time eight tutors for such subjects as " languages, music, dancing, writing and needle-work," but she had no interest in anything but reading.   She was taught French by her nurse, and Latin by her father's chaplain.   Her writings show that she also knew Greek and Hebrew, and was well read in classical and theological learning.

Like the Duchess she praises her mother's beauty.   The Duchess says:

I dare not commend my sisters, as to say they were handsome. But this I dare say, their beauty, if any they had, was not so lasting as my mother's.   Time making suddener ruin in their faces than in hers.[38]

Lucy Hutchinson says:

There were not in those days so many beautiful women found in any family as these, but my mother was by the most judgments preferred before all her elder sisters, who something envious at it, used her unkindly.[39]

Firth refers to the extraordinary mistake Lucy Hutchinson made as to her mother's age.[40]   She alleged that her mother was married at sixteen years, and yet she enumerates incidents in her mother's earlier life which would seem to indicate that she was so ardently wooed by suitors at the age of nine, that she was

---

38 *The True Relation* (ed. Everyman), p. 197.
39 *The Memoirs of Colonel Hutchinson*, containing the Fragmentary 'Life of Lucy Hutchinson' (Ed. Firth, 1885).
40 This point was raised, but left unexplained in *Notes and Queries.* July 19, 1884.

forced to take refuge in Jersey from her sisters' jealousy. This was no mistake on Lucy Hutchinson's part, but a stupid effort to have her cake and eat it. She wished to show the devastating effects of her mother's beauty, and yet to hide the fact that her mother did not marry until she was twenty seven.[41]

Lucy Hutchinson may have imagined that there was a great similarity between her disposition and that of the Duchess. Let us compare what each has to say of her young days:

> For I [says the Duchess] being addicted from my childhood to contemplation rather than conversation, to solitariness rather than society, to melancholy rather than mirth, to write with the pen rather than to work with a needle, passing my time with harmless fancies, their company being pleasing, their conversation innocent, in which I take such pleasure, as I neglect my health, for it is as great a grief to leave their society, as a joy to be in their company . . . likewise in playing at cards, or any other games, in which I neither have practised, nor have I any skill therein; as for dancing, although it be a graceful art, and becometh unmarried persons well, yet for those that are married, it is too light an action . . . and for revelling I am too dull a nature. [42]

Mrs. Hutchinson says:

> As for music and dancing, I profited very little in them, and would never practise my lute or harpsichords but when my masters were with me; and for my needle, I absolutely hated it. Play among other children I despised . . . and kept the children in such awe that they were glad when I entertained myself in elder company; to whom I was very acceptable . . . and very profitable discourses being frequent at my father's table and in my mother's drawingroom, I was very attentive to all, and gathered up things that I would utter again, to the great admiration of many that took my memory and imitation for wit. [43]

These characteristic accounts mark a great difference in the mental traits of the little Margaret Lucas and the little Lucy

---

[41] Lucy St. John's father died on September 20, 1594 according to the inscription on the outside of two large doors at the north side of the altar in the village of Lydiard Tregooge: (see *Notes and Queries*, July, 19, 1884); Lucy St. John was five years old when her father died (according to her daughter, Lucy Hutchinson, in her autobiography); therefore when she married twenty two years later, in 1616, she must have been twenty seven years.

[42] *The True Relation* (Ed. Everyman), p. 206.

[43] *Memoirs*, (ed. cit.), i. 25.

Apsley. The one was unobtrusively contemplative, a shy and awkward child feeding on thought; the other was a self-assertive prodigy, feeding on the praise which her facile parroting won from her elders. As women, both were convinced of their mental powers, and they were right, but the difference still remained between creative vision and very intelligent imitation.

Lucy Apsley married Colonel Hutchinson, then a widower, in 1638. The story of their meeting and courtship is very pleasantly and gracefully told. It stresses the fact that, like the Duchess, she was very bashful, and that none but this particular suitor could have persuaded her to marry. Her life with her husband was very happy, and he seems to have been tolerant of her literary ambitions. She found it possible during the early days of her married life to unite the care of her children with her translation of the six books of Lucretius' *De Rerum Natura*, which, long afterwards, she dedicated to the Earl of Anglesea, at a time when her views in regard to the doctrines of Epicurus and the atomic theory had suffered regeneration:

> 'Tis a lamentation and a horror [she says in 1675] that in these days of the gospel men should be found so presumptuously wicked to study and adhere to his and his master's ridiculous, impious, execrable doctrines, reviving the foppish, casual dance of the atoms, and denying the Sovereign wisdom of God in the great design of the whole universe. [44]

" This dog," she calls Lucretius finally, and she speaks of all worldly learning as " Those walks of wit which poor vain-glorious scholars call the Muses' groves, enchanted thickets . . . While they tipple at their celebrated Helicon, they lose their lives, and fill themselves with poison, drowning their spirits in their puddled waters, and neglecting the healing spring of truth." And this is the intimate confidante of the Duchess, to whom " Atomes " were dearer than life, who drank so deep of Helicon and wandered so long among the thickets that the sober were always shocked by the intoxicated dishevelment of her mind! That Lucy Hutchinson came to share not only her husband's moral principles but his political outlook, is abundantly clear

---

44 Dedication to the Earl of Anglesea, quoted by Firth, Appendix 37 to the *Memoirs*, p. 454.

in the *Memoirs*. These convictions made it inevitable that the Hutchinsons should take the Puritan side in the Civil War, and it must be said that, except for one somewhat pardonable vacillation, they adhered to their chosen path in the face of misery and death.

When the Duchess was confronted with the task of building up the political background of her husband's life, she relied on the sound information of the Duke's Secretary, John Rolleston. Lucy Hutchinson derived her background from May, but, unlike the Duchess, did not acknowledge her indebtedness. She sometimes objects to May's impartiality, but follows him rather closely nevertheless. In some respects, however, she was better informed than May. For example, she gives the true reason for the dissolution of the Long Parliament. May does not. For the account of the warfare in Nottinghamshire she revised manuscript No. 2, but was careful to omit certain facts which, on mature consideration, appeared to reflect unfavourably on her husband's conduct—such as, the story of Colonel Hutchinson's insulting message to Sir Roger Cooper, and his torturing of the spies from Newark. Sometimes, like the Duchess, she is apt to exaggerate the part played by her husband, and when she deals with the Colonel's escape from the immediate vengeance of the Restoration, she conceals and misrepresents much of the truth. As a regicide, Colonel Hutchinson's life was forfeit in 1660. He escaped by eating humble pie. His recantation was embodied in a letter to the Speaker in Parliament, and "no more humbling and dishonouring petition for life could be uttered." [45] Lucy Hutchinson says that she wrote that letter and signed it with her husband's name. This fact has been confirmed. But Colonel Hutchinson did not trust merely to his wife's expedient. He sent a second petition to the House of Commons six weeks later. He was regarded as a renegade by his old comrades, and this, coupled with the reproaches of his own conscience, made him repent his apostasy. When, after a few years of active Royalist enmity, he was again arrested, he greeted the prospect of his imprisonment with relief.

[45] *The Memoirs* (ed. Firth) Introd. p. xv.

From the moment that Colonel Hutchinson was arrested and taken to London, there is a different tone in the *Memoirs*. The style throughout has been admirably clear and forceful, but now there is a restrained emotion which raises it to a different level. We should be glad to claim this as Lucy Hutchinson's best writing—her own literary style vivified by deep feeling, and owing nothing to the compositions of any other writer. But the truth is that Colonel Hutchinson himself wrote an account of his arrest and imprisonment while he was in the Tower of London, and succeeded in getting it printed before he was removed to Sandown. It was reprinted in the Harleian Miscellany and is therefore accessible for comparison with this part of the *Memoirs*. It is quite clear that Lucy Hutchinson owed much to her husband's narrative. Some parts of it she copied with merely verbal changes. She did, however, incorporate Colonel Hutchinson's account in the *Memoirs* with such success that, were it not for evidence to the contrary, one would ascribe this part of the narrative entirely to her, and one would be inclined to explain the increased vitality of her style by the gathering force of the tragedy she is about to describe. It is an important fact that, though her husband's account ends before he was removed to Sandown, she continues the story to its conclusion, with no observable change of style, or diminution in force or imaginative insight. Despite all her imitations, she did not need help to describe her husband's death. She did the only thing which could have been of the slightest use—she poured out that part of the story from her heart.

Throughout the *Memoirs* Lucy Hutchinson speaks of her share in events always in the third person. This gives a peculiar dignity and grief to the latter part of the narrative. There is a detailed account of the political atmosphere prior to Colonel Hutchinson's arrest: the threats, the consciousness of impending danger, the insults, the raids on their house. No wonder that before the opening of the final stage the Colonel has a dream of ill-omen:

> He dreamt one night that he saw certain men in a boat upon
> the Thames, labouring against wind and tide, to bring their
> boat, which stuck in the sands, to shore; at which he, being

in the boat, was angry with them, and told them they toiled in vain, and would never effect their purpose; but, said he, let it alone and let me try; whereupon he laid him down in the boat, and applying his breast to the head of it, gently shoved it along, till he came to land on the Southwark side, and there, going out of the boat, walked in the most pleasant lovely fields so green and flourishing, and so embellished with the cheerful sun that shone upon them, as he never saw anything so delightful, and there he met his father, who gave him certain leaves of laurel which had many words written in them which he could not read. The Colonel was never superstitious of dreams. but this stuck a little in his mind. [46]

Finally he is arrested, despite all the Duke of Newcastle can do in his favour, and having been illegally imprisoned for four days, is taken to London. The long journey begins on October 28, 1663.

They were forced to stay a day at Owthorpe [the Colonel's own house] for the mending of the coach and coming in of soldiers, where the Colonel had the opportunity to take leave of his poor labourers, who wept all bitterly when he paid them off, but he comforted them and smiled, and without any regret went away from his bitterly weeping children, and servants, and tenants, his wife and his eldest son and daughter going with him. [47]

He was imprisoned in the Bloody Tower. His repeated examinations, the efforts to make him incriminate himself in conversation with his guards and fellow prisoners, the attempts to involve and to browbeat Mrs. Hutchinson are all excellently described. Robinson, the Lieutenant of the Tower, is a fine portrait of a scoundrel. Every deceit, every effort to extort money, every detail of his petty persecutions are recorded. Robinson refuses Mrs. Hutchinson access to her husband who is ill, and who is deliberately confined in the worst possible room because he cannot afford to bribe Robinson into more bearable treatment. Finally, Mrs. Hutchinson threatens to publish an account of Robinson's behaviour which the Colonel has committed to paper:

The next day, being the Lord's, he sent one of the warders to entreat her to come to her husband, and the *blood-hound*

[46] *Ibid*, (ed. cit.), p. 341 f.
[47] *Ibid*, p. 350 f.

Cresset, met her at the gate and led her to her husband, and left her all the day alone with him, which they had never before done . . . and in the evening Sir John Robinson sent for her, and partly expostulated and partly flattered. [48]

It must have been very strange for Lucy Hutchinson to find such suffering in the Tower of London where she was born, and which was bound up with the happy memories of her childhood.

At last, the Colonel is sent to Sandown Castle where his quarters and his treatment are even worse. The castle is dilapidated, and he is kept in a room with unglazed windows, a room with five doors, used as a thoroughfare, and swept by such damp winds from the sea that even in summer the walls and the wretched pieces of furniture are covered daily with mould. The walls ooze with damp, and salt lies like a perpetual sweat upon them. Notwithstanding all this, the Colonel is cheerful and endeavours to cheer his wife and daughter, who lodge at Deal and come to and fro every day to visit him.

His wife bore all her own toils joyfully enough for the love of him, but could not but be sad at the sight of his undeserved sufferings; and he would very sweetly and kindly chide her for it, and tell her that if she were but cheerful, he should think this suffering the happiest thing that ever befel him. [49]

One day she tells him that despite all his courage, she knows he will die in prison. He replied:

I think I shall not, but if I do, my blood will be so innocent, I shall advance the Cause more by my death, hasting the vengeance of God on my unjust enemies, than I could do by all the actions of my life. Another time when she was telling him she feared they had placed him on the seashore but in order to transport him to Tangier, he told her, if they had, God was the same God at Tangier as at Owthorpe; Prithee said he, trust God with me; if he carry me away, he will bring me back again.

Not long afterwards, Colonel Hutchinson died, while his wife was gone northward in an effort to raise enough money to secure him better treatment in prison.

48 *Ibid,* p. 367.
49 *Ibid,* p. 371.

From London he was brought down to Owthorpe, very seriously bewailed all the way he came along by all those who had been better acquainted with his worth than the strangers amongst whom he died, and was brought home with honour to his grave through the dominions of his murderers, who were ashamed of his glories, which all their tyrannies could not extinguish with his life. [50]

We have seen that the *Memoirs* written by Lucy Hutchinson were very far from being " a simple, unstudied utterance "; that they were, on the contrary, the result of long planning, steady labour and much imitation. We have noted that she modelled her work on that of the Duchess of Newcastle; based her political background on May, and relied on her husband's account for much of the latter part of her story. Even her character-portrait of her husband she wrote twice over, so earnestly was she studying how best to express what she had in mind. [51] But it would be a mistake to imagine that because Lucy Hutchinson used borrowed threads as well as those from her own distaff, and because she tried to imitate an existing pattern, that therefore she did not weave a sound reliable fabric. It is certainly no mean feat to recount in an interesting, thorough and systematic manner the events of forty-eight years. [52] A woman who could thus recount the complicated happenings of real life is well worth mentioning as a portent in the evolution in fiction. Julius Hutchinson showed some wisdom when he said of the *Memoirs* that the book " carries with it all the interest of a novel, strengthened with the authenticity of a real history." [53]

In 1643, when Margaret Lucas, awkward and unhappy, was striving to adapt herself to Court life in Oxford, another girl (one year younger than herself), lodging in a back-street in the same town, was striving to adapt herself to poverty. This was Anne Harrison, eighteen years old, fated also to lose everything

---

[50] *Ibid*, p. 382.

[51] The character-portrait itself came into possession of the Rev. Julius Hutchinson in two MS versions, of which he rejected the second as much more laboured and much less characteristic. (A. H. Upham, *ut supra*.)

[52] 1616-1664.

[53] *The Memoirs* (ed. Hutchinson, 1810), Introd. xxviii.

in the Royalist cause, to be a wanderer in far countries, to cleave to her husband through thick and thin, and to record her adventures in a biography.

Anne Harrison was the elder daughter and the fourth child of Sir John Harrison of Balls, Hertfordshire. She was born in 1625, in Hart Street, St. Olave's, London, and although her education gave her all the advantages that the time afforded, her interest in accomplishments was formal. Needlework, " French, singing, lute, the virginals and dancing " were well enough,

> Yet was I wild to that degree, that the hours of my beloved recreation took up too much of my time, for I loved riding in the first place, running, and all active pastimes; in short, I was that which we graver people call a hoyting girl; but to be just to myself, I never did mischief to myself or people, nor one immodest word or action in my life, though skipping and activity was my delight, but upon my mother's death, I then began to reflect, and, as an offering to her memory, I flung away those little childnesses that had formerly possessed me, and, by my father's command, took upon me charge of his house and family, which I so ordered by my excellent mother's example, as found acceptance in his sight. 54

When Anne became the mistress of her father's house she was fifteen—not a great age at which to assume the responsibilities of a woman. It was not long before her endurance and courage were fully tried. In 1641 her father, who had held a post in the customs, lent King Charles a large sum of money. In 1642 he was imprisoned by the Parliament and deprived of his property. Again at liberty, he attended the Court at Oxford in 1643, and sent for his children so that they might be near him. The Harrison family was then in such financial straits that Anne and her sister had to make shift as best they could.

> From as good a house as any gentleman of England had, we came to a baker's house in an obscure street, and from rooms well furnished, to lie in a very bad bed in a garret, to one dish of meat, and that not the best ordered, no money, for we were as poor as Job, nor clothes more than a man or two brought in their cloak bags : we had the perpetual discourse of losing and gaining towns and men; at the windows the sad spectacle

54 *Memoir of Lady Fanshawe* (ed. 1830), p. 35.

of war, sometimes plague, sometimes sicknesses of other kind, by reason of so many people being packed together, as, I believe, there never was before of that quality; always in want, yet I must needs say that most bore it with a martyr-like cheerfulness. For my own part, I began to think we should all, like Abraham, live in tents all the days of our lives. [55]

The beautiful and high-spirited Anne Harrison did not remain long in her garret. On May 18, 1644 (the year following her arrival in Oxford, and shortly after her brother William's death) she was married with her mother's wedding ring to Richard Fanshawe, her third cousin. Marriage to Prince Charles's Secretary of War could not mean " settling down." It involved every kind of uncertainty and danger, hardship and privation. It meant a restless and fugitive existence, home being merely wherever one happened to pause for a breathing space. In Anne Fanshawe's life only one thing was permanent—the faithful love between her and her husband. When, thirty-two years later, she set down the crowded events of her married life, her husband had been dead ten years; at fifty-five she was worn out by many griefs; poor, lonely and ignored; of her fourteen children born in various parts of England, Spain and France, nine were dead; and yet her devotion to her husband, ardent as ever, revived every detail of those strenuous years which were to her supremely worth while. Indeed she wrote the *Memoirs* so that her only surviving son, Richard, might properly appreciate his father's character and achievements.

The *Memoirs* were written in 1676, either by Lady Fanshawe herself or else at her dictation. [56] This manuscript was copied in 1776 by Charlotte Colman, said to be a great-granddaughter. Charlotte Colman's manuscript was copied in 1786, and this third manuscript was published in 1829. In 1830 there was a new edition with corrections and additional notes. One would expect mistakes in the second copy of a manuscript, particularly since Charlotte Colman was not a careful copyist, but even in

[55] *Ibid*, p. 57 f.
[56] S. L. Lee in D.N.B. speaks of "The original in *Lady Fanshawe's handwriting.*" The writer of the preface to the 1830 edition (one N.H.M.) says "The original . . . was written *under her Ladyship's inspection.*"

Lady Fanshawe's manuscript [57] the dates are not reliable, partly because she wrote from memory, partly because she sometimes used the old and sometimes the new style of computation. Occasionally, too, she mentioned events out of their proper sequence. The arrangement of the *Memoirs* is as follows:

(1) A portrait of her husband, Sir Richard Fanshawe.

(2) An account of his ancestors.

(3) A reference to their marriage, together with the names of their children alive and dead. Of the dead she mentions the burial places.

(4) A few pages dealing with the family of Sir Thomas Fanshawe of Jenkins, who was a near relative of her husband.

(5) An account of her own birth; of her mother, of her mother's death; and of her own brothers and sister.

(6) An account of her father's second marriage; of his birth and relatives.

(7) An account of her own childhood, and upbringing.

(8) A long and detailed account of the adventures which befell her husband and herself during their married life.

It is true that parts (1) to (7) are badly arranged, but this does not greatly matter, as, from the fictional point of view, the main interest is centred in the long narrative which constitutes section (8).

To the composition of the *Memoirs* Anne Fanshawe brought a most energetic, vivid and individual mind. She was a woman of great courage and directness, with a knack of adapting herself to any circumstances and of rising to any situation. We see her, fine and bejewelled, sweeping her curtsey to the Queen, or standing squarely on deck in the tarry clothes of a cabin-boy to meet the attack of Turkish pirates; gracing the brilliance of ambassadorial banquets, or gnawing a hunk of rotten cheese when shipwrecked off the coast of France; defending her husband's house from robbers, outwitting the passport authorities at Dover, fleeing through the streets of embattled Cork, or with her hair standing on end at the sight of a fearful ghost. She never wearies. She takes what comes with the simplicity and

57 This, the original manuscript, was never published, and remains or remained, in the possession of the Fanshawe family. See D.N.B.

verve of a child. She remains always the spontaneous and gallant
Anne Fanshawe. She retains always her tremendous gusto for
living. In the minuteness of her observation, in her interest
in clothes, customs, food, she is a very woman. When her
husband goes as English ambassador to the Spanish court, she
can tell us exactly the width of his coat-lacing, the colour of
his shoe-strings and the sort of ribbon which trimmed his gloves.
When she flees from Bristol to Barnstaple to escape the plague,
she notes (with delightful inconsequence) that " near Barnstaple
there is a fruit called a masard, like a cherry, but different in
taste, and makes the best pies with their sort of cream I ever
eat "; also that at the merchant's house where she lodged there
was a parrot a hundred years old. Such Pepysian particularity
adds greatly to the realism of the narrative. Like the great
diarist she has an insatiable appetite for curious facts. For example, the Spanish women " all paint white and red, from the
Queen to the cobbler's wife, old and young, widows excepted,
who never go out of close mourning, nor wear gloves, nor show
their hair after their husband's death "; and again, that in Spain
" they have a seed which they sow in the latter end of March,
like our sweet basil; but it grows up in their pots, which are
often of china, large, for their windows, so delicately, that it
is all the summer as round as a ball and as large as the circumference of the pot, of a most pleasant green, and very good
scent."[58] She loves also anything that is traditional or mysterious,
and tells with great relish how the prophecy written over the
entrance gate of the Alhambra came to be fulfilled. [59] She
describes further that through an iron grate fixed in the side
of a hill near the Alhambra, one could distinctly hear the clash-
ing of swords, and she adds that, according to a legend, it could
never be opened since the Moors left, and that all perished who
attempted it.

But although Anne Fanshawe's attention to detail gave a particular vividness to her narrative, she had a power of natural
realism quite independent of such touches. The vigorous simplicity of her style, and its worth as an expression of personality

[58] *Memoirs* (ed. 1830), p. 212.
[59] *Ibid*, p. 100.

can best be shown by extracts; and a brief resumé of the principal events will show the ability of this biographer to tell a gripping and, at times, a very moving story.

Anne Fanshawe's marriage to Richard Fanshawe was in itself an adventure, for though he was the Prince's Secretary for War, and had the King's promise of future preferment, the young couple were practically penniless. Both had large fortunes in expectation, and empty pockets for their present needs:

> We might truly be called merchant adventurers, for the stock we set up our trading with did not amount to twenty pounds betwixt us; but, however, it was to us as a little piece of armour is against a bullet, which if it be right placed, though no bigger than a shilling, serves as well as a whole suit of armour; so our stock bought pen, ink, and paper, which was your father's trade, and by it, I assure you, we lived better than those that were born to £2,000 a year as long as he had his liberty. [60]

When her first child was dying very soon after its birth, Anne Fanshawe's husband had to go to Bristol in performance of his duty. Three months later he sent for her to join him, and she, leaving her sick-room for the first time, set off for Bristol a few days afterwards, with a high heart; " but little thought I to leap into the sea that would toss me until it had racked me." When she arrives her husband greets her lovingly, and gives her a hundred pieces of gold saying:

> "I know thou that keeps my heart so well, will keep my fortune, which from this time I will ever put into thy hands as God shall bless me with increase." And now I thought myself a perfect queen, and my husband so glorious a crown, that I more valued myself to be called by his name than born a princess, for I knew him very wise and very good, and his soul dotes on me.

But, though his love for her is indeed great, she is very happy to prove that he loves honour more, and relates a vivid little story in proof thereof. Another lady, with whom she is very friendly, suggests that she should have a knowledge of state affairs, like other wives, and urges her to find out from her husband the contents of a packet that came post from the Queen in Paris that night.

[60] *Ibid*, p. 59.

I that was young and innocent, and to that day had never in my mouth what news, began to think there was more in inquiring into public affairs than I thought of, and that it being a fashionable thing would make me more beloved of my husband, if that had been possible, than I was. When my husband returned from Council, after welcoming him, as his custom ever was, he went with his handful of papers into his study for an hour or more; I followed him; he turned hastily and said, "What wouldst thou have, my life?" I told him, I heard the Prince had received a packet from the Queen, and I guessed it was that in his hand, and I desired to know what was in it; he smilingly replied, "My love, I will immediately come to thee, pray thee go, for I am very busy." When he came out of his closet I renewed my suit; he kissed me and talked of other things. At supper I would eat nothing; he as usual sat by me, and drank often to me, which was his custom, and was full of discourse to company that was at table. Going to bed I asked again, and said I could not believe he loved me if he refused to tell me all he knew; but he answered nothing and stopped my mouth with kisses.

She cries herself to sleep and refuses to speak to him even on the following day, but he takes her in his arms and explains his position in these words:

"My dearest soul . . . when you asked me of my business it was wholly out of my power to satisfy thee, for my life and fortune shall be thine, and every thought of my heart in which the trust I am in may not be revealed, but my honour is my own, which I cannot preserve if I communicate the Prince's affairs; and pray thee with this answer rest satisfied."

Such goodness makes her realise her folly and she never again troubles him so.

From Bristol she goes in her husband's (and the Prince's) train to Cornwall, and at Truro she defends the house against robbers in her husband's absence. Thence they proceed to the Scilly Isles, where they have almost no food, clothes, or fuel, and where their lodgings are so wretched that, when she wakes in the morning her bed is "near swimming in the sea." Three weeks later they go to Jersey, where a second child is born; from there, after fifteen days, to Caen, and then Anne Fanshawe returns to England to raise some money for her husband. He is allowed to join her, and for some time they live very privately in Portugal Row. During this time they visited King Charles, who was imprisoned in Hampton Court.   Anne Fanshawe thus describes the last visit:

> I went three times to pay my duty to him, both as I was the daughter of his servant, and wife of his servant. The last time I ever saw him, when I took my leave, I could not refrain weeping : when he had saluted me, I prayed to God to preserve his Majesty with long life and happy years; he stroked me on the cheek, and said, " Child, if God pleaseth, it shall be so, but both you and I must submit to God's will, and you know in what hands I am."

Soon they were in France again with letters from the King for Prince Charles and Queen Henrietta.   In September of the same year (1648) Sir Richard was ordered to embark in Prince Charles's ship in the Downs, to act as Treasurer of the Navy under Prince Rupert.   Later he joined Prince Charles in Holland, and was sent to Ireland to raise money.   There he was joined by Anne.   She landed in Youghal, and for six months they lived in Cork very happily, in Red Abbey, a house of Dean Boyle's.   They were on excellent terms with the Boyle family, as also with Lord Inchiquin, whose daughter Elkenna was christened by Anne.   But this pleasant interlude was soon to end.   Lady Fanshawe had only just got news of the death of her second son when Colonel Jeffries seized Cork on behalf of Cromwell.   Lady Fanshawe was most unhappily circumstanced at the time of this occurrence. Sir Richard was in Kinsale, and she was in bed with a broken wrist and an impending childbirth when the trouble began.   It was the 16th October, 1649.

> At midnight I heard the great guns go off, and thereupon I called up my family to rise which I did as well as I could in that condition. Hearing lamentable shrieks of men, women and children, I asked at a window the cause; they told me they were all Irish, stripped and wounded, and turned out of the town, and that Colonel Jeffries, with some others, had possessed themselves of the town for Cromwell.[61]

She at once determines to escape and writes a message to her husband, to tell him that she is securing his papers.   With this letter a faithful servant is lowered over the garden-wall of Red

---

61 *Memoirs*, p. 87 f.

Abbey, and he makes his escape in the darkness of the night. She packs up her husband's papers and all the valuables that can be carried, " and then, about three o'clock in the morning, by the light of a taper, and in that pain I was in, I went into the market-place, with only a man and a maid, and passing through an unruly tumult with their swords in their hands, searched for their chief commander Jeffries." [62] Jeffries who, while he had been loyal, had been well disposed towards the Fanshawes, gives her a pass.

> With this I came through thousands of naked swords to Red Abbey, and hired the next neighbour's cart, which carried all I could remove; and myself, sister and little girl Nan, with three maids and two men, set forth at five o'clock in November,[63] having but two horses amongst us all, which we rid on by turns. In this sad condition I left Red Abbey . . . We went ten miles to Kinsale, in perpetual fear of being fetched back again; but, by little and little, I thank God, we got safe to the garrison where I found your father.

Thence the Fanshawes went to Limerick where they were received with great kindness. They stayed three nights with the Lady Honor O'Brien, the youngest daughter of the Earl of Thomond. There Anne Fanshawe saw a ghost:

> About one o'clock I heard a voice that wakened me. I drew the curtain, and, in the casement of the window, I saw, by the light of the moon, a woman leaning into the window, through the casement, in white, with red hair and pale and ghastly complexion : She spoke loud, and in a tone I had never heard, thrice, "A horse," and then, with a sigh more like the wind than breath she vanished, and to me her body looked more like a thick cloud than substance. I was so much frightened, that my hair stood on end, and my night clothes fell off.[64]

She wakens her husband and they both observe that the window is still open. Next morning Lady Honor comes to tell them that a cousin of hers, whose ancestors owned the house, died during the night. She fears that they may have been disturbed, because whenever a member of the family was dying the appari-

---

[62] *Ibid,* p. 89.
[63] Lady Fanshawe is mistaken as to the month.
[64] *Memoirs,* p. 92.

tion of a woman always appeared at the window. It was a woman who had been wronged and murdered ages before by the owners of the house. Very naturally the Fanshawes left at once.

They are ordered to Spain, and sail from Galway—a Galway ruined by war and plague: " this disconsolate city, where now you see the streets grown over with grass, once the finest little city in the world." As the ship gathers way before the wind Lady Fanshawe puzzles over the unending misfortunes of the " brave Kingdom " of Ireland. But soon the threat of personal danger rouses her. A Turkish galley is sighted, and it draws nearer every moment. An engagement seems inevitable. The captain locks Lady Fanshawe in the cabin, but she has no intention of remaining there while her husband fights on deck. She beats on the door until the cabin-boy comes. Then

> I, all in tears, desired him to be so good as to give me his blue thrum cap he wore, and his tarred coat, which he did, and I gave him half-a-crown, and putting them on and flinging away my night clothes, I crept up softly and stood upon the deck by my husband's side, as free from sickness and fear, as, I confess, from discretion; but it was the effect of that passion, which I could never master.[65]

Her determination is not put to the final test, because the Turks, seeing the other vessel prepared, sail off.

Arrived in Spain they go from Malaga to Madrid by way of Granada, and are most kindly received, but the Spanish King shows no desire to help Prince Charles, and the Fanshawes leave Spain. Crossing to Nantes they are almost shipwrecked, and of this, as of everything else, Lady Fanshawe gives an excellent description. A terrible storm arises in the Bay of Biscay. Sails and mast are swept away, and the ship drives wildly on, while the crew " ran swearing about like devils," and finding all efforts useless, " ran into holes and left the ship drive as it would." On the third evening there comes a great calm, but they are still in peril of their lives, because the compass is lost.

> Thus, between hope and fear we passed the night, they protesting to us they knew not where they were, and truly we believed them; for with fear and drink I think they were

65 *Ibid,* p. 98.

bereaved of their senses. So soon as it was day, about six o'clock, the master cried out, " The land ! the land !" but we did not receive the news with the joy belonging to it, but sighing said God's will be done ! Thus the tide drove us until five o'clock in the afternoon, and drawing near the side of a small rock that had a creek by it, we ran aground.[66]

Anne Fanshawe well remembers their good cheer then. How (as no beds were to be had) they sat up all night around roaring fires regaling themselves with butter, walnuts, eggs, milk and some very bad cheese. "And," she says, " was not this enough, with the escape of shipwreck to be thought better than a feast."

Having seen the Queen-mother in Paris, the Fanshawes return to England. Sir Richard is captured at the Battle of Worcester and kept in solitary confinement in Whitehall (" in a little room yet standing in the bowling-green "), often examined, and all the time in expectation of death. He falls ill and nearly dies of scurvy.

During the time of his imprisonment, I failed not constantly to go, when the clock struck four in the morning, with a dark lantern in my hand, all alone and on foot, from my lodging in Chancery Lane, at my cousin's Young's, to Whitehall, in at the entry that went out of King's Street into the bowling-green. Then I would go under his window and softly call him : he, after the first time excepted, never failed to put out his head at the first call : thus we talked together, and sometimes I was so wet with the rain, that it went in at my neck and out at my heels.[67]

Finally Fanshawe is released on bail, and subsequently secures his full freedom. After a few years they go to France —Sir Richard first, but soon joined by Anne, who manages to escape the English authorities. They are at the Hague in May, 1660, and sail back to England triumphantly in the King's ship.

The king embarked at four of the clock, upon which we set sail, the shore being covered with people and shouts from all places of a good voyage, which was seconded with many volleys of shot interchanged : so favourable was the wind that the ships' wherries went from ship to ship to visit their friends all night long. But who can sufficiently express the joy and

66 *Ibid*, p. 105 f.
67 *Ibid*, p. 115.

gallantry of that voyage, to see so many great ships, the best
in the world, to hear the trumpets and all other music, to see
near a hundred brave ships sail before the wind with vast
cloths and streamers, the neatness and cleanness of the ships,
the strength of the commanders, the vast plenty of all sorts of
provisions; but above all, the glorious majesties of the King
and his two brothers, were so beyond man's expectation and
expression! The sea was calm, the moon shone at full, and the
sun suffered not a cloud to hinder his prospect of the best sight,
by whose light, and the merciful bounty of God, he was set
safely on shore at Dover in Kent, upon the 25th[68] of May,
1660.[69]

But although the Fanshawes gloried in the return of the
King whom they had served so faithfully, they had not much
cause for personal satisfaction. Charles had promised to make
Sir Richard one of his Secretaries of State, but this office he gave
instead to a Mr. Norris. Lady Fanshawe ascribed this reverse
to Clarendon whom she heartily disliked. S. L. Lee says[70] that
her dislike was unreasonable, since Clarendon always spoke of
Fanshawe's abilities and services in flattering terms. However
that may be, Lady Fanshawe had ample cause later to complain
of the treatment meted out to her. In 1662 Fanshawe was
appointed Ambassador to Portugal, and he and his wife remained
in Lisbon for a year. Back in England, they were graciously
received by the royal family, and in January, 1664, Sir Richard
was appointed Ambassador to Spain. He and his wife were in
high favour at the Spanish court when the King of Spain died,
on September 17th, 1665. They were present at the
proclamation of the new infant King, Charles II, and Lady
Fanshawe most vividly describes all these events, as well as the
general background of their life in Spain.

But now her husband entered into the final phase of his
fortunes. For some time he had been trying to negotiate a
treaty between Spain and England, and at length a draft treaty
was prepared by the Spanish council granting favourable terms
to English merchants, but it was presented to Fanshawe with
the proviso that it should either be confirmed by his sovereign

---

68 Actually on 26th May.
69 *Memoirs*, p. 151.
70 See D.N.B., Art. on Sir Richard Fanshawe.

within a fixed period or withdrawn. Fanshawe considered it right to sign the protocol without communicating with his government. On March 26th he was notified that Sandwich had been sent as Extraordinary Ambassador to supersede him. Clarendon said that Fanshawe's failure to communicate the terms of the Treaty to his home government while pledging it to confirm the articles stipulated therein, constituted so grave a breach of his duty that the English Council could not do otherwise than recall him. Fanshawe received his successor very kindly, introduced him to the King on June 10th, and sixteen days later was seized with a fatal illness. He died on June 26th, 1666, and was embalmed on the following day.

Fanshawe's recall was doubtless justified, but nothing can justify the attitude of the English authorities towards his widow. The Fanshawes had never had more money than was sufficient for their immediate needs, and very often not even that. On her husband's death, Lady Fanshawe was stranded in Spain without the money necessary for the journey to England, and she had to transport thither her husband's corpse and her family of five children. The home government gave her no help whatever.

> Much less found I that compassion I expected upon the view of myself, that had lost at once my husband, and fortune in him, with my son but twelve months old in my arms, four daughters, the eldest but thirteen years of age, with the body of my dear husband daily in my sight for near six months together, and a distressed family, all to be by me in honour and honesty provided for, and to add to my afflictions, neither persons sent to conduct me, nor pass, nor ship, nor money, to carry me one thousand miles, but some few letters of compliment from the chief ministers, bidding, "God help me!" as they do to beggars, and they might have added, "they had nothing for me," with great truth. But God did hear, and see, and help me, and brought my soul out of trouble.[71]

In this, the nadir of her fortunes, Anne Fanshawe acted with her usual fortitude. She sold more belongings to raise money, and left Spain owing not one shilling there or at home ("which every Ambassador cannot say"). Back in England, she found that the commissioners, by the instigation of one of them, Lord

[71] *Memoirs,* p. 250.

Shaftesbury ("the worst of men"), did all they could maliciously to oppress her in money matters.   She withdrew into the country where, under straitened circumstances, she reared her family.   She died in 1680, after fourteen years of poverty and loneliness quietly endured.

> How far that was from a reward, judge ye, for near thirty years' suffering by land and sea, and the hazard of our lives over and over, with the death and beggary of many eminent persons of our family, who when they first entered the King's service, had great and clear estates.[72]

No more is needed to attest the excellence of Anne Fanshawe's *Memoirs*. They are characterised not only by her complete realism and narrative power, but also by the sincerity of feeling.   Had she written fiction it could never have been Pastoral or Heroic.   To her the world around her was so colourful and so vitally interesting that she could never have found self-expression in fashioning a pale world of shepherds and knights.   She knew an exiled Prince and a slain King: she had experienced real wars, real shipwreck, real love, and real grief. She had a firm grip on facts.   If she were to create a story, one feels sure that she could never have subscribed to literary conventions which bore no relation to actual life.

As biographers Anne Fanshawe and the Duchess of Newcastle are immeasurably superior to Anne Clifford and Lucy Hutchinson.   It is not so easy to compare Anne Fanshawe's work with that of the Duchess.   In the construction of a narrative, in realism, in vivid descriptiveness, Anne Fanshawe was the superior, but the Duchess of Newcastle had—how shall one phrase it?—moments of greatness which somehow set her apart.   This aspect is most clearly seen in *The True Relation*. It is a subjective aspect, the value of which in the development of fiction is not perhaps so strikingly apparent as the more external qualities of Anne Fanshawe's writing.   Nor would it be just too greatly to stress Lady Fanshawe's objectiveness, lest one should seem to deny her that sensitive rightness of feeling so evident in many of the passages we have quoted.   One cannot

[72] *Ibid*, p. 249.

weigh different qualities against each other. It is best to think of the Duchess and Lady Fanshawe as two halves of a future whole—as contributing towards that mastery of narrative form and that expression of the inner being which finally fused in the modern novel.

Our female biographers were alike in one thing: they defied mortality. They were determined that not all of them should die, that they would erect a monument more lasting than brass to those events which were their pride and their heartbreak, which had devoured the years of their lives and demanded all their love, their faith and their endurance. Naturally it was essential for them to show that these sacrifices had been worth while, and so we find them exercising selectivity—not artistic, but merely human selectivity—in the use of their material. Anne Clifford never doubts that the law-suit was worth the contentions of a life-time, and she clenches her teeth on the humiliations of her married life; the Duchess ignores the slanders on the Duke's hasty exile; Lucy Hutchinson omits the details of the Colonel's lapse from valour; Anne Fanshawe refuses to consider that her husband's recall from Spain might have been deserved. Anne Fanshawe was nearest to the technique of fiction, but each woman told the story which she had lived in fact. Thus our female biographers' writings represent a phase in the evolution of the English novel which cannot be ignored.

CHAPTER IV

LIVING RESTORATION TRENDS.

" I have heard that some . . . say my Wit seemed as if it would overpower my Brain, especially when it works on Philosophical Opinions."

(Duchess of Newcastle, *Natures Pictures*, Bk. XI, Epistle).

1st Gentleman : But if a woman hath wit, or can write a good
             [tale] what will you say then?
2nd Gentleman : Why, I will say nobody will believe it, for if
             it be good they will think she did not write it,
             or at least say she did not . . . the very being
             a woman condemns it."

(*Duchess of Newcastle's Plays*, Final Introduction.)

" Thoughts [says the Duchess of Newcastle] are like stars in the firmament; some are fixed, others like the wandering planets, others again are only like meteors." By this simile the mind of the Duchess was like a chaos of the entire firmament; comets, meteors, fireballs, planets, stars—a blazing world, an astounding coruscation of dazzling confusion. They were, in particular, two fixed stars which shed a baneful influence upon her writings. One was her conviction of infallibility as an author. She was " Margaret the First," benevolent autocrat, subject to no laws of thought or of composition save those which she formulated for herself. Happy in the security that all she wrote would endure, she never revised her manuscripts. She considered it fairer to posterity not to waste valuable time in pruning her utterances, but to continue to pour out all her ideas exactly as they occurred to her. It is not surprising, therefore, that most of her writings are spoiled by this lack of judgment.

She considered originality to be the most important literary virtue. Every idea, every fancy, every whimsey, every metaphor was swept into the current of her style, as flowers, weeds and all sorts of flotsam are swept onward by a cataract. She undoubtedly had that concomitant of genius, a lofty and high confidence in herself, but she lacked an infinite capacity for taking pains. She did not even know that there were pains in authorship. She was an instinctive believer in the myth of continuous inspiration. She had no self-critical powers, and she was indifferent to the criticism of others. Her attitude to her readers is summed up in the nonchalant challenge:

" I hope you'll like it, if not, I'm still the same,
        Careless, since Truth will vindicate my Fame." [1]

The other fixed star which distracted the Duchess is best described by the one word "Atomes." Hobbes (of *Leviathan* fame) was at least in part responsible for this obsession. He was one of the Duke's friends. He visited at Welbeck, where extraordinary views on scientific and philosophical subjects were discussed without any poor-spirited hesitancies in regard to proof. In the *Treatise on Optics* (dedicated to the Duke) and in the *Decameron Physiologicum* the Duchess found the basis for her scientific poppycock. Where she did not know she felt free to invent. The only sanction she ever needed for her scientific and philosophic pronouncements was the sanction of her own approval. She did not feel daring when she published, in 1655, her *Philosophical and Physical Opinions*. She was sure that truth lay in her subconscious mind, and that the cream of such intuitions must rise naturally to the surface, and could therefore be enunciated with perfect safety. There was always more of artlessness than of arrogance in the Duchess.

If her literary egotism, her belief in the divine right of authorship, had remained quietly in the background, if her scientophilosophic propositions had confined themselves to her treatises, we could ignore them here. But these *idées fixes* disturb the balance of all except her biographical writings, and it is better to prepare ourselves for their intrusion.

[1] *Natures Pictures drawn by Fancie's Pencil to the Life* (1656). Dedication to Pastime.

In 1666, while the twin stars to which we have alluded were in the ascendant, the Duchess conceived a fictional work which in its nature gave free scope to her idiosyncracies. This was *The Description of a New Blazing World* which shared a volume with *Observations on Experimental Philosophy*. It was exactly the sort of invention which evoked all that was fantastic, exaggerated, and unstable in the mind of the Duchess. It conformed to a definite literary genre which had its origin in antiquity, and which has endured to the present day, but it was out of harmony with what is best in Margaret Newcastle's work. So little, indeed, does it conform to the most valuable trend in her writings, that we feel justified in ignoring chronology, and treating it at the beginning of the chapter, leaving until the end a volume which preceded it by ten years, but which we shall need as a sobering draught when we reel out of the *Blazing World*.

Since the days of Lucian, and even previous to that time, supposed journeys to imaginary countries had appealed greatly to the readers of feigned stories. In the beginning of the seventeenth century this vogue drew new life from the influence of Fontenelle. There was a variety of Lucianic writings in England, any one of which might have been the fuse to the Duchess's rocketing imagination. There was, for example, the essay of Francis Godwin, Bishop of Hereford, *The Man in the Moon, or a Discourse of a voyage thither by Domingo Gonzales, the speedy Messenger*, 1638, and that same year John Wilkins, Bishop of Chester, contributed *A Discovery of a New World in the Moone, with a discourse concerning the possibility of a passage thither*.

The Duchess sets out with the most sensible intentions, as she explains in her prefatory letter. She resolves to keep her fancy in check, to write a work of fiction that will embody some of her views on Experimental Philosophy. She is determined to set on paper a description of a New World, "Not such as Lucian's, or the French-man's World in the Moon," but a world of her own, a Blazing World which is situated at the North Pole. Let us not enquire why the Duchess should insist on a situation involving such a contradiction in temperatures. She did so in accordance with her own laws of ratiocination, and it is for us to suspend our disbelief. Suspicion does dawn upon us, however, when we hear that the first part of the work is to be "Romancical," the second philosophical, and the third "merely Fancy." We know Margaret Newcastle's attitude to romanceys, and we are not deceived by this leafy camouflage. We are to be lulled by security, coaxed to draw near, and then riddled by a fatal volley of "Atomes."

The story begins in a very promising manner as follows:

> A Merchant travelling into a forreign Country fell extremely in Love with a young Lady; but being a stranger in that Nation, and beneath her both in Birth and Wealth, he could have but little hopes of obtaining his desire; however, his love growing more and more vehement upon him, even to the slighting of all difficulties, he resolved at last to steal her away; which he had the better opportunity to do, because her Fathers house was not far from the Sea, and she often using to gather shells upon the shore, accompanied not with above two or three of her servants, it encouraged him the more to execute his design. Thus coming one time with a little light vessel . . . mann'd with some few Sea-men, and well victualled, for fear of some accidents, which might perhaps retard their journey, to the place where she used to repair, he forced her away: But when he fancied himself the happiest man of the World, he proved to be the most unfortunate; for Heaven frowning at his theft, raised such a Tempest, as they knew not what to do, or whither to steer their course; so that the Vessel, both by its own lightness, and the violent motion of the Wind, was carried as swift as an Arrow out of a Bow, towards the North-pole, and in a short time reached the Icy Sea, where the wind forced it amongst huge pieces of Ice; but being little and light, it did by assistance and favour of the Gods to this virtuous Lady, so turn and wind through those precipices as if it had been guided by some Experienced Pilot, and skilful Mariner: But alas! those few men which were in it, not knowing whither they went, nor what was to be done in so strange an adventure, and not being provided for so cold a Voyage, were all frozen to death, the young Lady onely, by the light of her Beauty, the heat of her youth, and Protection of the Gods, remaining alive: . . . . at last, the Boat still passing on, was forced into another World.[2]

She is rescued by the Bear-men, who live in the land of snow, and is carried to the Emperor of the Blazing World. He is overwhelmed by her loveliness and marries her, whereupon she is

[2] *Description of a New Blazing World* (1666), p. 13 f.

metamorphosed into Margaret the First, and holds endless conversations with her wise men as to the nature of Atomes, spirits, snails, air, lice, nettles, the sun, sight, and innumerable other problems. The arguments are somewhat enhanced by the appearance of the disputants:

> The Bear-men were . . . . her Experimental Philosophers, the Bird-men her Astronomers, the Fly-worm—and Fish-men—her Natural Philosophers, the Ape-men her Chymists, the Satyrs her Galenick Physicians, the Spider-and-Lice men her Mathematicians, the Jack-daw-Magpie and Parrot-men her Orators and Logicians, the Gyants her Architects . . . They were of several Complexions : not white, black, tawny, olive—or ash-coloured; but some appear'd of an Azure, some of a deep Purple, some of a Grass-green, some of a Scarlet, some of an Orange-colour, etc. Which Colours and Complexions, whether they were made by the bare reflection of light, without the assistance of small particles, or by the help of well-ranged and order'd Atomes; or by a continual agitation of little Globules; or by some pressing and reacting motion I am not able to determine.

The young Empress is also very much exercised as to the nature of spirits, and she wonders whether everything in the world is " soulified," and toys with the idea of soul-transmigration. She seeks a spiritual scribe to write down the esoteric mysteries divulged by the spirits. None of the ancient or modern philosophers would deign to perform such an office for a mere woman, " 'But, said [the Spirit] there's a Lady, The Duchess of Newcastle, which although she is not one of the most learned, eloquent, witty and ingenius, yet she is a plain and rational Writer, for the principle of her Writings, is Sense and Reason, and she will without question, be ready to do you all the service she can' . . . 'You say well, replied the Empress; wherefore I pray you send me the Duchess of Newcastle's Soul.' " The exponent of sense and reason at once arrives. Then follows a Tweedledum-and-Tweedledee conversation between the dis-severed halves of the Empress-Duchess. Finally the soul of the Empress follows the soul of the Duchess on a journey to this earth. They visit a theatre and the Court, and then set off for Nottinghamshire, one hundred and twelve miles from London, to visit the Duke of Newcastle. The Empress deplores so greatly the loss of his property that she decides to hear his grievance against Fortune. Each side is represented, the Duchess pleading for her husband and the Empress acting as judge. Ultimately the sister-souls part, the Empress returning to the Blazing World and the Duchess remaining in Nottinghamshire except when summoned by her majestic friend to confer on matters of state. During her periodic absences, the Duchess is still mindful of her husband's happiness. To show her devotion and to divert his mind from his misfortunes, she is careful to bring him back from the Blazing World just the very information he would like best:

> She . . . . related to her Lord what Magnificent Stables and Riding-Houses the Emperor had built, and what fine Horses were in the Blazing-World, of several shapes and sizes, and how exact their shapes were in each sort, and of many various Colours, and fine Marks as if they had been painted by Art . . . . Were there but a passage out of the Blazing-World into this, said she, you should not onely have some of these Horses, but such Materials, as the Emperor has, to build your Stables and Riding-Houses withal.[3]

We have omitted to mention many of the wonders which exist in the Blazing World. There is a youth-restorer, which is far more effective than monkey glands. A certain rock produces a gum which takes one hundred years to reach its full perfection. When heated, this gum melts into an oil which, swallowed in small quantities daily, changes the most ancient man into a youth of twenty. The treatment lasts nine months and causes, during that time, such a complication of bodily misery that none but an ancient lunatic could think the game worth the candle, unless indeed, he were fond of eagles' eggs and hinds' milk, which constitute the entire diet during rejuvenation.

There are many Utopian touches in the Duchess's description of her imagined world. She shows a country with few laws (because many laws lead to dissensions); a country which has only one form of religion, and which cannot have more because the people have "all but one opinion as to the Worship and

3 *Ibid*, p. 31.

Adoration of God." In such ways *The Blazing World* shows kinship with *Gulliver's Travels*.

During the Restoration period novelists and playwrights continued to be inspired by notions of imaginary worlds, but, as we have seen, this was already an established genre of writing, which gained nothing particularly characteristic from Restoration hands. The Duchess of Newcastle did not conform to Restoration fashions in prose fiction, and it is for that reason that we are justified in mentioning here separately not only *The Blazing World*, but also those other forms in which she contributed to the growth of the novel.

The Duchess of Newcastle kept clear of the entire school of the Heroic Romance. It offended her by its artificiality and by its false emphasis on the rhodomontade or the whining of lovers. She believed in love, but with a difference, and she assigned it a different value in the scheme of existence. She wrote feigned stories, but she made the distinction that they should not contain feigned estimates of life. She was a realist, not drawn towards the kind of realism in the *novelle*, but to a typically English expression of English life. She would have disowned allegiance to any school but that of Margaret the First; nevertheless, certain of her efforts at fiction show the same kind of native realism as we find in the writings of Greene, Nash, Breton and Deloney.

In 1656 appeared *Nature's Pictures drawn by Fancie's Pencil to the Life*. This work contains ten books consisting of moral tales, fables, dialogues, and some stories of varied lengths in which the moral is not explicit. At the end is " a true story in which there is no feigning" i.e., *The True Relation* . . .

The frontispiece of the volume containing *Experimental Philosophy* and the *Blazing World* prepares us somewhat for the contents. The Duchess there confronts one with a rakish air, her coronet askew to give place to the wreath of laurels with which she is being crowned by four fat cherubs. Literary and noble insignia thus precariously perched give an air of ill-balanced and ambitious distinction to the wearer. But if a frontispiece is symbolic of a book, then more normal entertainment awaits us in *Natures Pictures*. Diepenbeck's very rare

engraving shows us the Duke and Duchess of Newcastle,
crowned with bays, sitting comfortably before a roaring fire,
surrounded by their relations—all the children, wives and
husbands—who are listening spell-bound to the stories which
the Duchess relates. Underneath is the verse:

> " Thus in this Semi-Sircle wher they sitt,
>   Telling of Tales of pleasure and of witt,
>   Heer you may read without a Sinn or Crime,
>   And how more innocently pass your tyme."

We soon perceive, however, that even this fireside group is no
sanctuary from Margaret Newcastle's abstractions. When the
philosophic sock is on the Duchess proves herself without heart
or conscience, scrupling nothing to attract us with a very good
beginning and then to cheat us of the tale. For example, *The
Schools Quarrels, or Scholars Battles* commences thus:

> A man travelling, and being very weary, seeing a large House,
> alighted, and went to the Gates, which he found open for any
> to pass without any opposition; and entering therein, he came
> into a large paved Court; and walking about it, he heard a noyse
> or sound like a great Wind whereat he looks up towards the
> Clouds, and seeing the Air not much agitated, he wondered at
> it; at last he looked in at a Door that was open, but there was
> such a mist, that he could see no further than the entrance . . .4

But, alas! when he enters, he merely sees a library in which a
number of old men in tattered gowns are turning the leaves of
books, with a loud noise, and arguing about Grammar, Logic,
Moral Philosophy and kindred subjects.

Sometimes the Duchess's philosophising takes the form of a
witty conversation which much enlivens her didacticism. For
example:

> There was a grave Matron, who came to visit a young Virgin,
> whom she asked why she did not marry, since she was of mar-
> riageable years.   Truly, said she, I am best pleased with a
> single life.
> What! answered the Matron, will you lead Apes in Hell? The
> young lady said, it was better to lead Apes in Hell, than to live

4 *Natures Pictures* . . . Bk. 2.

I

like Devils on Earth, for, said she, I have heard that a married
Couple seldome or never agree, the Husband roars in his drink,
and the Wife scolds in her Choler, the Servants quarrell, the
Children cry, and all is disorder, than 'tis thought Hell is, and a
more confused noise.

Said the Matron, such are onely the poor meaner sort of people,
that live so; but the noble and rich men and their wives live
otherwise; for the better sort, as the noble and rich, when they
are drunk are carried straight to bed and laid to sleep, and their
wives dance until their husbands are sober. Said the Lady,
if they dance until their Husbands are sober, they will dance
until they are weary; so they do, replied the Matron.[5]

It is, of course, the Duchess who speaks through the lips of
the Discreet Virgin.   The action of the story is permanently
suspended while the Virgin delivers a diatribe on men and
their manners.   We are not surprised to find that the Virgin
eschews matrimony altogether, her final denunciation running
into two folio pages.   This is only one example of Margaret
Newcastle's habit of using her characters as mouthpieces for
her own opinions.   She herself is her favourite heroine, and
she stalks through all her plays and most of her stories, talking
commonsense about life or nonsense about philosophy,
challenging all comers to argument, fencing according to a wild
and whirling fashion of her own. Her opponents always leave
their guard open, and she drives her blade home to the very
hilt.   They are not dead, however.   They turn up again under
a different label to be further reduced to mincemeat. Often these
debates end in the opposers rolling the whites of their eyes
heavenwards in astounded appreciation of this female prodigy
who is invariably—the Duchess.

The supreme example of this kind of "story" is *The
Anchoret*.[6] Once upon a time there was a young woman who,
after her father's death, vows herself to a secluded and single
life, but gives leave to any to speak to her through the grating
of her cell. She has not long been enclosed when she grows
"as famed as Diogenes in his tub." All sorts of people come
to converse with her, or rather to listen to her. The face is
the face of the Anchoret, but the voice which discourses breath-

5 *Ibid*, Bk. 2, 'The Discreet Virgin.'
6 *Ibid*, Bk. 10.

lessly of "Atomes" could belong to nobody but the Duchess.
The rest of the story is a mere recital of the inspired replies
made by the Anchoret on a variety of subjects:

> Then they asked her what the Moon was?
> She answered a body of Water . . .
> Then they asked her, what Snow, Hail, Ice and Frost was.
> She answered, that Snow was curded water . . .
> As for Frost, said she, that is candied, or crusted vapour.
> Then they asked her what caused sleep in Animal figures.
> She said the tiredness or weariness of sensitive innated matter,
> which are called sensitive spirits, as of that part of the innated
> which works more to the use than to the consistence . . . . for
> though the sensitive spirits doth not desist from moving in any
> part, as to the consistence, or dissolution of the figure, yet all
> the sensitive spirits doth not work one and the same way . . . .
> but as some of the innated matter or spirits work in several
> parts of a figure on the dull part of matter to the consistence
> or dissolution of the figure, so others and sometimes one and
> the same degree works to the use, consistence, or necessities of
> the figure.

This inquisition continues for fifty-nine folio pages, and
embraces all possible and impossible subjects. Finally, the
fame of the Anchoret reaches the ears of a wicked monarch who
comes to see her and immediately becomes " a desperat Lover."
He has a wife, but when a man decides to marry an encyclopedia
all flesh is grass. Encyclopedias, however, are best on the shelf,
and sometimes they recognise their proper place. The Anchoret
scorns the tender passion. She makes an oration to a convenient multitude, and swallows poison before anyone can
prevent her, whether they would have done so being a con-
troverted point.

We have deliberately shown that the Duchess and her pseudo-
philosophy spoiled between them many of the tales in *Natures
Pictures*. There remains, however, more than sufficient
material to prove that, when the Duchess alights from her
hobby-horse and directs her attention to the world about her,
she is, beyond gainsaying, a very good story-teller.

Let us take first *The Matrimonial Agreement*. The characters
have no names; indeed, they are simply types, but it is nevertheless a very convincing story of real life. The events move

rapidly and clearly. There is not one redundant word. If the Duchess could more often have written thus nobody could deny her ability to fashion excellent, flexible prose, and to describe with humour and sincerity. It is a pity that space does not permit us to quote the tale in its entirety, but we must limit our wishes.

It is the story of a handsome young man and a fair young lady. He comes a-wooing, but she distrusts the permanency of love in matrimony. She agrees finally to marry him, but, as a proof of good faith, she asks that he settle on her part of his estate, so that, should he prove a false husband, she may be in a position to leave him. Confident of his fidelity, he agrees. They marry, and for some time all goes well. Then, after two years, the wife falls very ill, and recovers very slowly. At first, the husband is kind and sympathetic; then he becomes weary. Business calls him abroad and he embraces the opportunity. Henceforth he spends as much time as possible from home, and evades all his wife's questions as to the business (now entirely mythical) which so engages his attention:

The Husband returning home one day from jolly Company, whose discourse was merry and wanton, he met with his Wife's Maid at the door, and ask'd her how her Mistris did; she said, not very well; thou lookest well, said he and chucks her under the chin; she proud of her Masters kindness, smerks and smiles upon him, insomuch that the next time he met her he kiss'd her. Now she begins to despise her Mistris, and onely admires her self, and is allwayes the first person or servant that opens her Master the door; and through the diligence of the Maid, the Masters great affair abroad were ended, and his onely employment and busy care is now at home.

In the meantime his wife grew well, and his Maid grew pert and bold towardes her Mistris; and the Mistris wondered at it; began to observe more strictly what made her so; for perceiving the Wench came oftener than accustomed where her Husband and she were; also she found her Husband had allwayes some excuse to turn his head and eyes to that place where she was; and whenever the Wench came where they were, he would alter his discourse, talking extravagantly.

The wife realises her husband's infidelity, but nothing is said. He is sent on State affairs into another country, and lives there in a profligate manner: " Like a Horse that hath broken his reins, when he finds himself loose, skips over Hedges, Ditches and Pales . . . so wildly he runs about untill he is wearied." His wife goes to visit him while he is abroad. He feigns a welcome, shows her the sights, and hurries her home again: "So she, good woman, goeth home to care and spare, whil'st he spends." When he returns home at last, "Custom making Confidence, and Confidence Carelessness, [he] begins to be less shy, and more free, insomuch as . . . . his Maid, whom he did but eye, and friendly kiss, now he courts in every room; and were it not for his Estate he made over, even before his Wife's face; but that made him fawn and flatter, and somewhat for quietness sake."

At last, however, the wife has ocular proof of his back-sliding. She finds a letter from one of his mistresses. He cringes and promises amendment.

> No, said she, I never will trust in a broken Wheel; do you know what is in my power, said she? Yes, said he, a great part of my Estate. O how I adore Dame Nature, said she, that gave me those two Eyes, Prudence to foresee and Providence to provide; but I have not onely your Estate, but your Honour and Fame in my power; so that, if I please, all that see you shall hiss at you and condemn whatever you do.
> For if you had the beauty of Paris, they would say you were but a fair Cuckold.
> If you had the Courage of Hector, they would say you were but a desperate Cuckold.
> Had you the Wisdom of Ulysses, or Salomon, they would laugh and say, there goes he that is not so wise as to keep his wife honest.

With these words she embarks on a course as dissipated as her husband's, nor can he say her nay, because she has his example before her and his money to give her independence. "So they play like Children at bo-peep in Adultery; and face it out with fair looks, and smooth it over with sweet words, and live with false hearts and die with large Consciences. But these repenting, when they dyed, made a fair end."

Plain words for plain facts. Cupid does not aim his dart, Philander's soul does not burn, Elismonda does not languish, and pen grandiose epistles before yielding the last favour. The Duchess knows the jargon, but she will have none of it. In that loose age of sham and tinsel she knows the unequivocal English word for "Gallantry," and she does not hesitate to use it. Until we examine the contemporary Restoration literature we cannot estimate at its full worth the moral and literary realism of this highly individual woman.

But it is not always plain words which the Duchess gives us. When she feels beauty, then words flock to her like seraphs dropping from heaven. It is in words like these she relates *The Tale of the Lady in Elysium*. There was a Lord who made suit to a lady. She agrees to marry him and then hears a false report which wounds her to the heart. She falls into a swoon and for an hour is believed dead. When she recovers, she describes the country where she has lingered. She was not dead, " 'twas onely the sudden and violent passion which hurried my soul to Charon's Boat in a distracted Whirlwinde of Sighs, where in the Crowd I was ferried over to the Elyzium Fields . . . . such a place the Poets had described, pleasant green Fields, but as dark as a Shady Grove, or the dawning of the Day, or like a sweet Summer's evening when the Nightengale begins to sing."

We have referred to Margaret Newcastle's English realism and compared her in that respect to the best of the popular school. *The Marriage Contract* supported this claim, and *The Tale of the Traveller* definitely establishes it. This is the story of a man who tries many ways of life in succession, only to find that happiness was waiting for him always in the place from which he first set out. His education is described from horn-book to University, and it is continued in travel abroad. His observation of distant countries and the various aspects of life, civil governments, peace and war, military glory, all merely serve to convince him that country life on his own estate is best. Then follows a truly excellent description of the country squire, an ancestor from whom Sir Roger de Coverley would be very proud to have descended:

> Well, said he, I will now return to my native Soil again, leaving the flattering and dissembling Courts, the deboist Cities, the Cruell Warrs, and never take up Arms more, but when my King and Country sends me forth, but I will lead a Countrey life, study husbandry, follow my plows, sell my cattell and

corn, butter and cheese at markets and faires, kisse the
country Wenches, and carry my Neighbours Wife to a tavern
when market is done, live thriftily and grow rich; then . . . .
he returned to his own Countrey, where after he had visited
his friends, who had joyed to see him, and had welcomed him
home, he put himself into one of his Farm houses; stocking his
grounds, taking men-servants, and maid-servants to follow his
business, and he himself would oversee and direct, clothing
himself in a frize Jerkin, and a payre of frize breeches, a frize
pair of mittins and a frize mountier-cap, to keep out sharp
cold in Winter mornings, when the breath freezes between the
teeth; industrious to call up his servants, before day light, and
was the last a bed when their work was done. And in Summer-
time he would be up, with the Lark, to mow down his hay, to
reap down his harvest, to see his Carts loaded, riding from
cart to cart; and at noone would set down on his sheafs of
corne or hay-cocks, eating bread and cheese, and young oynions
with his regiment of Work-men, tossing the black leather-bottle,
drinking the healths of the Country Lasses and Goodwives,
that dwelt thereabouts; and after his harvest was brought into
his barnes; and his sheep-shearing-time done, make merry, as
the custome of the Countrey was, with good cheer, although
Countrey-fare, as Goose-pyes, Pudding-pyes, Furmity, Custards,
Aples, and march-beere, dancing to the horne-pipe, with the
lusty lasses and merry good Wives, who were drest in all
their bravery, in their stammell petticoats and their grey Cloth-
wascoates or white-wascoats wrought with black worsted, and
green aprons.
The men with cloth-breeches and leather doublets, with peuter
buttons, these and the like recreations the Countrey people hath
mixt with their hard labours; when their stomacks were full
and their leggs weary with dancing, or rather with running and
leaping; for their dances hath no nice and difficult measures
to tread, they disperse every one to their severall houses, which
are thatcht, and only holes cut for windows, unless it be the
rich farmers, and they most commonly have a chief room which
is glazed yet the poorer sort are seldom without bacon, cheese,
and butter to entertain a friend at any time.
Then giving thanks to the gentlemen for their good cheere,
and he shaking them every one by the hand, took their leave.[7]

Now follows his search for a suitable wife, which is described
with great simplicity and vividness. A young lady is found with
all the necessary qualities. Their first interview passes off very
well, and each retires to consider the situation and to come to a
decision. The Squire confides in his man, Jack, and the lady

[7] *Natures Pictures* . . . Bk. 9, 'The Tale of the Traveller.'

in her maid, Joan. There is much humour and raciness in these touches, but alas! there is space to quote only a little more:

> . . . Thus while the Master was trimming himself up, his man and he discoursed.
> In the meantime, the young lady was gone into her Chamber; and calling her Maid to bring her the Glass, and to view if the curls of her hair were in order. Lord, said she, Joan, how red my face is! I seem as if I were drunk, my cheeks burn like fire. You told me the other day I was in the Green-sickness, you cannot think so now.

They are married, and "Whilst he governed his outward Affairs, she governed the Family at home, where they lived plentifully, pleasantly and peaceably, not extravagantly, vaingloriously, and luxuriously; they lived neatly and cleanly, they loved passionately, thrived moderately, and happy they lived and piously died."

The fable was another kind of feigned story which the Duchess of Newcastle considered worth writing. From 1484, when Caxton published the first English translation, Aesop's Fables had been extremely popular, and that they continued to be so is proved by the great number of translations and paraphrases which constantly appeared up to the nineteenth century and beyond it. Before 1656 there had been numerous editions, and the Duchess, therefore, had ample opportunity to grow familiar with this literary form. It was natural that she should have a lively interest in this kind of story-telling. There was within her an irrepressible spring of simplicity, wonder and imagination—her secret of eternal youth—and she regarded Nature with the loving familiarity of a child. Like a child, she liked nothing better than to endue animals and birds with human personalities, to create conversations between them, and to record their supposed thoughts and adventures. Indeed, sometimes, she goes further and distinguishes their characters with circumstantial quirks and quiddities. Even in her poems, published in 1653, three years before *Natures Pictures*, there is clear evidence of this disposition.

Wat the Hare is not simply any member of the hare family. He is himself and none other. Whether he is lying, chin on paws, between a furrow, or sitting on his hindlegs washing his ears, or gazing obliquely out of his great grey eyes, or fleeing wildly before the pack, or dying without a cry—still he is Wat to the very last whisker. So it is with the Sparrow, that Bolshevik bird who piles up his arguments against human tyrants with the most ruthless and cocky logic. So it is with the "Oake Tree in the Grove," that mild and noble veteran. The Duchess had the power of making such characters live.

It is not surprising then that her fables, which constitute Book 4 of *Natures Pictures*, are all very good. They are four in number: three moral tales of the Ant and the Bee, and the moral tale of the Woodcock and the Cow. Since we have already described what the Duchess made of this sort of writing, there is no need to dissect these fables. Each exemplifies a moral truth which is, however, so skilfully interwoven that it never obtrudes itself dryly. The characters are spirited and are presented with humorous insight. Sometimes we are given a sudden revelation of style, as for example in *The Woodcock and the Cow*. The two are comparing their lives. One enjoys the freedom of the air; the other the security of the earth. Each envies the other. The Woodcock complains that in the air there is no food, whereas:

> You sit here all day chewing the Cud . . . and in the Summer
> you are put to rich Pasture, or lye in green Meadows
> growing thick with Cowslips and Daisies; or else for change,
> you walk up to the Mountain-tops to brouse on wilde Time,
> or sweet Margerum; and yet you rail against our good Mother
> Earth from whose Bowels we receive life, and food to main-
> tain the life she gives us; she is our kinde Nurse, from whence
> we suck out of her springing Brests fresh Water, and are fed
> by her Hand of Bounty, shaded under her spreading Boughs
> and sheltered from Storms in her thick Groves.

Surely it was a happy portent that a woman could, with inspired realism, bring to her narrative such strong, simple and melodious prose.

We cannot close an account of the Duchess's contributions to prose fiction, without commenting on her *Sociable Letters*.[8] It will be necessary later to discuss the growth of the Epistolary Novel, and to show that Richardson was by no means an innovator in form or in idea.   Among those who anticipated him were several women, and it is to such a discussion that the *Sociable Letters* are most cogent.   Let us here content ourselves in remarking with Jusserand: "She too may be credited with having anticipated Richardson in her *Sociable Letters* in which she tries to imitate real life, to describe scenes, very nearly to write an actual novel." [9]

Speaking still of the Duchess of Newcastle, Jusserand says: "Among the mass of her writings . . . ideas are scattered here and there which are destined to live, and through which she anticipated men of true and real genius."   Yes, but that is only a part of the truth.   It is not only by embryonic ideas that the Duchess contributed to the development of the novel, but also by such definite means as we have illustrated—in a word, by avoiding the decadent, and by showing in many forms her adherence to the living trend in story-telling.

8 *CCXL Sociable Letters* (1664).
9 J. J. Jusserand, *The English Novel in the time of Shakespeare* (1890), p. 378.

CHAPTER V

MAIN RESTORATION GENRES CONTRASTED.

> " Love in fantastic triumph sate
> While bleeding hearts around him flowed,
> For whom fresh pains he did create,
> And strange tyrannic power he showed."
>
> (Aphra Behn, *Abdelazar*.)

1660: fanfare of trumpets! Ring up the curtain on the literary tragi-comedy of the Restoration period. To describe the period from the literary point of view one would need the antithetical pen of Carlyle. Then one might say—it was an age of brilliance and an age of squalor; an age of vitality and an age of paralysis; an age of genius and an age of servile imitation. For drama it was a period of intense activity; for the novel it was a period of stagnation. It was an age when a large number of women forced their way into both fields, and at least held their own. Before we judge their work, let us consider the public they had to serve and the possibilities of developing prose fiction at that time.

The Restoration, coming after long years of bloodshed and rancour, found a certain section of the English people drained of idealism and sentiment. Events had made them cynics. They had seen England rebel against kingship only to groan under the heel of common men; now they heard the cry " Long live King Charles," and their minds sardonically revived the memory of one frosty morning in Whitehall. They had seen a revolt against what was termed licence in life and art, and had watched life being narrowed down to a mere preparation for death: for their part they were sick of death, coldly determined that life should pay them their arrears. For twenty years there had been too much dying, too much whispering, too much canting, too much wrestling with the spirit. It would take more than three score years and ten to wipe out the memory of those starved years of poverty and exile, to press into one lifetime all the luxury, the licence, the love, wit, beauty, shapes, colours, perfumes, sounds—all the richness of life to satisfy senses and brain—not heart nor conscience—those painful and demoded organs were no longer necessary to life. Necessary to happiness, whines the Puritan? Happiness—what thing is that? It is a word like so many other words that mean nothing—like love, for instance, or honour, or fidelity or fortune. When a man has seen governments rise and fall, love debased, honour shift with every wind, fortune crumble overnight, he cannot really be expected to regard them seriously, in the manner of good simple folk of twenty years ago. It is, after all, more amusing and more sensible and infinitely less ennuyant to take the world with careless elegance like a pinch of snuff.

This, in effect, was the philosophy which Charles II and his courtiers shared alike. It was by no means the philosophy of all England. The Puritans stood apart. Middle class citizens, steadily growing in power, regarded the new era with a suspicious or an indulgent eye, according to their dispositions, or their chance of worldly success. Dissenters from the Restoration spirit had no power to check it, or to moderate its effect on the literature of the age, and though they did express themselves in one immortal book, they cannot be considered in our present scheme.

At the Restoration, the people of England were passing through a phase of disillusionment and spiritual exhaustion. They might show energy in literary work, but it was not likely that they would show much initiative. It was, in fact, a time when imitation of French literary fashions reached a height unparalleled since the days when, between the Conquest and the rise of Chaucer, England forgot that she had a native genius and accepted the literary dominance of France. English Drama, which absorbed the main interest and activity at the Restoration, was to a great extent modelled on the French, although, indeed, France was not responsible for the depravity which became its peculiar characteristic. In fiction English writers gave to the French more than predominance: on the whole, they did not even compete, preferring to let French prose fiction satisfy the needs of English romance-readers. Drama was strangling prose fiction, and English writers had practically no interest at all in averting its doom.

Prior to 1660, English imitation of French Drama had been rendered impossible owing to Puritan oppression of the theatre, but for a considerable time before the Restoration (from the year 1647 onwards) a particular kind of French prose fiction had invaded England. This was the French Heroic Romance. Gomberville's *Polexandre* was the advance guard soon to be followed by the works of La Calprenède and Mlle. de Scudéry. Battalions continued to arrive even until the year 1677 when Mlle. de Scudéry's *Almahide* made its appearance. It is difficult now to understand how these ponderous romances, dragging on their wearisome and complicated narratives through tome after tome (sometimes through a dozen folio volumes), could possibly have won and retained the interest of the reading public. Apart from the unreality of their subject matter, one would have supposed it no small inconvenience to wait long years to discover whether the hero and heroine are finally united. For example in *Clélie*, published by Madeleine de Scudéry in January, 1649, the tale begins:

" There never shone such a fine day as the one which was to be the eve of the nuptials between the illustrious Aronce and the admirable Clélie." The marriage is delayed until the end of the tenth and last volume in September, 1654.

These heroic romances grew from the popularity of D'Urfé's *L'Astrée*, which was, however, like the *Arcadia*, a union of the pastoral and the chivalric romances. The pastoral trend of d'Urfé's romance was not much imitated, but the chivalric trend grew into the French Heroic Romance. *L'Astrée* bequeaths to the heroic romance three very important characteristics: authentication of background; the sovereignty of love, and a new conception of the relationship between men and women, whereby women were made the centre of society and the objects of respectful devotion.

These French Heroic Romances all had for their theme the love of a great hero for a lovely and discreet lady. He might be a Frenchman, a Roman, a Merovingian or a Turk, he might be the conqueror of the entire world, but he was still the captive of love. His love, the mainspring of all his actions, was of the most idealistic kind. He would endure for twenty years the most tremendous onslaughts of fate, perform the most heroic feats of valour, and then think himself mightily rewarded by one glance from the pure eyes of the fair one. A signal favour, such as a ribbon from the lady's wrist, or a scarf from the ivory column of her neck, was enough to spur him on there and then to another twenty years' hard labour. As the imagination of the authors, who were, after all, human, sank before the prospect of inventing sufficient exploits and obstacles to fill the customary succession of folio volumes, they adopted the device of making their characters write innumerable letters to each other, and constantly recount the stories of their lives. Sometimes, says Jusserand, we see them go to bed in order to listen more comfortably. In *Cassandre*, the eunuch Tireus has a story to tell Prince Oroondates: " 'The prince went to his bedroom and put himself to bed; he then had Tireus called to him, and having seats placed in the ruelle, he commanded us to sit,' [1] and then the story begins; and it goes on for pages; and when it is finished we observe that it was included in another story told by Araxe; wherefore instead of finding ourselves among the actors of the principal tale, we alight among those of Araxe's narratives. These stories are thus enclosed in one another like Chinese boxes." [2]

It is perhaps incredible, but it is none the less true, that even during the Civil War these French Heroic Romances were greedily devoured by the upper and the bourgeois classes in England. Charles I, on the eve of his execution, distributing some of his books as souvenirs, left *Polexandre* to the Earl of Lindsay. Dorothy Osborne, against the background of a convulsed England, constantly exchanges with Sir William Temple

---

[1] *Cassandre,* i, Bk. v.
[2] J. J. Jusserand, *The English Novel in the time of Shakespeare* (1890), p. 362.

volumes of *Cleopâtre* and *Le Grand Cyrus*. Mrs. Pepys, somewhat later, was an insatiable reader of French romances. Despite
her husband's avowed disapproval, he not only bought them
for her as a peace offering when he had been too attentive to
Pierce or Knipp, but actually stayed up late at night to read
them himself.   No doubt the immediate popularity of these
romances was due to the fact that they were a refuge from grim
reality, but it must be remembered that the *Arcadia* had left in
England a definite susceptibility to such fiction.

Whatever the attitude in England towards the Heroic Romance
up to 1660, one would not have expected the Restoration public
to tolerate such tedious accounts of a kind of love quite alien to
their cynicism. Probably they would not have done so if these
romances had been their only form of fictional amusement, but
in fact the main interest of the public and the main energies of
the best writers were all devoted to the drama.   It is true that
the two London playhouses were the only ones in England, and
that they were attended only by the corrupt, courtly clique and
the riff-raff of the town.   But this did not limit the influence
of the drama.   Plays were printed and widely circulated, and
they furnished a depraved eroticism far more titillating than the
meek pruderies of heroic love.   We have nothing to do with
the heroic tragedies which were partly modelled on French
Tragedy and partly a distortion of Shakespeare, but Restoration
Comedy, although at the time it stunted the writing of prose
fiction, nevertheless enriched it in the long run.   It was based
on imitation of Ben Jonson, but more particularly on Molière,
and though it was a depraved offspring of these sources, its
brilliance cannot be denied.   It was a comedy of manners, and
even if it represented the scavengings of human nature it
represented them in a very realistic way. It developed a flexible,
life-like prose, graphic description, excellent dialogue and
minute characterisation—*minute*, not deep.   It is interesting to
note how rapidly Restoration Comedy gained that verisimilitude
which was denied to the novel.   This was because the novel
was being ignored as a vehicle for story-telling, but also because
a story in action compels realism.   A novel though utterly
untrue to life, may by the very number and extravagance of its

episodes or by its style make us forget that we are being cheated
of reality, or at least make us willing to be so. With a play it is
far otherwise. However much our imagination is willing to be
imposed upon, it is continually being checked by the senses,
which insist that the little world on the stage must represent
the world we know. Comparing even in length the Heroic
Romance and the drama, the reversal of aim is apparent—one
endeavouring to concentrate action and the other incredibly to
prolong it. It was no wonder that Congreve, in his *Incognita*
tried to enclose a written story within the dramatic unities.

But it was really quite unnecessary to seek in the drama some
clue towards the concentration of action in prose fiction. The
astounding fact is that over a hundred years previously England
had been flooded with short, vivid, realistic stories—true novels
in miniature—and yet, although they proved a wonderful
inspiration to English drama, they were not accepted as models
by English writers of fiction. The *novelle* may be said to have
flowered simultaneously in France and Italy during the Middle
Ages. Italy hit on the form of the *novella*. France, meanwhile,
had been embodying similar material in the *fabliaux*, which
when made into prose, stood side by side with the Italian prose
tale as belonging to the same genre—that genre known as the
novella.[3] In 1566 and 1567, Painter and Fenton published their
collections of translated *novelle*,[4] but even before then, in 1563,
Roger Ascham had fulminated against the translation of such
harmful and " ungratious bookes." [5] England welcomed with
delight these pictures drawn from real life, these apparently
authentic stories which displayed " the possibilities of action to
which men and women, in pursuit of any passion, might be
driven by that force or virtu of the will, restrained neither by

---

3 "The fabliaux or fableaux were 'unrhymed' (i.e. made into prose)
and made their appearance in the famous form of the nouvelle or novella,
in regard to which it is hard to say whether Italy is most indebted to
France for substance or France to Italy for form." G. Saintsbury,
History of the French Novel (1917), p. 32.

4 William Painter, *The Palace of Pleasure*, i. (1566); ii (1567); additions
made in 1575. Geoffrey Fenton, *Certaine Tragical Discourses* (1567).
There were many other collections of translated *novelle*.

5 The *Scholemaster*, begun in 1563; left unfinished at Ascham's death
in 1568.

law nor conscience." [6]   But neither Bandello, Cinthio, Boccaccio, Margaret of Navarre, Straparola nor Fiorentino could induce the English to imitate their example and to write such stories as the *novelle*.   Possibly this was because a strong bent towards the drama caused English writers to ignore prose fiction, and to embody the influence of the *novelle* in dramatic form.   There was also the very important fact that prose writers had to please their powerful patrons, and that the aristocratic taste was entirely in favour of the Chivalric and the Pastoral Romances and their modifications.   England of the Elizabethan period was about two hundred years behind Italy in culture and in sophistication.   The English people had banished dragons from their romances, but they still preferred to live in a world of illusion which was merely an echo of medieval chivalry and Greek idylls, and which was a complete contrast to the surging life about them.   Also, they were not attracted by the intrigues which were the pivotal point in the *novelle*.   They preferred to adhere in fiction to the idea of constancy in love, a central theme which they had adopted from the Greek and Spanish romances.   From free fancy to realism is the road of development in fiction.   The Italians had arrived.   The English refused to be hurried, chiefly because they did not know where they were going.   They preferred to linger on the way, indulging in prolonged and complicated daydreams.   Indeed they were benighted, for when they had almost escaped from Arcadia they lost themselves again in the *pays du tendre*.

Suddenly, after this long period of quiescence, the *novelle* once more sprang into activity.   From about the year 1670 onwards it again commenced to attract attention.   From 1640, when they were first translated as a whole by Mappe, Cervantes' *Exemplary Novels* had engaged the interest of the reading public. They were reprinted in 1694, 1708 and 1728.[7]   In these Spanish tales the subject was generally the struggles of two lovers to be united in spite of cruel parents; or the determination of the deserted girl to pursue her recreant lover.   Both the

---

[6] Lord Earnle, *Light Reading of our Ancestors* (1921), p 112.
[7] Individual tales appeared much oftener in collections, such as *The Four Tragicomical Histories of Our late Times* (1638), *The Annals of Love* (1672), and the *Spanish Decameron* (1687).

K

Spanish and the Italian short stories were alike in the strata-
gems and surprises in which the plot worked itself out.
Both had also the great attraction of brevity.   This was one
reason for the revival of interest in the *novelle* after 1670.
Another and very powerful reason was that they were erotic, and
in this respect the Italian *novelle* far outdid the *Exemplary
Novels*.   The Italian *novella* had for its central theme sensual
love—all the subterfuges and scheming of infidelity. No wonder
that in the Restoration period, the *novella* had a new lease of
life, and that this time its influence was not indirect. It aroused
imitators.   The reading public was not only beginning to weary
of the tortuous prolixity of the Heroic Romance, but was at
last beginning to realise that, like the sandpiper in the proverb,
it could not fish both strands at once.   Gallant and fine lady
could not equally enjoy the intrigues of the drama (or of their
own experience) and the mawkish naïveté of Oroondates and
Cassandra.   They did not speak the same love-language as these
elevated spirits, and they preferred a tale which echoed their own
views and which was full of highly coloured adventures: "Come
near us," says Congreve, "and represent to us intrigues in
practice, delight us with accidents and odd events, but *not such
as are wholly unprecedented,* such which *not being so distant
from our belief,* brings also the pleasure nearer us. Romances
give more of wonder, novels more delight." [8]
    Now, this seems most promising. One would suppose that
the day of the Heroic Romance was ended, and that tales after
the realistic style of the *novelle* would now be written, tales
which would depict the London hurly-burly, the roystering
brilliance of the court, the stout adventures of merchants and
their wives—life in short, however much interwoven with love
intrigue. But alas! the Heroic Romance had not yet loosened
its grip. The short tales which now appeared were so sicklied
over with the romantic cast that they were not really imitations
of the *novella,* but actually sentimental novelettes. These
novelettes were a strange mixture of the worst elements in the
novella and in the Heroic Romance.   From the *novella* was
borrowed its central theme that passionate love justifies every

8 Congreve, Preface to *Incognita.*

means to its end. From the Heroic Romance was borrowed its blue-blooded characters, its grandiose sentimentality and its emotional exaggerations. The result was often farther than ever from reality and the best point in favour of the majority of these productions was their brevity. The Heroic Romance, however unreal, had a certain dignity—a quality which the romantic novelette frequently lacked. The effect which Restoration life and tastes had on most writers is well seen in Roger Boyle. His *Parthenissa*, a clumsy Heroic romance, appeared in six tomes, which were published separately at intervals from 1654 to 1669. In 1676, when court life and a desire to conform to the new fashion in novel writing had changed his outlook, he published a novel called *English Adventures*. It was a medley of the picaresque, the pastoral, scandal veiled as history, and sensual intrigue, all " related with . . . debauched cynicism." [9]

It was to be expected that the romantic vogue would produce a reaction. In France it had done so as early as 1627, when Sorel made fun of *L'Astrée*. Passing from satire he struck a blow for bourgeois realism in his *Francion*.[10] Scarron, Molière, Antony Hamilton, Subligny and Furetière all carried on the anti-romantic campaign. In England, although translations of the French anti-romantic works appeared, they did not inspire imitations until the day of the Heroic Drama was nearly over. And even then readers were still so enmeshed in romantic fiction that they ignored two really notable attempts[11] to disillusion them.

Nor was there wanting a precedent for a finer sort of fiction. In 1678, in the same year as the Pilgrim's Progress (which had no influence on the output of the literary period which it so completely surpassed), there appeared Mme. de la Fayette's *Princesse de Clèves*. This had for its theme renunciation, and it concentrated in its short form a reality, an insight and a power of characterisation which had never before shown themselves in

---

[9] E. A. Baker, *History of the English Novel*, iii, 102.
[10] Published 1622-1641.
[11] *The Adventures of Covent Garden* (1699); and *Zelinda* by T. D. Gent (1769). (T. Duffet, Jusserand suggests)..

French prose fiction. But neither in France nor in England had this any immediate effect.

The picaresque, coney-catching realism, and the imaginary journey drew a feeble life from the writings of Head and Kirkman. Popular fiction awaited the realism of Defoe to develop its powers.

Such were the genres of fiction which existed at the Restoration and in the days of James II. When we come to the women novelists and consider them against the social and literary background which it has been necessary to describe, several points at once suggest themselves. First, that no women unless under financial compulsion would write in such an age; secondly, that a woman hard pressed for money would not be content to sit and starve while she turned out a dozen volumes of Heroic romance; thirdly, that women would write plays as the most popular and paying concern, and write them like men for the depraved tastes of the period; also, that they would excel in the comedy of manners aided by the feminine power of minute observation, and perhaps of repartee; fourthly, that, if they wrote fiction at all (and the first woman writer of the age was possibly forced to it because she was " warned off " the stage), then they would concentrate on the romantic novelette, because it would exactly suit their public, and because it represented their outlook, and was within their literary scope; and, further, one would expect that their experience as dramatists would help them as fiction writers. All these facts are true of the women we shall discuss in this and subsequent chapters.

Aphra Behn was the first and the greatest of the literary swashbucklers who swept into prominence in Restoration and Post-Restoration days. She was one of a band of women early left to fend for themselves either because of moral transgression or lack of money. Many of them were of good family, a few (for example, Mrs. Trotter) led honest private lives. But their origin had nothing to do with their career as writers (Mrs. Pix, the author of the filthy *Spanish Wives*, was a clergyman's daughter). The reason was obvious. If one decides to be a miner one expects to be blackened from head to foot in the course of one's work. A fastidious miner in kid gloves and immaculate suiting, withdrawing delicately from contact with a coaly seam, would at once find that derision and starvation were the sole rewards of his particularity. So it was in the business of writing in Restoration days. The motto might have been "Get dirty or get out," and the women could not get out. They were writing to earn their bread. Their success depended on writing as the men wrote, and the men wrote to please the lewd and cynical tastes of the rich and leisured. The influential public wanted in plays or in stories a representation of life as they knew it, and life as they knew it stank to heaven. Theirs was a world hinging on open sexuality; a world which was, indeed, bored with ordinary immorality, and which insisted on themes of incest and perversion to relieve the monotony; a world in which men and women, even supposedly decent women, talked in an incredibly licentious manner; a world in which women considered it amusing to be mistaken for prostitutes, and in which certain diseases were considered a joke or a boast. Allardyce Nicol says:

All sorts of moral ties, all sense of decency had gone. Women had become as libidinous as the men. "Common women" were "public grown . . . . in this damn'd lewd town." "What a lewd world we live in!" says Aphra Behn, "Oh, London, London, how thou aboundest in iniquity! Thy young men are debauched, thy virgins deflowered, and thy matrons are turned bawds . . . ." Nothing was left to occupy the minds of this circumscribed clique but intrigue and sensuality. Every name and title given to a woman came, during this period, to have an evil significance. "Lady" as Pepys shows us, had become debased in meaning, as had "mother" and "Madam," "Miss" and "Mistress." The utter filth that marks many of the lyrics contained, for example, in such a collection as the *Poems on Affairs of State* is but the ordinary speech of women of this type and of their men companions, made a trifle more "poetical." It is evident from the dialogue in the comedies that the conversation of men with men, or women with men, reaches a freedom seen at no other period of our history. If we listen to the words of a couple of lovers of the time we wonder sometimes whether our ears be not deceiving us. Turn even to a work of one of the geniuses of the age, turn to John Dryden's *Secret Love,* and read the words of Celadon and Florimel; in spite of the wit we stand aghast. That such a conversation as appears in the fifth act of this play—and it was evidently realistic—could ever have taken place between two cultured persons in a civilised society, or that it could have been presented on the stage to a general audience shows us probably as clearly as anything the peculiar temper of the age with which we are dealing.[12]

That is the point we wish to drive home—the peculiar temper of the age, and the fact that it characterised women as well as men.   Moral decadence is never confined to the male members of a community.   If it were, it could not possibly persist unless there were segregation of the sexes.   It is necessary to emphasise another fact.   Aphra Behn and her followers wrote in the Restoration fashion, because they were Restoration women.   To listen to the criticisms levelled at them not only by elegant vipers like Pope, but also by kind and serious critics from that time to the present day, one would suppose that these women could have had the moral principles of Alice Meynell or Elizabeth Browning, but wilfully perverted their natures to write obscenely. Actually they wrote obscenely because their minds were already obscene, and their minds were obscene because they made no effort to resist the spirit of the time.   Could they have withdrawn from infection as did the Duchess of Newcastle?   Certainly, if they had had the Duchess of Newcastle's financial independence.   It is a vicious circle.   Let us, in the name of common sense, judge them as the product of that age, and not as if they could have been the product of the Hannah More era.   Madonna lilies did not flower in the literary London of Aphra Behn.   Tiger lilies did.   All novelists, women included, express some tendency of their period.   Many modern women write salacious fiction with far less external compulsion.

Aphra Behn was the first woman to earn her living by her pen.   The details of her life have been the subject of a controversy upon which a question in regard to her literary creativeness is supposed to hinge.   Since the problem makes itself felt in *Oroonoko*, one of her last works, we shall defer until then a discussion of the conflicting arguments, and here limit ourselves to the humble statement that as she really was born, she must have had parents, and must have had a birthplace.   She maintained that she spent part of her youth in Surinam.   She was

12 Allardyce Nicol, *Restoration Drama, 1660-1700* (2nd ed. 1928), p. 21 f.

certainly engaged in secret-service work in the interests of
Charles II. It is believed that she had been married to a
Dutch merchant in London. There is proof that she had also
been in a debtor's prison. We find her, after the
Restoration, established in London as a writer of plays, holding
her own with the best dramatists of her time. She took the
Tory side against the Whigs and attacked them roundly in her
plays. In revenge, the Whigs succeeded in getting a warrant
issued against her, and she was forced to abandon the theatre
in 1682. She may before then have experimented in novel-
writing, but circumstances now made it, for a while, her legitimate
literary outlet, and though, in 1688, she again took to plays, she
continued to write prose fiction of several kinds up to the time
of her death.

When Mme. de la Fayette wrote her short novel *La Princesse
de Clèves* the way to popular taste was indicated. But already
in England Aphra Behn had brought to the writing of short
novels the power of her personality and her literary prestige.
She created a new vogue which paved the way to important
developments in prose fiction. Not only did the short form give
fresh possibilities to story-telling, but in the hands of Aphra Behn
it showed distinctive trends which were of the utmost value in
the subsequent history of the novel. Mrs. Behn as a novelist,
says Jusserand, can only be studied with the authors of the middle
of the eighteenth century.[13] In her thirteen novels these trends
are sometimes distinct, but more often mingled curiously. There
is the influence of the Heroic Romance, there is the influence
of the continental *novelle*, and there is the urgent prompting of
everyday life. Chronological classification of Mrs. Behn's stories
is very doubtful, and so it is not really necessary to review them
in the order in which they are supposed to have been written,
nor would it be easy since these dates vary so much. It will be
more helpful to consider them as far as possible in relation to
their most predominant trend. Even this, however, is not easy,
since romance and realism are often so interwoven as to defy
classification, and also since it is not always possible to define
whether Aphra Behn's realism is imaginative or genuine.

[13] J. J. Jusserand, *The English Novel in the time of Shakespeare* (1890),
p. 416 f.

It seems very probable that Aphra Behn's first novel was *The Adventures of the Black Lady*.[14]   This tale has signs of immaturity not observable in her other novels.   It is original not only in its brevity, but also in its subject matter which shows clearly that Mrs. Behn had been browsing on anti-romantic literature.   *The Black Lady* is one of the three novels to which Aphra Behn gave a London background and which truly represent the world in which she lives.

The story begins: "About the beginning of last June (as near as I can remember) Bellamora came to town from Hampshire and was obliged to lodge the first night at the same inn where the stage-coach set up." She wishes to spend about six months with Madam Brightly, a kinswoman of hers, undiscovered, if possible, by her friends in the country. She seeks Madam Brightly all over St. Anne's parish, but in vain. And she is so foolish as to entrust her trunk to a porter she saw in the street. She is behaving like the typical country bumpkin; she wanders about, expecting everyone she meets to know the whereabouts of her relative. She is exasperating, but we are sympathetic, and our curiosity is aroused.   How will she extricate herself from this predicament? She does so by a surprising stroke of what we can only call fool's luck. She seeks Madam Brightly in the house of a decayed gentlewoman, and encounters there a lady who knows her, but whom she herself does not know. Next morning

---

[14] Miss Charlotte Morgan *(The Rise of the Novel of Manners,* Columbia Univ. Press, 1911, p. 78) says that *The Little Black Lady* appeared in 1663. No doubt she means that it was then published. She gives no reasons for assigning this very early date, and facts connected with Aphra Behn's biography make it appear improbable. The Calendar of State Papers proves that she went to Holland in August, 1666, on her secret mission, and returned in the following December or January. It was after her return to London that her plays began to be acted and her works published. No doubt, as in the case of *The Young King,* some of them may have been written earlier, but nobody except Miss Morgan has claimed that Aphra Behn published a work of any kind as early as 1663. Could this possibly be a misprint for 1683—a very probable date, since Mrs. Behn had been obliged to abandon the stage temporarily in 1682, and then turned to fiction as her *Love Letters between a, nobleman and his sister,* 1683, testifies? Gosse (in D.N.B.) gives 1684 as the date of *The Adventure of the Black Lady.* It is all the more probable that Miss Morgan's date is a misprint, since, on page 76, there are two similar mistakes, i.e. 1671 (instead of 1670) as the date of Aphra Behn's first play; and 1691 (instead of 1689) as the date of Aphra Behn's death.

she reveals that she came to town to conceal the disgrace brought on her by one Mr. Fairlove who loves her, but whom she refuses to marry. The lady who recognises her is Fairlove's sister. She and the decayed gentlewoman concoct a benevolent plot. They summon Fairlove to town, and, to detain Bellamora until his arrival, they pretend that her trunk (which has been safely delivered) has been lost. By the time Fairlove appears, Bellamora is so distracted with anxiety and misery that she is willing to marry him—and does.

The story is told in a simple, conversational style. It is not of intrinsic value. Its significance is in its background of London life, and in the fact that it was to the familiar scenes around her that Aphra Behn instinctively turned when she decided to write a novel.

When, struck (no doubt) by the realism of *The Black Lady*, some friends of Mrs. Behn's challenged her to imitate Scarron, she wrote *The Court of the King of Bantam*. As it was based on the *Roman Comique*[15] one would naturally expect to find it an anti-romantic, witty tale of London life. This is exactly what it is. The story, which is excellently told, hinges on an elaborate practical joke. It plunges us directly into the fortunes of the principal characters:

This money certainly is a devilish thing! I am sure the Want of it had like to have ruined my dear Philibella in her love to Valentine Goodland; who was really a pretty deserving Gentleman, Heir to about fifteen hundred Pounds a Year; which however did not so much recommend him, as the Sweetness of his Temper, the Comeliness of his Person, and the Excellency of his Parts. In all which Circumstances my obliging Acquaintance equall'd him, unless in the Advantage of their Fortune. Old Sir George Goodland knew his Son's passion for Philibella and tho' he was generous and full of a Humour sufficiently complying yet he could by no means think it convenient that his only Son should marry with a young Lady of so slender a Fortune.

[15] (a) Scarron, *Roman Comique* (Paris), 1651. (b) *Scarron's "Comical Romance: or a facetious history of a company of strolling stage-players* (London), 1676, fol. The latter was not merely a translation, but also an Anglicised version of the *Roman Comique*. The translator substituted London where Scarron spoke of Paris, etc. This work was available at the time when Aphra Behn wrote.

Here with admirable directness, economy and spirit we have the key to the situation which arises. Philibella lives at Charing Cross with an uncle on whom she is dependent, and is adored by a wealthy nincompoop called Mr. Would-be-King. Although married, Mr. Would-be-King is a gay Lothario, and in addition suffers from a *folie de grandeur* which leads him to shower expensive presents on his feminine acquaintances, not, however, in the spirit of pure philanthropy. Philibella steadily ignores his advances, but he continues to visit at her uncle's house. On a particular evening, Sir Philip, his niece and her lover, Valentine Goodland, sit playing cards, with Sir Philip's wife and Lucy, his quondam mistress—a juxtaposition which would amaze anyone given to straining at gnats. Mr. Would-be arrives to find them " very merry, with a flask or two of Claret before 'em and Oranges roasting by a large fire for it was Christmas time." They win a considerable sum of money from him, and Sir Philip urges him to come again on Twelfth Night to renew the famous and ancient solemnity of choosing king and queen. This invitation is given in furtherance of a scheme which Sir Philip has devised, by which Would-be shall be parted from £3,000, and Philibella shall be united to Valentine. Valentine is instructed that on Twelfth Night he shall pick a quarrel with Would-be, and Lucy is to pretend that she is simply a niece to Sir Philip. On the appointed evening, Would-be-King arrives, and is entertained most royally. In fact, so that nothing shall be lacking in his splendid illusion, it has been arranged that by the lots in the cake, he shall be chosen king. To the surprise of the household, he has brought musicians who play all the more merrily for the money he lavishes on them " for gold and wine doubtless are the best rosin for musicians." In comes the mighty cake "teeming with the Fate of this extraordinary Personage." Would-be discovers the bean which indicates that he is King of the revels, and Lucy (by a similar prearrangement) is the Queen. Healths are drunk amid laughter and huzzas, and the dupe becomes intoxicated, chiefly with magnificence. He gives costly presents to Lucy and Philibella, and incautiously offers Valentine enough money to marry whomever he likes. He is enraged to hear that Lucy is " that not impossible she," and turns furiously on Valentine, thus relieving him of the necessity of picking a quarrel. They exchange insults, Valentine playing his role with a zest derived from Would-be's attentions to Philibella. After an eruption of rhodomontade he departs, breathing vengeance. " Let him go " cries Would-be, " like a pragmatical captious, giddy fool he is! I shall take a time to see him." Sir Philip ingeniously points out that Valentine cannot fail to have the upper hand as he is to be married to Lucy before Easter. Would-be falls into the trap, and led by amorousness, vanity and spite, reacts exactly as Sir Philip had hoped he would. This worthy knight explains that Lucy has a fortune of £3000, and that accordingly Valentine means to marry her although he loves Philibella. But how diverting it would be if Lucy could be induced to become Would-be's mistress before becoming Valentine's wife! The King of Bantam is enchanted at the prospect. That it is to be achieved by giving Philibella a fortune of £3,000 does not deter him, because, as Sir Philip points out, he can recover the sum in gaming with her future husband, a young fop appropriately called Sir Philip Flygold. In fact, this is a doubly useful scheme because it will give him future power over Philibella. To while away the time until morning the intriguing pair play piquet, and Sir Philip, with unaccountable luck, wins three thousand two hundred guineas, for which Would-be gives him a bond witnessed by Will Watchful and Sim Slyboots, Sir Philip's servants, " a couple of delicate beagles," as Mrs. Behn inimitably calls them. The next day Sir Philip receives Valentine, reports progress and instructs him now to make his peace with Would-be, which he does to the great relief of that regal personage, who, in contemplation of a duel, has already died a thousand deaths. Sir Philip returns the bond to Would-be on condition that he pays £3,000 to Philibella. This is done. A few days later Would-be achieves his supposed vengeance only to discover that Philibella and Valentine have married on the strength of the money he has so obligingly provided.

The *King of Bantam* is surprisingly modern in form, and we see in it a proof of what Aphra Behn could have achieved had she been brave enough to abandon more frequently and more

fully the Heroic tradition, and to depict life as she knew it. Here
we have a glimpse of Restoration London, not an edifying
glimpse, but if we are to walk with Aphra Behn we must be
prepared to take things in our stride. How real it is, how completely alive—the jostling crowds, the eating houses, the plying
coaches, the theatre (described with authentic particulars of the
very plays being acted at the time and with familiar references to
the King's box), not to mention the ways of the reckless gallants.
the drinking-bouts, the gaming, the balls! We know so well
already all these people to whom we are introduced: "The Lady
Flippant, the Lady Harpy, the Lady Crocodile, Madam Tattlemore, Miss Medler, Mrs. Gingerly, a rich Grocer's wife, and
some others besides Knights and gentlemen of as good humours
as the ladies." "There can be no mistaking Madam Tattlemore
with a secret: "How wondrous hasty was she to be gone, as
soon as she heard it! It was not in her power, because it
was not in her nature, to stay long enough to take a civil leave
of the company, but away she flew . . . proclaiming it to every
one of her acquaintance."

   The Unfortunate Happy Lady is the third[16] of these novels
that reflect a London background. It is less characteristic of
this background than are *The Adventures of the Black Lady* and
the *King of Bantam,* and it is more like an Italian or Spanish
novella. The ironic style is rather in the manner of Scarron.
The story begins:

> I cannot omit giving the World an account of the uncommon
> villainy a Gentleman of a good Family in England practis'd
> upon his sister, which was attested to me by one who liv'd in
> the Family, and from whom I had the whole truth of the story.
> I shall conceal the unhappy Gentleman's own under the bor-
> row'd Names of Sir William Wilding, who succeeded his father,
> Sir Edward, in an estate of near £4,000 a Year, inheriting all
> that belong'd to him, except his Virtues.

To avoid paying his sister, Philadelphia, her portion of £6,000
(which he cannot afford owing to his extravagance) he takes her
to London and under the pretence of putting her under the

---

16 These three novels are *The Black Lady; The Court of the King of
Bantam;* and *The Unfortunate Happy Lady.* All three were published
together in 1697, eight years after Aphra Behn's death.

protection of a friendly old lady, he puts her into a brothel. To the old beldame he pretends that Philadelphia is his cast-off mistress. The sardonic tone of the narrative is well seen in the following description of the relations between the harridan and the as yet undeceived girl:

> Not long after, they went to Dinner; and in the Afternoon, three or four young ladies came to visit the Right Reverend the Lady Beldam; who told her new Guest that these were all her Relations, and no less than her own sister's Children. The Discourse among 'em was general and very modest, which lasted for some Hours : for, our Sex seldom wants matter of Tattle. But, whether their Tongues were then miraculously wearied, or that they were tir'd with one continual Scene of Place, I won't Pretend to determine : but they left the Parlour for the Garden, where after about an Hour's Walk, there was a very fine Desert of Sweetmeats and Fruits brought into one of the Arbours. Cherbetts Ros Solis, rich and small Wines, with Tea, Chocolate, etc., compleated the Old Lady's Treat; the pleasure of which was much heighten'd by the voices of two of her Ladyship's Sham-Nieces, who sung very charmingly. The Dear, sweet Creature, thought she had happily got into the Company of Angels; but (alas!) they were Angels that had fallen more than once.

Fortunately Philadelphia's character is realised by a young man called Gracelove. He removes her to the protection of an honest family, and calls the wicked brother to account. Sir William goes abroad hastily, and changes his name. Philadelphia refuses to marry Gracelove until her fortune has been paid. He also has to cross the seas. When he returns Philadelphia has been married and widowed. She is now very rich. At the same moment her brother reappears in the story. Debts drive him back to England and finally into prison, "where he learnt the Art of Peg-making, a Mystery to which he had been a Stranger all his Life long 'till then." Philadelphia now buries the wicked William under an avalanche of coals of fire, paying all his debts to the extent of over £25,000. She marries Gracelove, William marries an heiress, and all ends with a deplorable lack of poetic justice.

We now come to a group of novels in which Heroic sentiment makes a strange veneer for the intrigues so dear to Restoration tastes. In her more usual code of sexual morality, the divine

Astrea was a true child of her epoch.   Her two main principles
she thus defines:

"Conscience: a cheap pretence to cozen fools withal."

"Constancy, that current coin for fools." [17]

She has read her Bandello, and she shows sometimes that she
has benefited by his example, but for the most part she is satisfied
to smother the dramatic directness of the *novella* in a suffocating
jargon of gallantry.   It is interesting to note that she is not
really at ease with the sophisticated roués and demi-rips whom
she so often depicts.   Her muse was more direct and colloquial.
She is certain that love and sexual indulgence are the same
thing, and she is comfortably determined that every Jack shall
have his Jill.   But she spreads a smoke screen, in the fashion
of the day.   Desire must not be too crudely naked.   It must
say:

> 'Tis you deny me life: 'tis you that forbid my flame; 'tis you
> will have me die, and seek my remedy in my grave, when I
> complain of tortures, wounds and flames.   O Cruel Charmer!
> 'tis for you I languish.[18]

The Heroic Romance showed the mighty champions of the
world as the slaves of their pure goddesses.   The romance of
gallantry showed every man and woman the slave of passion.
Oroondates with high-souled ecstasy cherished the hope of one
kind look.   Lysander languished, and cherished the certainty of
obtaining all he desired.   If he did not obtain it, he, like
Oroondates, went to death's door, but first he was careful to
exhaust every means of success.   It was the law of Love that all
obstacles could be removed and that the end justified every
possible means.   Seduction, abduction, murder, were not
criminal nor even blameworthy if only they were undertaken in
the service of the sacred flame.   Lysander was as one devoted—no
more responsible for his excesses than a dervish or an epileptic.
The God of Love inspired, justified and rewarded all the actions
of its helpless victims.

---

[17] Miss V. Sackville-West quotes these lines in this connection in *Aphra
Behn* (1927).
[18] *The Fair Jilt.*

Mrs. Behn wrote three stories in which the heroine was a nun. In this, as in her *Love Letters between a Nobleman and his Sister* (1683), she was influenced by the *Portuguese Letters,* which appealed to the public. It was not to be supposed that the essential purity and dignity of these letters would at that time be understood. It was characteristic of Restoration writers that they depraved all they touched. Their ideas in regard to convents are so ludicrously ignorant that we can but laugh. Generally the nun is an incredibly immoral woman, and the convent a kind of elegant brothel with the added piquancy of a grille. Occasionally, however, the convent is a retreat for harassed damsels fleeing from a plethora of lovers. They take the veil for a few days merely while they get their second wind, and then proceed to repel the naughty villian and to encourage the true adorer from the top of the garden wall. Soon they are off again into the world which their fatal loveliness makes so perilous.

In *The Fair Jilt, or Tarquin and Miranda,*[19] we have the more sinister view of convent life. Mrs. Behn begins with a preamble which puts us in mind of the argument with which Bandello prefaces his *novelle.* Only in this case there is no moralising, but instead an excellent little disquisition on love and lovers, which could well stand alone as a miniature essay in which complete truth is presented with mordant wit, in which every word expresses vividly a close observation of life and manners. But for the story: Miranda is a member of a religious community in Antwerp, a curious community whose inmates coruscate with diamonds, and who spend their time coquetting with their languishing admirers. This nun is young, wealthy, witty, accomplished and beautiful. "She was admirably shaped: she had a bright hair and hazel-eyes, all full of love and sweetness." She conceals under a modest exterior an insatiable lust, which, weary of too easy conquests, finds provocation in the purity of a young friar called Hendrik. Her interest is all the stronger when she hears Hendrik's story from her maid.

[19] Published in 1688. Ten years earlier there is advertised for R. Tonson *The Amorous Convert; being a true relation of what happened in Holland.* Summers believes that this may have been the first sketch.

Now, Hendrik's story is a complete digression, and in fact
Hendrik himself is more of a hindrance than a help to the main
narrative, but Aphra wished to show a nun trying to seduce a
friar, and would not be deprived of this artless pleasure. It is
unnecessary to recount Hendrik's sad past. Suffice it to say that
he once loved innocently, was robbed of his betrothed, and
narrowly escaped being murdered by a wicked rival. He then
decided to become a monk. He repels the foul Miranda's
advances without the slightest difficulty, and she is so infuriated
that she accuses him of the evil he has refused. He is cast into
prison and condemned to be burned, but there is a delay in his
execution.

Meanwhile Miranda, cured of her love and triumphing in her
revenge, secures in marriage the great Prince Tarquin, whose
title and fame have attracted her, and who is so besotted with
love for her that neither the Bishop nor the nobles of Antwerp can
dissuade him from his ruin. The married pair live in great
splendour, partly supported by the embezzled fortune of
Alcidiana, Miranda's young sister. But soon Alcidiana wishes to
marry, and a gulf yawns at Miranda's feet—because the necessity
of a marriage portion will reveal her theft. She does everything
in her power to discourage her sister's suitors, but finally
Alcidiana invokes the aid of a powerful kinsman who arranges a
marriage for her. The day is appointed, the portion is
demanded, and Miranda sees only one way out of the impasse.
She sets on to the murder of her sister a young page who is her
adoring tool. His ingenuity, however, is as deficient as his
morals, and he bungles his attempt to poison Alcidiana.
Condemned to death, he reveals the complicity of Miranda who
is apprehended. However, with her genius for being served by
every situation, she throws all the blame on the page, makes a
triumph of her imprisonment, and so far from slinking in chains,
surrounds herself with royal pomp, and uses Tarquin as a buttress
for her prestige. Still, she is forced, with a halter around her
neck, to witness the page's execution and to see him for the last
time hanging on her words. But her final release does not
relieve the situation because Alcidiana's suitor is still intent on
the marriage, undeterred by the fact that his future bride has

" lost the finest hair in the world, and the complexion of her face ever after," not to mention that her eyes are " starting out of her face black and all deformed." Completely cornered, Miranda, woman-like, seeks refuge in bed. She refuses " to eat, or sleep or see the light." The Prince, raving with love and compassion, implores that she will suffer herself to live. She graciously consents, on condition that the Prince will assassinate Alcidiana. Seeing the reasonableness of this request, Tarquin puts two bullets into his pistol and later into Alcidiana's petti-coats. She escapes without a scratch. Tarquin is captured and sentenced to be beheaded. Miranda, under pressure, confesses all her wickedness. Tarquin escapes death, through an error on the part of the headsman. He is pardoned and goes to Holland, where presently he is joined by the indefatigable Miranda and they live happily ever after. Aphra Behn is not content to omit Hendrik the friar from the final unity of action. During his long imprisonment we lost sight of him, but he influences the dénouement. Tarquin's pardon is secured by the confession of Miranda, and Miranda confesses only under compulsion, Hendrik's fellow monks insisting that she shall clear him and all the others whom she has implicated.

This story is an excellent example of Aphra Behn's amoral romanticism. It is really more than immorality: it is a complete absence of moral sense. Throughout the narrative her sympathy is entirely with the evil-doers. It is as if she believed them to be the hypnotised slaves of love. Sometimes in listening to her observations, we can hardly believe our ears.

Having described Miranda's effort to seduce the friar in the confessional, Mrs. Behn comfortably refers to her as " the charm-ing wanton." Later, when Miranda's false accusation has condemned Hendrik to death, Mrs. Behn, with an indulgent cluck, calls her " the implacable beauty." Prince Tarquin, after his attempted murder, is spoken of as " the poor unfortunate gentleman ", and his imprisonment is described as follows:

> In an Hour's Time, the whole fatal Adventure was carried all over the City, and everyone knew that Tarquin was the in-tended Murderer of Alcidiana, and not one but had a real Sorrow and Compassion for him. They heard how bravely he had defended himself, how many he had wounded before he

could be taken, and what numbers he had fought through. And even those who saw his Valour and Bravery and who had assisted at his being seiz'd, now repented from the Bottom of their Hearts their having any Hand in the ruin of so gallant a Man . . . . He was eternally visited by his friends and acquaintance and this last action of bravery, had got him more than all his former conduct had lost.

This attitude to murder seems entirely fantastic, until we remember that since Tarquin's attempt at crime was prompted by his passion for Miranda, he was not a murderer but a martyr to the sacred flame. Similarly, in describing the execution of the page, Aphra recounts how he approached the scaffold " fair as an angel but languishing and pale "; and when Miranda joins her husband in captivity, both criminals are referred to as " the amorous prisoners."

Now, even in this artificial tale certain characteristics are apparent—characteristics which are of the first importance in our final assessment of Aphra Behn as a novelist. Passing over the influence of heroic sentiment, we observe first the influence of the drama, sometimes exaggerated to melodrama, sometimes more rightly displayed in the focussing of attention on a dramatic situation for which she carefully sets the scene. Witness the stage directions for Miranda's love-making: "On one side of him, she kneel'd down, over-against a little altar where the priests' robes lye, on which were placed some lighted wax-candles . . . which shone full upon Miranda." Another note-worthy point is Aphra Behn's occasional aptness of phrase. When Hendrik is unjustly suspected by a jealous husband, who plots to murder him, it is unfortunate that he persists in his innocent visits for " every visit more and more confirmed his death." And when the murderers came on Hendrik in a wood: " One of the men advanced, and cried ' Prince, you must die—I do believe thee (reply'd Hendrik) but not by a Hand as base as thine.' " And when Miranda is cozening Tarquin to murder Alcidiana, "She kissed him to an oath, a solemn oath to perform what he had promised." This aptness is part of a pithy collo-quialism which breaks now and then through the rococo style of her hyper-romantic stories, and of which we shall find much more later on. Aphra Behn could not maintain her high-flown artificialities for long. The real woman, the woman of racy, vigorous diction, was forever tearing her way through the tinsel. Even when Prince Tarquin's heroics are at their height, he must come down to take water. When, loaded with debt and summoned to pay Alcidiana's fortune he sought for bail among his friends, he could get none for " Every one slunk their heads out of the Collar when it came to that."

Not only in this, but in all Aphra Behn's novels we observe her determined effort to make them appear the records of real events. It is that same trick which Defoe afterwards used so lavishly and in which he was certainly anticipated by Aphra Behn. There is no length to which she will not go to render her stories credible. She is forever telling us that the characters were known to her personally, and that she was present at the time of the occurrence, and that she saw the correspondence to which she refers; or, at the very least, that the tale was recounted to her by one who could vouch for its authenticity. In *The Dumb Virgin* she takes the greatest pains to prove that, although she herself knew only English, yet by a lucky accident the heroine's sister (a Venetian) spoke English also, and thus the narrator got a first hand account of all that happened. One of the most amusing of Mrs. Behn's efforts at authentication occurs in *The History of the Nun, or the Fair Vow-breaker.* Supporting her views on the seriousness of taking the veil, she says: " I once was design'd a humble Votary in the House of Devotion, but fancying myself endued with an obstinacy of Mind great enough to secure one from the Efforts and Vanities of the World, I rather chose to deny myself that Content I could not certainly promise myself, than to languish . . . in a certain affliction." If she had been describing the hunting of elephants she would have written as a quondam elephant-hunter. Such was her particular technique. It was an important part of her efforts towards realism, which we shall have to analyse more fully at the end of this chapter. And it was not only by her persistent claims to first-hand information that Mrs. Behn achieved verisimilitude. She did so by a thousand tricks of detailed description. Witness Prince Tarquin's execution:

When he came to the Market-Place, whither he walked on

foot, follow'd by his own Domesticks, and some bearing a black Velvet Coffin with Silver Hinges; the Head's-man before him with his fatal Scimiter drawn, his Confessor by his Side . . . he mounted the Scaffold; which was strewed with some Sawdust, about the place where he was to kneel, to receive the Blood: the scaffold had a low Rail about it that every body might more conveniently see . . . He was some time in Prayer, and a very short time in speaking to his Confessor; then he turned to the Head's-man, and desired him to do his Office well, and gave him twenty Louis d'Ors; and undressing himself with the Help of his Valet and Page, he pull'd off his Coat and had underneath had a white Sattin Waistcoat: He took off his Periwig, and put on a white Sattin Cap, with a Holland one done with Point under it, which he pulled over his Eyes; then took a cheerful Leave of all, and kneel'd down, and said. " When he lifted up his Hands the third Time, the Head's-man should do his Office." Which accordingly was done, and the Head's-man gave him his last stroke, and the Prince fell on the Scaffold. . . . and murmurs and Sighs were heard from the whole Multitude, who scrambled for some of the bloody Sawdust, to keep for his Memory.

Such passages support Macaulay's view that *Roxana, Moll Flanders,* or *Colonel Jack* would have been well within the scope of Aphra Behn.

Another tale of a coifed adventuress is *The Nun or the Perjured Beauty.*[20] Two friends, Antonio and Henrique love the same woman—Dona Ardelia, a miracle of beauty and falsehood. Antonio loved her first, but her family forbade the marriage, so Don Henrique plays John to Antonio's Miles Standish, and with the same result. Ardelia falls in love with the eloquent newcomer, but he, torn between love and friendship, resolves to sacrifice Ardelia to Antonio, and Ardelia agrees to marry Antonio as proof of her adoration for Henrique. This seems devoid of sense or meaning, but we presume that it must have appeared logical in the days of high romance. The fatal charmer points her generosity by telling Antonio why she is marrying him. Antonio recoils as if stung, as indeed he has been. All three rant for the length of three pages, their hearts burn, their eyes start and they give every sign of mental disturbance. Finally the rivals escort Ardelia to a convent where she is to remain for a few hours. They then retire, still

20 Not published until 1697, eight years after Aphra Behn's death.

ranting, and fight a duel. Antonio is slain, and having kissed his cheek Henrique withdraws from the scene as he is himself bleeding to death. He decides to bleed in the house of Ardelia's father, who, delighted that Antonio is dead, receives him cordially and permits him to stay there in hiding until he has recovered.

Meanwhile, Ardelia has fallen into a high fever, and no wonder. She continues to languish until Henrique's wounds are healed, and then, because she loves Henrique and they are now free to marry, she decides to become a nun. No sooner has she donned the veil, however, than she wishes to doff it again. Accordingly she and Henrique plan an elopement. But an enemy out of Henrique's past now comes on the scene—Don Sebastian, whose sister Elvira Henrique had wronged. By a surprising coincidence this sister is now a nun in the same convent as Ardelia. When Sebastian comes to the convent Ardelia remembers that when she was ten years old she loved him to madness, and now this tender feeling revives. Sebastian's sister warns Henrique that her brother intends to slay him, but Henrique, persuaded that Ardelia still loves him, comes to the convent with high hopes and a rope ladder. Ardelia descends, confident that Sebastian awaits her at the other side of the wall. Actually both her lovers are there in concealment. They fight, and the sword passes "quite through Ardelia's body." With great presence of mind, but singular inappropriateness, she says: "Alas, poor maid!" In a final access, Henrique and Sebastian stab each other, and they all die simultaneously and with suitable farewell speeches. Elvira dies also (of a violent fever in twenty-four hours) and the moral is—but we are too dazed to find a moral. We only know that nothing in life became any of them like the leaving it. Aphra Behn described this as "a true novel." Mr. Baker calls it "a debased novella." [21]

For a long time it was supposed that this story, *The Nun, or the Perjured Beauty* was the source of Southerne's tragedy, *The Fatal Marriage, or the Innocent Adultery*. In the dedication to Antony Hammond with which Southerne prefaced his play he acknowledged his indebtedness to " a novel of Mrs. Behn's called

[21] E. A. Baker, *History of the English Novel*, iii, 97.

The Fair Vow-breaker." It seemed to be accepted[22] without further question that this was the same story as *The Nun, or the Perjured Beauty.* It was pointed out that Aphra Behn had muddled her titles in one definite case, i.e., in the 1689 edition of *The Fair Jilt,* the title-pages bore the double title: *The Fair Jilt, or the history of Prince Tarquin and Miranda,* whereas the half-title of the same was: *The Fair Hypocrite, or the Amours of Prince Tarquin and Miranda.* In view of this, and because people did not appear to remember that Aphra Behn had really written two tales called *The Nun,* opinion concentrated on the better known tale of the two, i.e., *The Nun, or, the Perjured Beauty,* which we have just summarised. In 1909, however, Dr. Paul Hamelius of Liége pointed out that the plot of Southerne's *Fatal Marriage* was not at all like Aphra Behn's *Perjured Beauty* which was supposed to be its source. Dr. Hamelius, however, took it for granted that the two novels were one and the same, only under two different names.[23] It was the Rev. Dr. Montague Summers who, in 1916, elucidated the mystery.[24] Aphra Behn wrote two tales both of which had as the main title: *The Nun. The Nun, or, the Perjured Beauty,* published in 1697, was not the source of Southerne's play, which he really derived from *The Nun or the Fair Vow-breaker*[25] published in 1689.

This last mentioned work is greatly superior to *The Perjured Beauty.* Although liberally coated with heroics, it does convey the impression that Aphra Behn had in mind some genuine Italian *novella,* which, however, has not been identified. In the introductory passages she is on the side of the angels and she maintains this attitude in the tale that follows: In Iper lived Count Hendrick de Vallery, who, on the death of his wife,

22 By such critics as the following: Ward, *History of Dramatic Literature* (1899), iii, 42, and Article on 'Southerne' in D.N.B.; Charlotte Morgan, *Rise of the Novel of Manners* (Columbia Univ. Press, 1911); *Cambridge History of English Literature* (1912), viii, chap. 7 (by A. T. Bartholomew); Joseph Knight, *David Garrick* (1894).

23 Dr. Paul Hamelius, 'The Source of Southerne's Fatal Marriage,' *Mod. Lang. Rev.* (1909), iv, 352.

24 Rev. Dr. M. Summers, 'The Source of Southerne's Fatal Marriage,' *ibid,* April, 1916.

25 C. E. Morgan had been of opinion that *The Fair Vow-breaker* (12mo, 1689) was the name of the *editio princeps* of *The Nun, or, The Perjured Beauty.* See *The Rise of the Novel of Manners* (Columbia Univ. Press, 1911), p. 83, note 63.

decides to be a Jesuit, and arranges that his daughter Isabella shall be reared in a convent, with the proviso that at the age of thirteen she shall decide whether to marry or to become a nun. Despite the just efforts of the Abbess who counsels her to think carefully before renouncing the world, she takes the veil, thereby dooming to misery her many suitors, one of whom is Villenoys. He goes to the wars. She becomes so holy a nun that her name becomes a proverb.

In this same convent was a young nun, Sister Katherina, Isabella's dearest friend. Katherina's brother, Henault, when visiting the convent falls in love with Isabella, and despite all her efforts to resist, she returns his love. Katherina pleads with Isabella that she remember her vows. Henault's father threatens to disinherit him. All is vain; Henault plans an elopement and after an inward struggle Isabella agrees, her father's death removing one obstacle from her path. Henault's father, how- ever, is in flourishing health, and ready to cut him off with a shilling at the least breath of scandal, so the sensible creature bridles his impetuosity, and suddenly points out that one cannot live on air. Isabella is wounded by his mercenary thoughts. She says: " I thought of living in some lonely Cottage far from the noise of crowded busie Cities, to walk with thee in Groves, and silent shades . . . my Monarch thou, and I thy Sovereign Queen." They do elope finally. They change their names, marry and live on a farm near the Rhine. They write for pardon. Henault is duly disinherited; bad luck dogs them; crops fail, cattle die; for a while they appear to be under a curse. Then they are pardoned by church and state. Henault's father offers to forgive him if he will leave Isabella and go to the wars. To the wars Henault goes, but merely to humour his father. He has no notion of abandoning Isabella. During the campaign he meets Villenoys, Isabella's old suitor, and shortly after he falls in battle entrusting Villenoys with a dying message to Isabella. Villenoys delivers the message, and later prevails on Isabella to marry him. They live happily for some years, and then one day a ragged man comes to the door. One glance is enough for Isabella. Henault has returned.

Throughout the story Mrs. Behn has shown clear insight into

the workings of a woman's heart, but at this point her imaginative power raises the narrative to a far higher level. Her style is now no longer sentimental. It is grimly realistic. We are shown Isabella's horror on finding that she has quite innocently committed bigamy. Amid the whirling confusion of her mind one thought prevails: she now loves Villenoys, and she will not return to Henault. She meditates killing herself, but that will not mean happiness for Villenoys and herself, so in a sudden access of despair she smothers Henault in his sleep. Villenoys comes in at that moment, and filled with remorse and horror, she tells him that Henault has returned and has died of shock on learning that she had remarried. Villenoys sees that they will be suspected of foul play, although he does not realise that it has actually taken place. He puts the body in a sack with the intention of throwing it into the river:

> Isabella all this time said but little, but filled with thoughts all black and hellish, she ponder'd within, while the fond and passionate Villenoys was endeavouring to hide her shame, and to make this an absolute secret: she imagin'd, that could she live after a deed so black, Villenoys would be eternal reproaching her, if not with his tongue, at least with his heart, and embolden'd by one wickedness, she was the readier for another, and another of such a nature, as has, in my opinion, far less excuse than the first; but when fate begins to afflict, she goes through stitch with her black work.

Through stitch—that is the secret of the dénouement, because when Villenoys has the sack on his back, ready to bear it to the river, Isabella bids him tarry a moment whils she tucks in some of the corpse's clothes which, she says, are sticking out. To make all sure, she will sew them inside the sack. With a packing-needle and strong thread she sews the sack to the collar of Villenoys' coat, and bids him go now " and when you come to the bridge," said she, " and that you are throwing him over the rail, which is not above breast high, be sure you give him a good swing, lest the sack should hang on anything at the side of the bridge, and not fall into the stream." " I'll warrant you," said Villenoys, " I know how to secure his falling." At the bridge he gives one mighty swing and, carried over by the weight of the dead body which is sewn to his coat, he is borne down to drown with Isabella's other victim. She is so tortured by remorse that she brings suspicion on herself and is executed.

This story is remarkable in that it is not merely shot through with realism as are so many of Mrs. Behn's romantic tales. It shows an abrupt change of style. This change comes at the point where the dramatic interest is heightened, at the point where the author really lived her subject. The result is valuable, as might be expected, and it proves that Aphra Behn turned to realism when she was most in earnest. It was her natural medium.

It was not often, however, that Mrs Behn, in high-falutin' vein, so completely deviated into reality. In *Agnes de Castro, or the Force of Generous Blood*, [26] she is again on the side of morality, but her adherence to the convention of aristocratic characters and romantic attitudinising is once more evident. *Agnes de Castro* is based on the true story of Ines de Castro, who lived in the earlier part of the fourteenth century. That her life was a very popular subject with writers is seen in J. de Araujo's huge *Bibliographia Inesiana* (1897). Aphra Behn, no doubt, borrowed the tale from Peter Ballon's translation[27] of Mlle. de Brillac's *Agnes de Castro, nouvelle portugaise.* [28] Mrs. Behn's novel is far better than her source.

The story begins in the reign of Alphonso IV of Portugal. Although, on the whole, the construction is sound, Aphra Behn again repeats her mistake of concentrating interest on unimportant preliminary details. First we see Don Pedro, the Prince of Portugal, marry Bianca, Princess of Castile. After a short time Bianca is afflicted with the palsy, the marriage is dissolved, and Bianca departs to languish in a melancholy retreat. We never hear of her again, and there is really no reason why we should have heard of her at all. A marriage is then arranged between Don Pedro and Constantia Manuel, daughter of Don John Manuel, a prince of the blood of Castile, and

---

[26] Published in 1688, dramatised by Mrs. Trotter in 1690.

[27] P.B.G., *Two New Novels* (1688).

[28] Charles Gildon says that Aphra Behn's *Agnes de Castro* was a translation from "the French Lady's" novel, but this is incorrect. See Gildon's Langbaine (*The Lives and Characters of the English Dramatic Poets*, 1699) s.v. Mrs. Trotter.

famous for the enmity he has towards his king. But this marriage is scarcely more fortunate, because although Constantia is devoted to her husband, he is secretly interested in Agnes de Castro, his wife's maid of honour. Agnes is quite unconscious of the Prince's love for her; indeed, she is the faithful friend of the Princess, and the Prince's love might well have remained a secret but for the spiteful interference of Elvira Gonsalez, who had hoped to become his wife. Elvira discovers the Prince's secret to the Princess, who, although deeply grieved, blames neither her husband nor Agnes de Castro. In fact, she herself tells the innocent Agnes of the Prince's love for her. But Elvira is determined to revenge herself on the Prince for his indifference to her charms, so she determines that the king shall learn of his infatuation. This she achieves through her brother Don Alvaro, the king's favourite, but she is enraged to discover that her brother also is in love with Agnes de Castro. " Don Alvaro was one of those ambitious men, that are fierce without moderation, and proud without generosity: of a melancholy, cloudy humour, and of a cruel inclination; and to effect his ends he found nothing difficult or unlawful." He hates the Prince because he considers him his rival in the affections of the king, but particularly in the love of Agnes. The king learns of his son's unwise devotion, and promises to help Don Alvaro in his courtship. To please his favourite he orders a tournament and commands that everything shall be magnificent. The rival lovers enter the lists. The Prince, out of respect for his wife, abstains from wearing Agnes's colours, but though Don Alvaro has almost as little right to them, no scruples withhold him. Don Alvaro " appear'd there all shining with gold mix'd with stones of blue, which were the colours of Agnes; and there were embroider'd all over his equipage, flaming hearts of gold on blue and velvet, and nets for the snares of love with abundance of double A's." However, we find with some pleasure that " the pride of Don Alvaro was soon humbled at the feet of the Prince of Portugal, who threw him against the ground with twenty others." But Don Alvaro is not a whit deterred from his pursuit of Agnes. She desires to leave the court, but is dissuaded by the Princess who loves her dearly:

"What ails you, Agnes? (said the Princess to her, in a soft tone, and with her ordinary sweetness). And what new misfortune causes that sadness in thy looks?" "Madam (reply'd Agnes, shedding a rivulet of tears) the obligation and ties I have to you, put me upon a cruel trial. I had bounded the felicity of my life in hope of passing it near your highness, yet I must carry to some other part of the world this unhappy face of mine, which renders me nothing but ill-offices."

She is persuaded to remain, but still has some scruples as to the effect of her presence on the Prince. What if he should speak to her of his flame? The tale goes on to show the Princess and Agnes treating the love-lorn prince as if he were an infant that the wife bids the young girl not to repulse her husband's to be kept from crying by any means, and we are asked to believe avowals of love. That this is not lovers' psychology nobody should have known better than Aphra Behn, but if it is a faulty portrayal of women in love, it is entirely consistent with Aphra's philosophy. Elvira unsuccessfully plots against Agnes's abduction, and then forges a guilty note purporting to be from the Prince to Agnes. The handwriting would not deceive a child, but nevertheless it deceives the Princess who now dies of grief at a supposed infidelity which but a short time before she appeared willing to overlook. Before she expires she advises and blesses the future marriage of Agnes and the Prince, and with relief we feel that the web is broken. By no means; Agnes has serious scruples, and considers that in respect of Constantia's memory they should part forever. "Go, Madam," replied the Prince, growing pale, " go and expect the news of my death . . . I will go seek it in those wars which reign among my neighbours . . . Follow the motions which barbarous virtue inspires you with . . . enjoy the glory of having cruelly refused me." For a moment Agnes meditates marrying Don Alvaro because she loves the Prince. Then she decides to leave the court. But alas! the king insists that she shall remain and marry Don Alvaro, which does not at the last moment appear so romantic a solution of the tangle. The Prince is now falling into a decline from thwarted love, so Agnes finally agrees to marry him secretly. Their joy is brief. Don Alvaro's passion leads him to discover the truth. His fury is unbounded, and one night in the absence of Don Pedro, and abandoning all hope of otherwise touching the heart of the fair Agnes, he pierces it with his poignard.   Don Pedro's vengeance leads him to wage a terrible war against the assassin, but with what success we are not told. He succeeds to the throne of his fathers, and, one supposes, reigns in single blessedness.   With such a matrimonial record a fourth marriage would have been a proof of demented optimism.

Space makes it impossible to deal fully with more than one other novel—*Oroonoko*, and therefore we can only refer in passing to five novels of Mrs. Behn's as yet unmentioned.   Three of these are in the romantic tradition: sentimental in tone, and based on stock themes of intrigue.   These are: *The Unfortunate Bride;* [29] *The Unhappy Mistake, or, The Impious Vow Punished;* and *The Lucky Mistake.*   There is a tendency towards real life in *The Wandering Beauty*, which is noteworthy as the sort of tale that, in some form or other, appears to have pleased the public long before Richardson immortalised it.   Mrs. Behn shows a beautiful girl, Peregrina, who, to escape marriage with an aged suitor, leaves home and becomes a servant in a far-off country.   She is sought in marriage by a young gentleman whose lack of snobbishness is later rewarded by the discovery that Peregrina's family is as good as his own.   A clergyman appears also, but unlike Richardson's clergyman, this divine considers it beneath him to contemplate marriage with a servant, however much her beauty attracts him.   He is well punished by having to perform the marriage-ceremony which unites her to one far more important than himself.   *The Dumb Virgin* is a very close approach to the real Italian *novella*.   It is told with much power and dramatic intensity.   Incest is the theme.

We now come to Mrs. Behn's great novel *Oroonoko*, which carried her far beyond all the novelists of the age.   Published in

29 *The Unfortunate Bride, or the Blind Lady a Beauty; The Dumb Virgin, or the Force of Imagination;* and *The Wandering Beauty* were published in 1687; *The Lucky Mistake* was published in 1688.   These dates are given by Miss V. Sackville-West, *Aphra Behn* (Rep. Women Series, 1927).   E. A. Baker simply says that they were written between 1671 and *Oroonoko* which was published in 1688.   (See E. A. Baker, *History of the English Novel*, iii, 86).

1688, it is unique in being the apotheosis of her three main characteristics as a novelist, and yet in possessing also something which differed essentially from all else she wrote. In her other novels she is the romantic; the realist deriving her power from the drama, from the continental *novella* or from the life about her; the fanatical fabricator of evidence calculated to prove the truth of her stories. In *Oroonoko* these three qualities are very marked. Indeed as for authentication, never did Mrs. Behn so whole-heartedly vouch for every fact, to the immense satisfaction of her immediate public and to the despair of modern critics.

In 1696, just after Aphra Behn's death, appeared Charles Gildon's *Account of the Life of the Incomparable Mrs. Behn*,[30] to be followed in the same year by *The Life and Memoirs written by one of the Fair Sex*. [31] The *Memoirs* state that Mrs. Behn's maiden name was Johnson, that her father was a gentleman of good family in Canterbury, that when she was a young girl her father was appointed lieutenant-general of Surinam and that she, with her parents and family, went to Surinam, where, although her father had died on the outward voyage, they settled in the best house in the colony. She returned to England, and married a Dutch merchant; she went to court and diverted King Charles II with her descriptions of Surinam and of one Oroonoko. On the death of her husband she went on a secret service mission to Holland, and actually warned the English authorities of De Witt's intended attack on the Medway. She was neither thanked nor paid for her services, returned to England in a destitute condition, saw the inside of a debtors' prison, and took to writing so as to earn her living. In 1884 Gosse struck the first blow at the truth of the above biographical details. A note by Lady Winchilsea in a volume in his possession (to the effect that Aphra Behn was born at Wye and that her father was a barber) led him to seek confirmation of these remarks from the vicar of Wye. The vicar undertook the examination of the parish register, and verified Lady Winchilsea's statements.

[30] Prefixed to *The Younger Brother* (1696).
[31] Prefixed to *The Histories and Novels* (1696). *The Life and Memoirs* was probably also written by Charles Gildon, and gives a more detailed account.

In 1913, Dr. Ernest Bernbaum[32] not only discovered glaring inconsistencies in the accepted facts of Aphra Behn's life, but endeavoured to show that his discoveries definitely proved certain facts about her powers as a writer.   In another article[33] published that same year he concentrated his discoveries to prove that, as Mrs. Behn had never been to Surinam, certain claims could no longer be made for her as a narrator.   Before we discuss the bearing that Dr. Bernbaum's conclusions might have on Aphra Behn's status as a novelist, it is as well to show that his dogmatism as to her putative visit to Surinam is quite baseless. If Dr. Bernbaum had possessed all available information on the Surinam question, that is to say if he had known and adduced the evidence later offered by the Rev. Dr. Montague Summers[34] and Miss Sackville-West,[35] it would still have been impossible for him to prove by honest logic that Aphra Behn had never been to Surinam.   A complete review of this matter which has engaged the attention of Gosse, Dr. Bernbaum, the Rev. Dr. Montague Summers, and Miss Sackville-West proves only that all the evidence adduced so far on either side is insufficient to establish any final decision.   In 1913 Dr. Bernbaum accepted unquestioningly the statement that Aphra Behn's father was a barber named Johnson, and stated that, as such an individual could not have been made lieutenant-general of Surinam, Aphra Behn most certainly could not have accompanied him there. In 1915 the Rev. Dr. Montague Summers, by the simple process of examining for himself the parish register at Wye, discovered there an entry recording the baptism of Ayfara, the daughter of John and Amy Amis, July 10, 1640; and he noted the fact that so far from there being proof that Ayfara's father was a barber, there was actually no column in the register for "Quality, Trade and Profession."   Some years later Miss Sackville-West, although on the whole satisfied by the evidence of the

32 E. Bernbaum, Mrs. Behn's Biography a Fiction' (*Mod. Lang. Assoc. of America,* XXVlll).

33 E. Bernbaum, 'Mrs. Behn's Oronooko,' *Anniversary Papers by Colleagues and Pupils of G. L. Kittredge* (1913)

34 Aphra Behn's Works (ed. Rev. Montague Summers, 1915), i, Memoir of Mrs. Behn.

35 V. Sackville-West, *Aphra Behn, 1640—1689* (Representative Women Series, 1927).

parish register, referred [36] to a surprising passage in James Rodway's *Chronological History of the Discovery and Settlement of Guiana*, 1493-1668 (Georgetown, Demerara, 1888). Rodway makes the curious statement that Aphra Behn was the adopted daughter of the man (a relative of Lord Willoughby's) who was sent as lieutenant-governor to Surinam; and further states that this lieutenant-governor died on the outward voyage, and that Aphra and the rest of the family continued their journey to Surinam, and lived there for two or three years. One might, in view of Rodway's remarks, try to reconcile these conflicting pieces of evidence by deciding that Aphra really was a barber's daughter and that she was adopted by Lord Willoughby's relative, but whatever the barber's name may have been, Rodway states definitely that the lieutenant-governor's name was— Johnson! This brings us back again to Lady Winchilsea's marginal note, and it is clear that this vicious circle cannot solve the question of Aphra's visit. The same confusion exists as to the date when Aphra Behn went to Surinam and returned therefrom. Dr. Bernbaum makes out an interesting case here, but not a conclusive one. He begins by noting that if Aphra Behn returned from Surinam at eighteen years (as she claimed) she must have returned in 1658, and he finds this an impossible date. Actually there is no need to accept Aphra Behn's statement as to her age, as women's accounts of their age generally err on the side of youth. Dr. Bernbaum says that if Aphra Behn was right in claiming that she knew certain officers in Surinam, then she must have been there within the period 1665-1666, because this was the period during which these officers served in Surinam. Aphra Behn also said that the Dutch took over the colony immediately after Oroonoko's death. Therefore, Dr. Bernbaum argues, in consideration of these facts, Aphra Behn could not have returned to England earlier than December, 1665; but, he continues, State Papers prove that she went to Holland in August, 1666, so it is necessary to believe that in the intervening eight months she was married, widowed, and had her famous interview with King Charles II. Dr. Bernbaum

[36] V. Sackville-West, *Aphra Behn, 1640—1689* (Representative Women Series), Appendix 1.

says it is impossible to believe that such a programme could be crowded into eight months. It is improbable, but it is not impossible. These contentions do not disprove Aphra Behn's visit to Surinam. The Rev. Dr. Summers believes that Aphra Behn returned to England in 1663, despite the question of the officers. Miss Sackville-West also agrees that Aphra Behn returned to England earlier than 1664, and supports this view by dates given in Rodway's *Chronological History . . . of Guiana*. It is clear that these irreconcilable arguments as to the dates of Aphra's journey to Surinam and her return therefrom do not point to any definite conclusion. Leaving the realm of attempted chronology, Dr. Bernbaum, because the background of *Oroonoko* resembles George Warren's *Impartial Description of Surinam*, 1667, is certain that she was never in that country, and that she depended on Warren for her facts. He piles up a marvellous accretion of alleged evidence: Mrs. Behn's descriptions are correct only when she imitates Warren; the moment she raises her eyes from *The Impartial Description* she introduces white marble cliffs where they do not exist, and omits the twenty-eight waterfalls. Mr. Baker agrees with Dr. Bernbaum in this (and indeed is inclined to believe that Mrs. Behn never did go to Surinam). However, the Rev. Dr. Summers and Miss Sackville-West point out that as Mrs. Behn was about fifty years when she wrote *Oroonoko* it was quite natural that she would revive in Warren's book the background which had grown dim. It is stalemate again. And when Miss Sackville-West and Dr. Summers point out the unanimous opinion of Aphra Behn's contemporaries, and the peculiar coincidences of testimony which, however confused, do indicate Mrs. Behn's visit to Surinam, the anti-Surinamians may reply that these hypotheses do not constitute proof.

We have mentioned some of the pros and cons of this argument simply to show that Dr. Bernbaum's conclusions on Aphra Behn's kind of realism are based on no decisive proofs. But this problem does not arouse one's enthusiasm, because even if the fundamental proofs were decisive, Dr. Bernbaum's inferences therefrom, so far as they concern Aphra Behn's powers as a novelist, are altogether incomplete and faulty. Dr. Bernbaum delighting in his excavations, insists on investing them with excessive and disorientated literary significance, and this is quite in keeping with the distinct lack of balanced judgment which both of his articles on Aphra Behn display. Dr. Bernbaum is not really concerned with the literary value of *Oroonoko*. He merely uses it as a stick to beat Sir Walter Raleigh and any others who may share Raleigh's belief that " realistic fiction in this country was first written by way of direct imitation of truthful record." In his anxiety to disprove Raleigh's theory, he sets himself to show that the pseudo-biographies of the seventeenth century, which, he says, were generally accepted as fact, are, on the contrary, fiction. His work on the *Mary Carleton* narratives is interesting, but discretion should have kept him from the quagmire of Aphra Behn's works. His insistence that *The Fair Jilt* is not a record of facts would seem to indicate that Dr. Bernbaum has a genius for the obvious, but unfortunately the obvious conclusions of his Surinam arguments escape him utterly. Dr. Bernbaum is like some amateur archaeologist who having dug up shards, coins and knives, cannot arrive at any estimate as to their value or significance. When, in regard to *Oroonoko*, he outlines the effect which his discoveries may have on future estimates of Aphra Behn's art as a novelist, then it is that he so curiously stops short of those final conclusions towards which his basic arguments inevitably direct themselves. To explode a myth means so often the discrediting of its originator that exploding the myth of *Oroonoko's* " genuine " realism has blinded Dr. Bernbaum to the true significance of his discoveries in relation to Aphra Behn's powers. He claims to show that *Oroonoko* was not the result of Aphra Behn's personal experiences; from that it follows that she was not what Dr. Bernbaum calls a genuine realist, and therefore he erroneously concludes that whatever she substituted for genuine realism must be inferior to it. There his conclusion ends. But it cannot end there. On the contrary, that is only the first link in the chain of conclusions which cannot be broken if Dr. Bernbaum's Surinam claim is correct. He says Mrs. Behn was not a genuine realist. Very well; let us say that she was not. We must still take into account that, despite the

M

romantic tinge in *Oroonoko*, it contained a particular kind of realism which carried conviction to readers and critics for two hundred and twenty-five years. This was not merely the sort of verisimilitude attempted by the pretence that a narrative was a record of real events, because, although Aphra Behn made this claim in almost all her novels, it is *Oroonoko* alone which carried conviction to the critics. Assuming that Aphra Behn was not in Surinam, what is this realism which for so long completely hoodwinked everyone? Since it is not genuine realism it must be then a sort of realism at which she arrived by using her imagination on collected facts and ideas—it must be imaginative realism. What is the difference between these two kinds of realism? Genuine realism, that is reproductive realism, regurgitates experiences as they have occurred; imaginative realism builds up from a thousand scenes, hints, emotions and concepts something which appears convincingly real. The genuine realist is a mere narrator. The imaginative realist is a creator. It is surely unnecessary to indicate which is the superior kind of realism, and yet Dr. Bernbaum seems to consider that somehow in abolishing the Surinam visit, he detracts from Aphra Behn's status as a novelist. On the contrary, he establishes it on a far higher plane—so much so that no true friend of the Divine Astrea should dream of contesting Dr. Bernbaum's claim that she invented *Oroonoko* and her trip to Surinam. When Dr. Bernbaum raised this hare (and a long-lived, prolific animal it will prove) he really should have trained it to run in the right direction.

When Raleigh said that realistic fiction in England was first written by way of direct imitation of truthful records he never meant that fiction was the better for being a mere narration of real events, but merely that (in common with the majority of literary authorities) he believed that this was a stage in the development of realistic fiction. It seemed natural to suppose that, as an infant cannot walk alone at first, so in the beginning story tellers might have needed the support of actual events. This was considered to be a phase in the development of realistic prose fiction pending the evolution of a superior growth of novelists who could spin reality out of imagination plus experience, instead of merely describing experience seriatim or with slight embroideries. If, as Dr. Bernbaum appears to claim, realistic fiction did not pass through this phase, then the writers of realistic fiction in the seventeenth and early eighteenth centuries deserve nothing short of reverence for dispensing with the slow process of evolution.

Speaking of Congreve's romantic[37] novel *Incognita,* Mr. Baker says: " It *does not detract* a whit from its ingenuity if the plot is based on actual experience as Congreve himself avers. His biographer of 1730, the *Biographica Britannica,* and Mr. Brett Smith himself, the recent editor of *Incognita,* make unnecessary fuss about this point." [38] So? It does not detract from the *Incognita* that its plot is not original, and yet (in Dr. Bernbaum's view) it does detract from *Oroonoko* that its plot *is* original. Again, speaking of Green's cony-catching pamphlets of which the avowed object was to show up scandals, Mr. Baker says: " *From the literary point of view, however, we are concerned solely with his success in painting a realistic picture . . . It is, of course, no business of the realistic painter of life to provide any evidence save that of verisimilitude.*" [39] Since Mrs. Behn provided that to an unusual extent, why are we concerned with anything except her success as a realistic painter of life? Would Jane Austen be a better kind of novelist if it could be proved that she knew Elizabeth Bennet, Darcy and Mr. Collins in real life, and that she had actually lived at Longbourne and visited Rosings? Is Charlotte Brontë superior to Jane Austen because we can identify segments of her life in *Villette, Jane Eyre* and *Shirley?* Mrs. Ann Radcliffe is praised by literary critics for her ingenuity in creating convincing backgrounds of travel and letting her imagination play around them. [40] Mrs. Aphra Behn is not in the least praised for doing the same thing one hundred years before. When it is found that Mrs. Radcliffe for her descriptions in *The Mysteries of Udolpho* and *The*

---

[37] Although anti-romantic in purpose, *Incognita* is romantic in tone.

[38] E. A. Baker, *History of the English Novel,* iii, 104, footnote. The italics are the present writer's.

[39] E. A. Baker, *History of the English Novel,* ii, 144. The italics are the present writer's.

[40] See C. F. McIntyre, *Anne Radcliffe in relation to her time* (New Haven, 1920), chap. 2.

Italian took as a basis Mrs. Piozzi's *Journey through France and Italy* and de Carbonièrres' *Observations faites dans les Pyrénées*[41] her imaginative power is rightly commended. When it is found that Mrs. Behn drew on Warren she is treated like a child who has been found stealing jam. Is there, after all, any reason why literary criticism should not be consistent? Dr. Bernbaum's researches are interesting, but he seems to have been more engrossed in making them than in determining their use or pursuing his inferences to their conclusion.

Oroonoko was published in 1688. It was written by an Aphra Behn with whom we are not familiar—not the woman whose bawdy dialogue kept the pit in a roar, not the woman who deified the passions—and yet the same, so many soul-sides have we all. Aphra Behn had a lyrical genius, and a generous nature. Her profession showed her at her worst, but, as Gosse said, she was "not degraded although she might be lamentably unconventional."[42] Within the rombustious Aphra Behn there was the woman who wrote: "He began to tell her how short life was and how transitory its joys; how soon she would grow weary of vice and how often change to find repose in it, but never arrive to it;"[43] and who wrote in her paraphrase of the Lord's Prayer:

> Oh that this grateful, little Charity,
> Forgiving others all their sins to me,
> May with my God for mine atoning be,
> I've sought around, and found no foe in view,
> With whom the least revenge I would pursue,
> My God, my God, dispense thy Mercies too.[44]

This is the Aphra Behn who shows herself in *Oroonoko*.

In her other novels Mrs. Behn does no more than indicate the background of the action, but in *Oroonoko* she takes pains to show us the country in which this tragedy is enacted. Her initial description of Surinam is in the nature of an inventory.

---

41 Also other sources mentioned in J. S. M. Tompkins' excellent article, 'Raymond de Carbonnières, Grosley and Mrs. Radcliffe,' *Review of English Studies* (July, 1929).
42 D.B.N.
43 *The Fair Jilt.*
44 *The Works of Aphra Behn* (ed. Rev. M. Summers), vi, 375.

She tells us of " marmosets, a sort of monkey, as big as a rat or a weasel, but of a marvellous and delicate shape, having face and hands like a human creature . . . then . . . little parakeets, great parrots, mackaws and a thousand other birds and beasts of wonderful and surprising forms . . . rare flies . . . various excellences, such as art cannot imitate." But later on, when the emotion of her story has kindled her imagination, she situates as follows the house in which she claims to have lived in Surinam:

> It stood on a vast rock of white marble, at the foot of which the river ran a vast depth down, and not to be descended on that side; the little waves still dashing and washing the foot of this rock, made the softest murmurs and purlings in the world; and the opposite bank was adorned with such vast quantities of different flowers eternally blowing, and every day and hour new, fenced behind them with lofty trees of a thousand rare forms and colours, that the prospect was the most ravishing that fancy can create. On the edge of this white rock, towards the river, was a walk, or grove, of orange and lemon trees, about half the length of the Mall here, whose flowery and fruit-bearing branches met at the top, and hindered the sun, whose rays are very fierce there, from entering a beam into the grove; and the cool air that came from the river made it . . . fit to entertain people in, at all the hottest hours of the day . . . and it is a marvel to see how such vast trees, as big as English oaks, could take footing on so solid a rock, and in so little earth as covered that rock. But all things by nature there are rare, delightful and wonderful.

In this description we see very clearly the romantic and the realistic struggling for supremacy. That the romantic strain should appear is not surprising when we consider the age in which it was written and the idyllic nature of the story. Let us observe also the vivid and circumstantial precision of the details given.

To this paradise, a slave, came Oroonoko, the Prince of Coramantien. In his own country he had loved and married the beautiful Imoinda, but by an evil chance the king, his grandfather, demanded her for his harem. Oroonoko, despite great difficulty, succeeded in visiting Omoinda. He is discovered, and, certain that she can mollify the king, Imoinda bids him return to camp. He obeys her, and in his absence the vengeful king sells Imoinda into slavery. Oroonoko believes her dead. Some time later he is lured aboard an English ship and brought as a slave to Surinam. But, although he is nominally a slave, his captors and all the people who see him are so impressed by his princely air that he is treated like a free man. By a remarkable coincidence he finds again in Surinam the beautiful and chaste Imoinda, and for a little while they are happy together. But soon it becomes clear that the white rulers of the colony have promised them freedom only to secure their submission. Oroonoko tries to escape. He is overtaken, and he surrenders on the condition that he shall not be punished. He is tortured, but greater far than any bodily suffering is the knowledge that a dreadful fate awaits his unprotected wife. He wins free for a little time; he kills Imoinda so that she shall not fall into the hands of the white men. He is recaptured and put to death by being hacked to pieces.

Such is the story and we can see that there are several ways in which it could be treated. Mrs. Behn's way is half heroic and half realistic. For example, Oroonoko loses some of his reality by being presented as a lofty hero. Miss Sackville-West very well describes the impression we receive: " Oroonoko resembles those seventeenth century paintings of negroes in plumes and satins, rather than an actual slave on a practical plantation. She dresses him, it is true, in a suit of brown hollands; but none the less the plumes continue to wave in the breeze and the satins to glisten in the sun. She could not wholly escape from ' Le Grand Cyrus.' " [45] Very unlikely also is the picture of Oroonoko sitting at meat with the white men and even with the white women in those days of racial prejudice; and the fact that he was, if only nominally, a slave makes the improbability all the greater. Still, that Mrs. Behn should have written thus of a negro proves very thoroughly her novel point of view. It is novel in our age, not to mention hers, because even in this century we are assured of white superiority. It would be interesting to discover why she chose a negro as her hero, but this is a point entirely beyond proof. It is also note-

---

[45] V. Sackville-West, *Aphra Behn, 1640-1689* (Rep. Women Series, 1927), p. 74.

worthy and very characteristic of Aphra Behn that, having chosen him, she did not by the fraction of a shade abate his negritude, as Mrs. Kavenagh believed Mme. de la Fayette or Mlle. de Scudéry would have done. [46]

Many critics have said that this is the first novel which champions the emancipation of the coloured races. This is true in effect, but (as the present writer believes) not in intention. If Mrs. Behn intended her story as a polemic against slavery she would hardly have shown her hero in agreement with the practice. In contrast with Oroonoko's leadership of his fellow slaves in an attempted escape we must set his offer to deliver many of his countrymen into bondage in exchange for his own freedom and that of Imoinda: " He was every day treating with Trefry for his and [Imoinda's] liberty, and offered either gold, or a *vast quantity of slaves*, which should be paid before they let him go, provided he could have any security that he should go when his ransom was paid." This offer is refused and Oroonoko's slavery confirmed, so he incites his fellow prisoners to escape. Then he uses arguments which, however, incontestable, did not deter him from making his previous offer to Trefry:

> [Oroonoko] having singled out these men from the women and children, made a harangue to them of the miseries and ignominies of slavery; counting up all their toils and sufferings, under such loads, burdens and drudgeries, as were fitter for beasts than men . . . He told them, it was not for days, months or years, but for eternity; there was no end to be of their misfortunes. They suffered not like men, who might find glory and fortitude in oppression; but like dogs, that loved the whip and bell, and fawned the more they were beaten; that they had lost the divine quality of men, and were become insensible asses, fit only to bear: nay, worse; an ass, or dog, or horse, having done his duty, could lie down in retreat, and rise to work again, and while he did his duty, endured no stripes; but men, villainous, senseless men, such as they, toiled on all the tedious week till Black Friday; and then, whether they worked or not, whether they were faulty or meriting, they, promiscuously, the innocent with the guilty, suffered the infamous whip, the sordid stripes, from their fellow-slaves, till their blood trickled from all parts of their body; blood, whose every drop ought to be revenged with a life of some of those tyrants that

[46] Julia Kavenagh, *English Women of Letters* (1863), chapter on Aphra Behn.

impose it . . . "And why," said he, "my dear friends
and fellow-sufferers, should we be slaves to an unknown
people? Have they vanquished us nobly in fight? Have
they won us in honourable battle? And are we by the
chance of war become their slaves? . . . No, but we are bought
and sold like apes or monkeys, to be the sport of women, fools
and cowards; and the support of rogues and runagates, that
have abandoned their own countries for rapine, murders, theft
and villainies. Do you not hear every day how they upbraid
each other with infamy of life, below the wildest savages? And
shall we render obedience to such a degenerate race who have
no human virtue left, to distinguish them from the vilest creatures?"

And again:

[Oroonoka] told him [Byam] there was no faith in the white
men, or the gods they adored; who instructed them in principles
so false, that honest men could not live amongst them; though
no people professed so much, none performed so little : that
he knew what he had to do when he dealt with men of honour;
and with them a man ought to be eternally on his guard, and
never to eat and drink with Christians without his weapon of
defence in his hand; and, for his own security, never to credit
one word they spoke.

These are the vehement words of one deeply moved by a
grievous wrong. They are the words of Mrs. Behn, speaking
through Oroonoko. But if she had wished to launch an attack
upon the slave-trade would she not have considered Oroonoko's
offer to Trefry as a serious lowering of his character? One is
inclined to believe that Mrs. Behn's feelings are entirely centred
in her hero, that it is, primarily, *his* enslavement which arouses
her sympathy. Then the depth of her feeling for her own creation leads her, in denouncing his oppressors, to denounce the
entire abomination of slavery. She brings to her story a strong
conviction that civilisation is a curse which achieves only de-
generacy, and which connotes only misdirected cleverness, hypocrisy, avarice, cruelty and lip-religion. Her proofs are all about
her in the society of her time, and suddenly the life she knows
nauseates her, a stench rises from its corrupt heart, its teeming
life seems to feed only on decay, and from this aggregation of
evil she recoils, and she escapes into a different world. Here
is a purer air; here is " eternal Spring, always the very months

of April, May and June; the shades are perpetual, the trees
bearing at once all degrees of leaves, and fruits." Here are
people who have retained innocence and dignity because their
desires are no more than their needs:

> These people represented to me an absolute idea of the first
> state of innocence, before man knew how to sin: And 'tis most
> evident and plain, that simple Nature is the most harmless,
> inoffensive and virtuous mistress. 'Tis she alone, if she were
> permitted, that better instructs the world, than all the inventions
> of man: religion would here but destroy that tranquillity they
> possess by ignorance; and laws would but teach 'em to know
> offences, of which now they have no notion.

It is interesting to note how in this story Aphra Behn's emotion
mounts with the action. Here she finds her spiritual centre;
she speaks deeper truths than she knows; she overleaps time; she
anticipates the theories of Rousseau, the fierce satire of Swift,
the abolition of slavery, and she does all this because the gap
between her experience and her idealism, realised suddenly with
deadly clarity, wrings from her something nobler than she guessed.
Oroonoko is as far above the rest of her writings as the real
Aphra Behn was above the stamp life put upon her. How often
in her other novels and in her plays, are our feelings shocked,
not even so much by the lack of morality, as by her deviations
from aesthetic taste, her inability to hit the truth! But in
Oroonoko all this is changed. Some excess of romanticism there
may be, but since it is expended on an epical subject it does
not offend our sense of probability. Nor is it a sterile romanticism; it is really the effect of an enthusiasm which raises the theme
to the height of ideality.

Where now is her trolloping muse, her cynical material-
ism? One would have thought that she could not resist the
chance of erotic writing offered by that part of the story which
deals with the harem of the King of Coramantien, but even that
she invests with considerable dignity. Thereafter, transformed
for once in her life by a noble inspiration, she exercises on her
subject an instinctive mesure. Most notable as a proof of this
is Oroonoko's farewell to Imoinda, whom he is about to kill.
We have had so many ranting farewells in Aphra Behn's stories

that we may be pardoned for suspecting one here. It is the fatal climax of many misfortunes; it is the end of a great love. How will she describe it? What words can she possibly ascribe to them which will not offend one's sense of fitness? Listen:

> It is not to be doubted, but the parting, the eternal leave-taking of two such lovers, so greatly born, so sensible, so beautiful, so young, and so fond, must be very moving, as the relation of it was to me afterwards. All that love could say in such cases being ended . . . .

No more. Mrs. Behn has faced her problem with the ease of sincere feeling, and in her refusal to intrude on that scene she achieves her finest artistic effect. Dr. Bernbaum has taken much trouble to point out the impossibilities and improbabilities in *Oroonoko*. The story of the electric eel is unlikely, the healing of the hero's abdominal wound is possible, but not probable, and we are told this on the authority of a doctor whose opinion Dr. Bernbaum has sought to reinforce his own; the natives of Surinam must have known how to tell a lie because their language at that time had five distinct words meaning falsehood— these are but a few of Dr. Bernbaum's objections. Since they add nothing to the Surinam question, and have no bearing on literary criticism, it is unnecessary to consider them. We have in *Oroonoko* a story which is universally judged to be of worth. It seems a pity to destroy, for the sake of mental gymnastics, something of permanent worth in the history of the novel.

Similarly, because in this story we are concerned with the hero's personality, we do not trouble to ask ourselves whether Oroonoko could actually continue to smoke while his body was being hacked to pieces. That is what Oroonoko would have wished to do, and therefore it does not ring false. It is a truth in art. Thus Aphra Behn describes Oroonoko's end:

> And turning to the men that had bound him, he said "My friends, am I to die, or to be whipt?" And they cried "Whipt! no, you shall not escape so well!" And then he replied, smiling, "A blessing on thee!" and assured them they need not tie him, for he would stand fixed like a rock, and endure death so as would encourage them to die: "But if you whip me," said he, "be sure you tie me fast."

He had learned to take tobacco; and when he was assured he should die, he desired they would give him a pipe in his mouth, ready lighted; which they did. And the executioner came, and first cut off his members, and threw them into the fire: after that, with an ill-favoured knife they cut off his ears and his nose, and burned them; he still smoked on, as if nothing had touched him; then they hacked off one of his arms, and still he bore up and held his pipe; but at the cutting off of the other arm, his head sunk, and his pipe dropped, and he gave up the ghost, without a groan, or a reproach . . . They cut [Oroonoko] into quarters, and sent them to several of the chief plantations: one quarter was sent to Colonel Martin; who refused it, and swore he had rather see the quarters of Banister, and the Governor himself, than those of [Oroonoko] on his plantations; and that he could govern his negroes, without terrifying and grieving them with frightful spectacles of a mangled king.
Thus died this great man, worthy of a better fate, and a more sublime wit than mine to write his praise. Yet, I hope, the reputation of my pen is considerable enough to make his glorious name to survive to all ages, with that of the brave, the beautiful and the constant Imoinda.

Southerne in his dedication of the dramatised version of *Oroonoko* expressed his amazement that Mrs. Behn, having so great a command of the stage, " would bury her favourite hero in a novel, when she might have revived him in the scene. She thought either that no actor could represent him, or she could not bear him represented; and I believe the last, when I remember what I have heard from a friend of hers that she always told his story more feelingly than she writ it."[47]

Charles Gildon, however, in comparing Southerne's version with the novel *Oroonoko* makes an illuminating remark which hints a reason for Mrs. Behn's choice of medium, and which shows that the essential difference between the drama and the novel was commencing to be understood: " But as to this play *Oroonoko*," says Gildon, " you find our poet [Southerne] has allowed the Plot of it to Mrs. Behn; for on that Prince she has composed the best of her novels: and as it must be confess'd that the Play had not its mighty Success without an innate Excellence; so in my Opinion, the necessary regularities a Drama-tick Poet is obliged to observe, has left many Beauties in the Novel which our Author could not transfer to his Poem." [48]

[47] Southerne, Dedication of *Oroonoko*.
[48] Gildon's Langbaine (*The Lives of the Poets,* 1699), p. 136.

It is necessary to sum up what we already know of Aphra
Behn's prose fiction if we are to judge the value of her contribution.   So far we have seen that she was influenced by the Heroic
tradition and that she sought to escape from it; that she alternately subscribed to and rejected the code of gallantry; that
she anticipated the method by which Defoe vouched for the
truth of his narratives; that she could create backgrounds of
natural scenery when nobody else attempted it, foreshadowing,
even though feebly, as Mr. Baker says, [49] the prose epics of
Chateaubriand; that she wrote the first eulogy of the Natural
Man—a subject which was later to become a distinct genre of
literature, and a cult in the hands of Bernardin de St. Pierre
and Rousseau; that she wrote the first novel which anathematised
the slave-trade, and that her savage indignation taught her to
write as scathing a satire as any of Swift's.   We have seen something also of her realism.   Sometimes we know that it is imaginative realism (as in the case of the latter half of *The Nun; or, the
Fair Vow-breaker*); sometimes, as in the novels with a London
background, we see, not " genuine realism " but the weaving
of Mrs. Behn's actual surroundings into invented tales.   On this
very subject Miss Sackville-West says: " It is a pity that Mrs.
Behn, as a novelist, thought her London experiences beneath the
dignity of her pen.   She had that gift of God, a free, rapid,
and colloquial style, and she neglected to turn it to its best
advantage." [50]   We shall see that she did turn it to excellent
advantage in that ruthlessly realistic satire: *The Ten Pleasures
of Marriage.*

---

[49] E. A. Baker: (ed.), Aphra Behn's Novels, p. xxiii f.
[50] V. Sackville-West, *Aphra Behn, 1640-1689* (Rep. Women Series,
1927), p. 72.

CHAPTER VI.

SATIRE—ENGLISH REALISM.

" If there be nothing that will lay me in my Tomb till Love brings
me thither, I shall live to all eternity."

(Aphra Behn, *Lycidas, or, the Lover in Fashion.*)

Some years ago in an antiquarian bookseller's shop in the
heart of London was found a book which the Navarre Society
considered well worth publishing. This was *The Ten Pleasures
of Marriage and the Second Part, the Confession of the New
Married Couple.* On the title page appears the name A. Marsh,
Typogr. It has not been possible to trace the identity of
A. Marsh, nor is the book included in the Stationers' Register
for the period, i.e., 1682-1683. It has been suggested that
Marsh may have thought the book too licentious for registration,
but this explanation does not seem probable in view of the
material which poured from the printing presses in Restoration
times, and more particularly since, in 1682, there was registered
a book of the same parent-stock as *The Ten Pleasures*, and at
least as loose in tone. It is thought that *The Ten Pleasures of
Marriage* was published abroad—probably, Hazlitt thinks, [1] at
the Hague or Amsterdam. In the very first page of the original
edition there appears one of several hints of Batavian origin:
" younger " is printed " jounger." But the mystery of this book
is not confined merely to its printer. No author's name appears
on the title-page of *The Ten Pleasures of Marriage.* There is,
however, a clue as to its authorship: a letter in the first part
is signed A.B., and in view of many facts which seem to support
the contention, the work (including both first and second parts)

[1] See introd. Navarre Soc. ed *The Ten Pleasures of Marriage.*

is ascribed to Aphra Behn.   Before we examine the arguments
in favour of her authorship let us glance at the ancestry of this
book.

The Ten Pleasures of Marriage, a vigorous satire on marriage
and women, springs from an ancient root.   It is based on *Les
Quinze Joyes de Mariage*, attributed to Antoine de la Salle, but
he in turn must have been acquainted with three important
satires against women which were published in France in the
thirteenth and fourteenth centuries.   The earliest and most
influential writing of this kind was that part of the *Roman de
la Rose* written by Jean de Meun, who attacked the idealised
conception of women so dear to the hearts of the troubadours.
Another anti-feminist work was *The Lamentations* of Mathieu
(1295-1300) written in Latin verses, and translated c. 1370 by
Jean Le Fevre.   A third important French satire against women
was *Le Miroir de Mariage* by Eustache Deschamps. [2]   *Les
Quinze Joyes de Mariage* was written between 1448-1456.   The
idea of the title was irreverently borrowed from one of the prayers
which terminated the Book of Hours—a pious composition
entitled *Les Quinze Joyes de Notre Dame, Mère de Dieu*.

> *Les Quinze Joies de Mariage ou la Nasse* forment une suite
> de litanies dans laquelle sont longuement enumerées avec le
> repons, le final invariable
> > Ainsi vivra en languissant tousjours
> > Et finira miserablement ses jours
> > Les tribulations infinies de l'homme marié. [3]

The first English translation of *Les Quinze Joyes de Mariage*,
printed by Wynkyn de Worde in 1509, was entitled : *The Fifteen
Joyes of Maryage*.   It was a poor verse rendering of de la Salle's
excellent prose work.   Other translations and adaptations followed.   In 1599 Adam Islip's *The XV Joyes of Marriage* was
burnt at Stationers' Hall.   For the greater part of the seventeenth
century the popular translation of *Les Quinze Joyes de Mariage*
was *The Batchelars Banquet* [4] which is generally ascribed to

---

2 A poem of 12,103 lines.
3 *Nouvelle Biographie Universelle* (1859).   See 'Antoine de la Salle.'
4 *The Batchelars Banquet* is included in the collected non-dramatic
works of Dekker.   See also J. J. Jusserand, *The English Novel in the
time of Shakespeare* (1890), p. 339.

Dekker, but which may have been the work of Robert Tofte. [5]
The earliest extant edition of *The Batchelars Banquet* was published in 1603 and the last in 1677. In Restoration times it
is not surprising to observe that *Les Quinze Joyes de Mariage*
took a fresh lease of life. In 1682 there appeared a new translation: *The XV Comforts of Rash and Inconsiderate Marriage
or select Animadversions upon the Miscarriage of the Wedded
State. Done out of French.* " In this the Frenchman's delicate
irony is here debased to a broad leer, the dialogue is mean and
slovenly, though in places pert and lively. The grossest passages
in *Les Quinze Joyes*, omitted in *The Batchelars Banquet*, are
given with advantages." [6] It is not surprising, therefore, that
The XV Comforts ran into three editions in one year, and continued to be reprinted up to 1760. It gave rise to a spate of
pamphlets for and against women. For example, *The Fifteen
Real Comforts of Matrimony, by a person of Quality of the
Female Sex*, 1683. In 1682 appeared *The Ten Pleasures of
Marriage* mentioned above, followed in 1683 by its second part
The Confession of the New Married Couple. We believe that
both parts were written by Aphra Behn.

Some of the arguments which support Aphra Behn's authorship can be briefly stated. Others require more lengthy consideration. First, it is remarkable that *The Ten Pleasures* was
published in 1682—that very year when Aphra Behn had been
obliged to intermit the writing of plays. We know that she
turned to prose fiction between 1682 and 1688, when she resumed
her dramatic work. Indeed, in 1683 she published *Love Letters
between a Nobleman and his Sister*, and it is natural to suppose
that she did not allow a year to elapse before trying her hand
at this new kind of work which could be essayed without peril
of the law. Presuming that Aphra Behn wrote *The Ten Pleasures
and the Second Part, the Confession* why did she not acknowledge her authorship? In the first place, there appears to have
been a tradition of anonymity connected not only with all the
translations and modifications of *Les Quinze Joyes*, but also with
Les Quinze Joyes itself, and we have seen that these writings

5 *The Batchelars Banquet* (ed. F. P. Wilson, 1929), Introd.
6 *Ibid.*

had always been regarded as daring and disreputable, as the fate
of Adam Islip's book amply demonstrates.   But, it will be argued,
Aphra Behn was not a squeamish author, and she was writing
for a debauched age, therefore there was no reason why she
should not have published *The Ten Pleasures* boldly over her
own name. On the contrary, there was a most urgent reason
for her anonymity.   In 1682 she had been summoned for her
dramatic writings, and debarred from continuing such work.
The Ten Pleasures could not shock the Restoration public. Indeed, to tell the truth, it was more broad than salacious.   Still
Aphra Behn had already been condemned, and knew herself an
object of suspicion.   She could not risk a further embroilment
with the law, particularly within the selfsame year.   It is easy,
therefore, to understand why she preferred *The Ten Pleasures*
to be anonymous.   She could nevertheless give a clue as to the
authorship, to stir the interest of the reading public, and perhaps
to mock slyly the very authorities she feared.   Possibly it was
for these reasons that we find the letter at the end of *The Ten
Pleasures* signed A.B.   In Restoration times there was only one
writer of note whose initials were A.B., and so far, at least, no
other writer has been suggested as the author of *The Ten
Pleasures*. To seek among the obscure writers is unprofitable,
because *The Ten Pleasures* is obviously the work of an original,
witty and vigorous mind.   No mediocre A.B. could possibly
have produced it.   The fact that the publisher of the book cannot
be traced and that the book appears to have been printed in
Holland is in accordance with Aphra Behn's predicament.
Negotiations with a London publisher through a third party
would involve a strong possibility of her secret leaking out.   She
was too well-known a literary figure for such an experiment to
ensure anonymity.   Nothing then remained for her except to
publish abroad.   She had spent some time in Holland, and had
friends there.   All things considered it is not in the least surprising that she should decide to publish her book at The
Hague or Amsterdam.   Apart from the fact that it contains
clues which point to Dutch publishing, there is another factor
which strangely links *The Ten Pleasures* to Holland.   The
illustrations bound up in the copy of the 1621 edition of *Les*

Quinze Joyes in the Bodleian Library indicate that this book is in some way related to the Dutch *De Tien Delicatessen des Houwelicks*. If these illustrations are contemporaneous with the 1621 edition or previous to it, then *De Tien Delicatessen* was a Dutch version of *Les Quinze Joyes*, and Aphra Behn's *Ten Pleasures* would most likely be based on the Dutch book. But there is no evidence whatever as to the date of *De Tien Delicatessen*, of which there appears to be no extant copy. There is, moreover, no means of ascertaining when these illustrations were bound up in the Bodleian copy of the 1621 edition of *Les Quinze Joyes*. It may have been done even a century later by some private owner of *Les Quinze Joyes* who considered the illustrations of *De Tien Delicatessen* applicable to the subject matter of the French book. It is, indeed, quite possible that *De Tien Delicatessen des Houwelicks* was simply a Dutch translation of *The Ten Pleasures of Marriage*. It would not be the only translation of Aphra Behn's works published in Holland or in Germany. [7]

The Ten Pleasures must have been written by someone who knew French and who was familiar with French literature, because although there were numerous English translations of *Les Quinze Joyes*, *The Ten Pleasures* contains an allusion to the French poet Clément Marot, which would require more than a passing acquaintance with Marot's works. The reference probably alludes to the fact that in 1526 the Sorbonne condemned Marot and his poem *Colloque de l'Abbé et de la femme sçavante*. Mr. Harvey in his introduction to *The Ten Pleasures* points out that Marot " is not a 'stock figure' in English literary allusion, either learned or popular, and the fact suggests at least familiarity with the literature of other countries." [8] Mrs. Behn's mastery of the French language is proved by her excellent translation or rather adaptation of Fontenelle's *Entretiens sur la pluralité des*

[7] E.g. *Oroonoko, traduit de l'Anglois de Mme. Behn par P.A. de la Place* (Amsterdam, 1745).
Lebens-und Liebes-Geschichte des Königlichen Schlaven Oroonoko in West-Indien . . . Verteuscht durch M.V. (Hamburg, 1709).
Oroonoko, ein Trauerspiel, by W. H. Von Dalberg? or—Von Eisenthal? (1789).
[8] *The Ten Pleasures.* Privately printed by the Navarre Soc. Ltd. Introd. by John Harvey.

mondes as also her free paraphrase of the Abbé Tallemant des Réaux's *Voyage de l'Isle d'Amour.*[9]

But the person who wrote *The Ten Pleasures* must also have known some German, because in the second part of the book, *The Confession of the New Married Couple,* a High German doctor makes his diagnosis and his recommendations in High German. Aphra Behn must have learned Dutch, since she was considered a suitable person to send on a secret mission to Holland. It is, moreover, a very significant fact that the speech of the High German doctor in *The Ten Pleasures* contains a few misspellings due to Dutch.

Normally speaking, it might be suggested that a woman would not be likely to launch upon her fellow-women such a virulent attack as is to be found in part of *The Ten Pleasures.* Such a contention does not apply to such women as Aphra Behn. Not only was the Restoration attitude towards women entirely cynical, but Aphra Behn and her female followers were all the more relentless, because they themselves were outlawed by feminine society. It was comforting for them to mock at their more cautious sisters and to assert, self-justifyingly, that the courtesan, the wife and the *jeune fille bien élevée* were all sisters under the skin. Indeed (they cried) what is the difference between wife and mistress except that one has patented her claim to a man's protection and the other must rely solely on her own powers to retain it? When Mrs. Pix could write as follows there is no room to doubt that these women writers sharpened their claws for their own sex:

> Sir Francis: As for the Damosels, three sorts make a Bushel, and will be uppermost: First, there's your common Jilts will oblige every body.
> Beaumont: These are Monsters sure.
> Sir Francis: You may call 'em what you please, but they are very plentiful, I promise you; The next is your kept Mistress, she's a degree modester, if not kind to each, appears in her dress like Quality, whilst her ogling eye, and too frequent Debauches discovers her the youngest sister only to the first . . . The third is not a Whore, but a brisk, airy, noisy Coquette that lives upon treating, one Spark has her

9 *Lycidas, or the Lover in Fashion . . . His Voyage from the Island of Love* (1688).

to the Play, another to the Park, a third to Windsor, a
fourth to some other place of Diversion; She has not the
heart to grant 'em all favours, for that's their design at
the bottom of the Treats, and they have not the heart to
marry her, for that's her design too, Poor Creature. So
perhaps a year, or it may be two, the gaudy Butterfly flut-
ters round the Kingdom, then if a foolish Citt does not take
compassion, sneaks into a Corner, dies an Old Maid, de-
spised and forgotten . . . The men that fit those Ladies are
your Rake, your Cully, and your Beaux. [10]

In *Sir Patient Fancy* Aphra Behn puts into the mouth of Isabella
these words:

Keeping begins to be as ridiculous as matrimony . . . The
insolence and expense of their mistresses has almost tired out
all but the old and doting part of mankind.

But indeed it would be difficult to exhaust the quotations from
Aphra Behn's works which reveal her cynical attitude to women.
In her *Lycidas, or the Lover in Fashion* (which is no mere translation, but rather a reply to Tallemant des Réaux's slight but
graceful work) Aphra Behn makes her general attitude clear.
Lycidas begins by condoling with Lysander on the death of his
Aminte. Personally he takes such matters philosophically. He
knows the game of love from A to Z, and considers it not worth
the stakes. "After you have heard," he says, " My account of
the Voyage I made [to the Island of Love], with my more lucky
one back again . . . you will by my Example become of my
Opinion, (notwithstanding upon dismal Tales of Death and the
eternal Shades), which is, that if there be nothing that will lay
me in my Tomb till Love brings me thither, I shall live to all
Eternity." [11]   Lysander speaks of love as if it were a mere
devitalising enslavement to women:

I have seen a Man, handsom, well shap'd, and of a great deal
of Wit, with the advantage of a thousand happy adventures,
yet finds himself in the end fitter for a hospital than the Eleva-
tion of Fortune: And the Women are not contented we should
give them as much Love as they give us (which is but reasonable) but they compel us all to Present and Treat 'em lavishly,
till a Man hath consumed both Estate and Body in their service.

[10] Mary Pix, *The Innocent Mistress* (1697), Act 1.
[11] *The Works of Aphra Behn* (ed. Summers, 1915), vi. 299 f.

This is the subject of the Second Pleasure in *The Confessions of the New Married Couple*. On his voyage to the Island of Love Lycidas was accompanied by " abundance of young Heirs, Cadets, Coxcombs, Wits, Blockheads and Politicians, with a whole Cargo of Cullies all, nameless and numberless." He says:

Heaven keep me from being a Woman's Property. There are Cullies enough besides you or I, Lysander. One would think, now that I, who can talk thus Learnedly and Gravely, had never been any of the number of those wretched, whining, sighing, dying Fops, I speak of, never been jilted and cozen'd of both my Heart and Reason; but let me tell you that think so, they are mistaken, and that all this Wisdom and Discretion I now seem replenish'd with, I have as dearly bought as any keeping Fool of 'em all. I was ly'd and flattered into Wit, jilted and cozen'd into Prudence, and, by ten thousand broken Vows and perjured Oaths, reduced to Sense again; and can laugh at all my past Follies now. [12]

He recounts that when he fell in love with Sylvia, a paragon of beauty and grace, she

found my Weakness and her own Power; and using all the Arts of her Sex, played the Woman all over: she wou'd be scornful and kind by turns, as she saw convenient, This to check my Presumption and too easy hope: That to preserve me from the brink of Despair. Thus was I tost in the Blanket of Love, sometimes up and sometimes down, as her Wit and Humour was in or out of tune, all which I watch'd, and waited like a Dog, that still the oftener kick'd would fawn the more. Oh, 'tis an excellent Art this managing of a Coxcomb, the Serpent first taught it to our Grandam Eve; and Adam was the first kind Cully: E're since they have kept their Empire over Men, and we have, e're since, been slaves. [13]

" Women," says the author of *The Ten Pleasures*, " are in effect of less value than old Iron, Boots and Shoes, etc., for we find both merchants and money always ready to buy these commodities." There is no lack of evidence in Aphra Behn's accredited works that this was her view of women, and that she held downright views on "the quarrelsome, crabbed, lavish, proud, opinionated, domineering and unbridled nature of the female sex." [14]

12 *Ibid*, p. 300.
13 *Ibid*, p. 301.
14 *The Ten Pleasures*.

To argue that *The Ten Pleasures* is so scathing a satire on women that no woman could possibly have written it is simply to demonstrate a touching but undeserved confidence in women's mutual loyalty. Such an argument collapses not only in view of the peculiar temper of Restoration women, but also because women of any age, in life or in print, tend to be more merciless towards each other than any man could be towards them. And yet it is interesting to observe that when a woman has rent her sex for the diversion of the men whom she proportionately praises or pities, some deep, primitive antagonism within her awakens, and drives her to execute a final *volte face*. She watches, as it were, the faces of men creased with laughter at her sardonic revelations of women, and then, unable to shed her own sex, she stands branded with the very brand she has forged for her sisters. She stands a self-confessed traitor, and she stands alone, having withdrawn momentarily from the objects of her scorn. Every man knows that a woman will deride other women up to the moment when he joins in her derision; then she turns swiftly and, by a curious metamorphosis, becomes the protagonist of her sex. A tamed lioness will lower her dignity by jumping through hoops and climbing on stools, and then, just when her keeper feels that she knows her place at last, she fells him to the ground with one contemptuous stroke of her paw. So it is with women, those " Drawcansirs that maul both friend and foe." So it was with Aphra Behn in *The Ten Pleasures*.

Mr. Harvey in his introduction to the Navarre Society edition, says: " The irony [of *The Ten Pleasures*] is less well sustained in the sequel, *The Confession of The New Married Couple*." But this is not the main difference between *The Ten Pleasures* and *The Confession*. The fact is that whereas *The Ten Pleasures* is violently condemnatory of women and marriage, *The Confession* chiefly defends women and, showing that all marriages are not alike, pleads for reconciliation rather than divorce. The introduction to *The Confession* says: "Of those [joys] we have before demonstrated unto you Ten Pleasant Tables: But because the Scale of Marriage may hang somewhat evener and not fall too light on the women's side, we shall for the Courteous Reader add unto them Ten Pleasures more." In these additional pleasures a different point of view is very apparent, illustrated with innumerable touches which reveal a woman's mind. Many of the feminine grievances in *The Confession* concern matters of which a man would not be alertly conscious, as we shall see when we come to consider them in more detail. And it is worthy of careful note that whereas the *Quinze Joyes* and its English versions devote one episode only to satirising the vagaries and extravagances which are represented as characterising the expectant mother, no less than seven of the ten episodes in *The Ten Pleasures* are devoted to this subject. Since *The Ten Pleasures* depicts merely the first year in the life of a young married couple, it is obvious that the maeutic outlook supervenes at a very early stage, and it progresses with the most detailed and forthright consideration of every phase until the moment when the neighbours gather to celebrate the birth. If a man wrote *The Ten Pleasures,* he could surely have found a wealth of masculine grievances to depict without committing himself to describe the first married year almost entirely from an obstetrical point of view. Furthermore the feminine touch is evident in these descriptions. It is evident in the gusto, albeit the sardonic gusto, with which the author depicts these women deriving intense pleasure from their garrulous reminiscences of child-bearing, closing their ranks as they sit gossiping together, sinking their voices to mysterious whispers and raising them to dogmatic assertion, forming a temporary cabal against mere husbands, finding a brief unison in their common maternity. She despises the homely vulgarity of such séances, but she understands it; and she understands also the dogged strength which underlies the apparent weakness of the pettish, complaining, attitudinising woman. That is why, when she has shown us these people she pulverises them before our eyes. These chapters do not lend themselves to detailed exposition, but readers will find in them confirmation of the feminine authorship of this book.

For all the reasons, therefore, which we have mentioned, we believe that Aphra Behn wrote *The Ten Pleasures of Marriage and the Second Part, the Confession of the New Married Couple.* Let us see now how far she was indebted to the sources at her disposal. No doubt she was familiar with the original *Quinze*

Joyes and with some of its English renderings, certainly with *The Batchelars Banquet,* but although she took from them the general, basic idea, *The Ten Pleasures . . . . and the Confession* is in no sense a translation, paraphrase, or version of any of these works. It would be very simple indeed to show by collated columns that Aphra Behn's twenty pleasures do not adhere to the material or the sequence of the fifteen joys. One might expect that she would have given some characteristic twist to the fifteen joys and then added five joys or pleasures more. But this is not so. It is true that in the first ten pleasures there is the main principle of *Quinze Joyes*—that a married man is like a squirrel in a cage and that woman entraps and exploits him for her own selfish purposes, but Aphra Behn does not follow the material or the structure of the *Quinze Joyes* to illustrate this principle; instead she drives it home with ten sardonic pleasures which are ten nails in the coffin of a married man's happiness. Echoes from the *Quinze Joyes* are occasionally to be observed but they come and go as they will, and do not detract from the original character of *The Ten Pleasures.* Mr. Harvey remarked that the letter at the end of *The Ten Pleasures* (first part) was a savage attack on women. So it is, but this letter is only an improved version of the preface to de la Salle's *Quinze Joyes.* For her letter (in which one friend asks another whether it is advisable to marry) Aphra Behn seems to have taken for her text these words in the preface of *Les Quinze Joyes* and of its translation *The XV Comforts*: " The report is current of a famous Physician, Valere by name, who being ask'd by one of his Friends (that had the misfortune to be catched in the Nooze of Wedlock) whether he had done well in changing his condition of single Life, returned him this bitter, tho' true Answer; Friend (said he) could you not find some Precipice[15] to cast yourself from thence into the sea?" De la Salle's argument continues:

It is certainly a greater Happiness for a Man to enjoy Freedom uncontroul'd, than to enslave himself for ever without compulsion . . . That man is unquestionably senseless who enjoys his Freedom in the Vigour and Sprightliness of his youth, living

[15] De la Salle used the word *fenestre* : "Amy, n'avez vous peu trouver une haute fenestre pour vous laisser tresbucher en une rivière la teste devant?" (1607 ed., p. 11)

in the stream of Wealth and the high Tide of Pleasure and Delight [who] throws himself into an Abyss of misery, confines himself to a person (a Wife) whose best qualification is Peevishness, forfeits his Freedom, Reason, Content, and Satisfaction and loseth his own to enslave himself to the Humour of another, and this too for Life . . . Would not any rational creature judge him guilty of Statute-madness, who being shewn the Loathsomeness and Horror of a Dungeon, views the maigre and Ghost-like Aspect of the famished Prisoner, hears the hideous Shrieks and Groans of shackled Malefactors, the ratling noise of whose heavy Irons is a Harmony only fit to drive a serious Man out of his Wits; would not, I say, any Person gifted with reason look upon him to be mad beyond the cure of Drugs or Medicines, who shall . . . cast himself in a Goal [sic] with a resolution never to be discharged, but to lie there and perish . . It is a saying of the learned Scaliger, that a Wife is a Hectic Fever never to be cur'd by any thing but Death, nor can any wise man deny it."[16]

Aphra Behn's letter incorporates these views:

But the Tortures of Marriage are such a burthen, that I never saw no man, let him be as couragious as he would, which it hath not brought under the yoke of her Tyranny. Marry then, you shall have a thousand vexations, a thousand torments, a thousand dissatisfactions, a thousand plagues; and in a word, a thousand sorts of repentings, which will accompany you to your Grave.[17]

And there are more direct echoes in Aphra Behn's letter. She says to the prospective husband: "You shall never be at quiet till you are in your grave.[18]   In *The XV Comforts* the pouting wife says: "I'm sure I shall never rest but in that place of undisturbed Rest (the only Dormitory of Mortals) the Grave." [19] *The XV Comforts* says: "Yet for all that is premention'd, I do not blame the State of Matrimony (as now instituted by the Church) for beyond all dispute Marriage is an Ecclesiastical and Religious tye." [20]   Aphra Behn says: "Yet I would not have you to believe, tho' I so much discommend it that it is no waies usefully profitable.   I esteem it to be a holy institution ordained

16 The version of the preface to *Les Quinze Joyes* given in *The XV Comforts of Rash and Inconsiderate Marriage* (4th ed., 1694).
17 Letter at the end of *The Ten pleasures*.
18 *Ibid.*
19 *The XV Comforts*, 1st Comfort.
20 *Ibid*, Preface.

by God Almighty," but, she adds, "that which makes it bad is the woman in whom there is no good." [21]

These quotations may convey a false impression of Mrs. Behn's indebtedness. She adhered to the general procedure of such writings: she took such hints as were useful to her purpose, but in the grip of her originality they become part of an entirely different fabric. For example, she embodies the introduction of the *Quinze Joyes* in a letter, but the episodes or pleasures which constitute her book are quite individual and, from the point of view of fictional development, very much superior. Although the first three joys in de la Salle's work might be episodes in the same marriage, the remainder could not. But Aphra Behn, apparently with the idea of producing something which would approximate to an integral whole, rejects de la Salle's disjointed episodes, and in the first half of her book (the part entitled *The Ten Pleasures*) attempts to write a sequential narrative, beginning with the preparations for the marriage, recounting the events of the first year of married life, and ending with the picture of the young daughter growing up and being married in her turn. " It is an early instance of the stringing together, in a connected narrative, of the material previously used only in short sketches or ' characters'; and so it is directly in the succession which in the end produced what is perhaps the most enduring and individual phenomenon in our language—the English novel." [22]   It is accepted that the character-sketches and episodic accounts given in the *Spectator* and the *Rambler* played an important part in the development of prose fiction, but such contributions were merely the culmination of a trend which had long given proof of its existence in such works as Thomas Overbury's *The Wife* (1614), John Earl's *Microcosmographie* (1628), Thomas Bastard's *Chrestoleras* (1598) and the Duchess of Newcastle's *CCXL Sociable Letters* (1664).   These works, though most valuable for their embryonic delineations of character and for their scenes from real life, lacked a connecting thread.   Indeed the *Spectator* and *Rambler* contributions were very loosely strung together, and as sequential narratives were in no way superior to *The Ten*

---

[21] Letter. *The Ten Pleasures.*
[22] *The Ten Pleasures* (Navarre Soc. ed.) Introd by John Harvey, p. ix.

Pleasures. An even more important contribution to the novel was the realism of *The Ten Pleasures*. Here there is no need for cautious hairsplitting as to the kind of realism involved. *The Ten Pleasures* and *The Confession* are a striking example of realism in a most artificial literary age. As Green, Breton, Nash and Deloney showed the England of their time, as the Duchess of Newcastle in *The Traveller* and in her *CCXL Sociable Letters* gave a glimpse of the uncorrupted side of Restoration life, so Aphra Behn takes us into the very heart of English middle-class life in the reign of James II. With complete fidelity, with immense energy, vivacity and colour she depicts for us the daily round of a young husband and wife. We know the details of their house, their furnishings, their clothes, their food, their customs, their friends, their servant-problem, their money troubles, their quarrels and their reconciliations. We see the husband busy in the shop, or chaffering in the City or drinking with his cronies. When, flown with Dutch courage, he brings them home unexpectedly to supper we watch the wife bite her lips with temper, and we gather the fluent acidities of her curtain lecture. Then the sun comes out again, and we see her in her finery going to market, followed by her hand-maid who carries a basket and the baby " finically dressed "—a proud display for the neighbours. *The Ten Pleasures* and *The Confession* are an on-looker's account of Restoration bourgeois life, told with robustious humour and an astonishing facility of phrase. It is alive; it sweeps us along in a tide of vigorous words. It does not trouble itself with the subtleties of character, but it makes the stock-characters of the husband and wife seem rich by virtue of their universality. They are as good as bread, as sound as ale, as pungent as an onion.

Mrs. Behn, as we have said, took her general idea and some definite hints from the *Quinze Joyes* or its English versions, but this was not the end of her indebtedness. To *The Batchelars Banquet* she owes the style of *The Ten Pleasures*, that style which loses some of its intensity in the second part (*The Confession of the New Married Couple*). Whether or not Dekker was responsible for *The Batchelars Banquet*, it is characterised by the very same style as *Guls Horne-booke* which was Dekker's rendering of Dedekind's *Grobianus*. In *Guls Horne-booke* and in *The Batchelars Banquet* Dekker maintained Dedekind's peculiar manner of writing which is known as Grobianism. The *Grobianus* consisted of a number of scenes not connected by a definite story, but giving an opportunity of describing various kinds of men and manners. It had for its subject bad manners reduced to a code, and its style consisted in a savagely sardonic agreement with all the idiocies described. The style of *The Batchelars Banquet* is an excellent example of Grobianism, and it is this self-same attitude which Aphra Behn adopts towards the objects of her satire. Any part of *The Ten Pleasures* might be quoted as an example. Let us take at random a passage from the First Pleasure. The wooing is successful. The parents have consented and the match is concluded. The wedding is at hand and all is bustle and preparation:

Oh call the Bride, time will deceive us! The Semstress, Gorget-maker, and Starcher, must be sent for, and the linnen must be bought and ordered for the Bridegroom's shirts, the Bride's Smocks, Cuffs, Bands and Handkerchiefs; and do but see, the day is at an end again: my brains are almost addle, addle, and nothing goes forward: For Mrs. Smug said she would bring linnen, and Mrs. Smooth laces, but neither of them both are yet come. Run now, men and maids, as if the Devil were in you, and comfort yourselves that the Bride will reward you liberally for your pains.

Well, Mrs. Bride, how's your head so out of order! Might not you now do (as once a Schoolmaster did) hang out a sign of a troubled pate with a Crown on it? How glad you'l be when this confusion is once over? Could you ever have thought that there was so much work to be found in it? But comfort yourself . . . it is not your case alone, to be in all this trouble, for the Bride-groom is running up and down like a dog, in taking care that the Banns of Matrimony may be proclaimed. And now he's a run-ning to and again through the City to see if he can get Brides-men to his mind that are capacitated to entertain the Brides-maids and Gentleman with pretty discourses, waiting upon them and the rest of the Company. Besides that he's taking care for the getting of some good Canary, Rhenish and French Wines, that those friends which come to wish the Bride and Bridegroom much joy may be presented with a delicate glass of Wine. And principally, that those who are busy about the Bride's adorn-ments may tast the Brides tears.

But really friends, if you come to tast the Brides tears now, tis a great while too soon : But if you'll have of the right and unfeigned ones, you must come some months hence.[23]

The Second Pleasure shows the young wife going to buy household stuff. The maid-servant goes with her and " neighbour John, that good careful labourer must follow them softly with his wheel-barrow, that the things which are bought may be carefully and immediately brought home." [24]   Heart-burnings have begun. The husband is secretly distracted at his wife's extravagance, and she is displeased at the ingratitude of some of the wedding-guests. The Third Pleasure is in happier vein. The young couple walk daily abroad being entertained by their friends and travel into the country for their pleasure.   The writer considers all these diversions with withering irony, and no wonder, because in the following seven Pleasures the husband is about to welter in a sea of troubles, no sooner breasting one wave than another takes his breath away.   This part of the book is a very fine piece of sustained Grobianism, but although there is not really much occasion " to make use of the gesture of turning up the whites of the eyes," we must limit ourselves to two quotations. Some of the most notable effects are achieved by a deadly reduction of what appears unique to the commonplace.   Mr. Pecksniff's nocturnal quest for Sarah Gamp deserves its immortality, but not more so than this wretched husband's frantic predicament.

There's now no small alarm in the Watch. Who is there that is but near, or by the hand that is not set a work !   Oh, was Dorothy the Semstress and Jane the Laundress now here, what a helping hand we might have of them ! Where are now the two Chair women also, they were commonly every day about the house and now we stand in such terrible need of them, they are not to be found?   Herewith must the poor Drone very unexpectedly get out of bed . . . having hardly time to put on his shoes and stockings . . . and it is nothing but hast, hast, hast, fetch the Midwife with all possible Speed . . .
      Therefore without denial away the good man himself must to fetch the Midwife : for who knows whether or no she would come if the maid went; nay it is a question also, being so late in the night, whether she would come along with the maid alone, because she dwells in a very solitary corner clearly at th' other

23 *The Ten Pleasures of Marriage* (Navarre Soc. ed.), p. 19 f.
24 *Ibid*, p. 26 f.

end of the City: (for, after a ripe deliberation of the good woman [the wife] the lot fell so that she made choice of this grave and experienced midwife).

Away runs the poor man without stop or stay, as if he were running for a Wager of some great concern. And though it be never so cold, the Sweat trickles down by the hair of his head, for fear he should not find the Midwife at home; or that perhaps she might be fetcht out to some other place, from whence she could not come. And if it should happen so, we are all undone, for the good woman must have this Midwife, or else she dies; neither can or dare she condescend to take any other for the reasons afore mentioned . . . Be not discomforted although she doth thus unexpectedly force you out of bed, before you have hardly slept an hour, for you see there's great occasion for 't; and now is the time to show that you truly love your wife. This first time will make it more accustomary, the first is also commonly the worst. And if you be so fortunate that at the very first you happen to meet with this prudent and grave Matron Midwife, and do bring her to your longing-for dearly beloved Wife; yet nevertheless you may assure your self, that before you can arrive to have the full scope and height of this Pleasure you'll find some thing more to do: For the Midwife is not able alone to govern and take care of all things that must be fetched brought and carried to and again: therefore of necessity the friends must be fetched with all the Speed imaginable, viz Sisters, Wives, Aunts, Cousins, and several familiar good acquaintances must have notice of it, and be defraied to come to her quickly, quickly, without delay: and if you do not invite them very ceremonially, every one according to their degrees, it is taken as no small affront. 25

Expense now comes like an avalanche upon the unhappy father; hordes of dictatorial women entrench themselves in his house, and treat him like a worm. They enjoy themselves to their hearts' content, gossiping and consuming incredible quantities of food and drink. " But stay a little, tomorrow or next day the Nurse goes away. This seems to be a merriment indeed for then you'll have an Eater, a Stroy-good, a Stuf-gut, a Spoil-all, and a Prittle-pattler less than you had before." 26

So the narrative goes on, and the time is anticipated when the little daughter is grown up:

25 *The Ten Pleasures,* p. 77 ff.
26 *Ibid,* p. 122.

Both you and her mother will reap an extraordinary pleasure in seeing your daughter grow up in all manner of comely and civil deportment; and that she begins to study in the book of *French Manners and Behaviours;* and knows also how to dress up her self so finically with all manner of trinkum trankums, that all the neighbouring young Gentlewomen, and your rich Neeces esteem themselves very much honoured with the injoiment of her company; where they, following the examples of their Predecessors, do by degrees, instruct one another in the newest fashions, finest Flanders Laces, the difference and richness of Stuffs, the neatest cut Gorgets, and many more such Incombobs as these. Nay, and what's more, they begin also to invite and treat each other like grave persons, according as the opportunity will allow them, first with some Cherries and Plums; then with some Filbuds and Small Nuts; or Wallnuts and Figs; and afterwards with some Chestnuts and new Wine; or to a game at Cards with a dish of Tee; or else to eat some Pancakes and Fritters or a Tansie; nay if the Coast be clear to their minds to a good joint of meat and a Sallad. Till at last it comes so far, that through these delicious conversations, they happen to get a Sweetheart. [27]

In a word, another squirrel enters the cage to wear out his distracted existence in the captivity he was too stupid to avoid.

The conclusion of *The Quinze Joyes* (written probably as a last-moment attempt to appease feminine readers) appears to reverse the author's ill-opinion of the female sex. We quote from *The XV Comforts of Rash and Inconsiderate Marriage* (1682):

Nor on the other hand do I say it is ill done to Marry; but it is not well done certainly, for a man to be so Stupid and Insensible, as those we here discourse of apparently declare themselves to be, and so are enslaved with a self-procured Bondage. I would not willingly disoblige the Female Sex; nor indeed do I, if read without Prejudice, and rightly understood, the Contents of this Treatise, tending much to their Honour and Commendation, in all which Rencounters the Women win the day, come off triumphantly, and man is most shamefully worsted by the Weaker Sex: and 'tis but reason it should be so considering the wrongs that they suffer by the Oppression and Severity of their Husbands, by Violence, and without Reason; only because they are not of so Robustious Constitu-

[27] *Ibid.*

tion, and are sent into the World with no other weapon but
the Tongue, nor any other defence but their Chastity, though
daily exposed to the crafty assaults of Wily Man : Nature have
sent them so weakly arm'd into the World, it is a prodigious
shame, that Man should so barbarously insult over them, who
are so ready to serve and obey, without whose Society the World
would soon be a Desart, nay Men could not, did not, nor cannot
live happily. [28]

Possibly these words are sardonic in intention. At any rate,
they did not placate the " Person of Quality of the Female Sex "
who, in the year following *The XV Comforts*, replied with *The
XV Real Comforts*. Whether or not it was possible for Aphra
Behn to be influenced by this latter work, she may have taken
the hint of feminine defence in the passage above quoted, and
rallied to the cause of worthy wives as enthusiastically as she
had pilloried the vapid opportunists.

In *The Confession of the New Married Couple* she parts
company with those who asperse women and matrimony:

Here they are cited to appear who display the married estate
too monstrously as if there were nothing but horrors and terrors
to be found in it. Now they would see how that Love in her
curious Crusible, melteth two hearts and ten sences together.
To this all Chymists vail their Bonnets, though they brag of
their making the hardest Minerals as soft as Milk and Butter.
This Art surpasseth all others. [29]

She applies herself to proving that it is not matrimony, but the
abuse of matrimony which causes so much misery. Marriages
made for money are foredoomed, and she flays the matchmakers
" who negotiate with a very Close intelligence in this sort of
Flesh-Trade," and who draw a commission on the good bargains
they arrange:

You, O Lovers, who seek to be Livry Men of the great
Company, and aim to possess the pleasures of Marriage, have
a care of the inchanting Voices of these crafty Syrens, because
they intend to batter you upon the Scylla and Charibdis where
the Hellish Furies seem to keep their habitation. These are
the onely Occasioners of bad Matches, and such as raise a

[28] *The XV Comforts* . . . (4th ed. 1694), p. 127 f.
[29] *The Ten Pleasures* . . . *and the Confession of the New Married
Couple*, p. 152 f.

Scandal of that Estate, which at once affords both Pleasure, Mirth and Joy. [30]

The young couple in *The Confession* may or may not be identical with the young couple in the *Ten Pleasures*. They are a good-hearted pair, who set up a shop and are determined to live happy ever after. But alas! happiness does not come at the whistle of determination. They experience all the usual vicissitudes. We leave them at the end sunk in debt, short in temper, confused by the blows of life, wanting a divorce. Aphra Behn uses this couple to give continuity to her description of the storms which so often drive " the marriage-ship " on the rocks. She presents them to us as the average faulty but well-meaning husband and wife, and then, by a thousand examples, she shows us how, without love and with initial faults aggravated, men and women can make of marriage a hell upon earth. Now, however, it is the husband whom she lashes with scorpions. It is a curious fact that it is not the major vices which are shown as most objectionable in a husband. Aphra Behn does not greatly dwell, for example, on the loose livers who automatically outlaw themselves from the covenant of marriage. No, her purpose is to show the countless ways in which a man, although fundamentally sound, may be a maddening husband. In her writing there is all the stringency and the minute observation of exacerbated feminine nerves. She shows, in effect, that a wife's nerves, strung taut by her subservient position, may suffer exquisitely through the arrogance, stupidity or selfishness of her lord and master. How can she be supposed to acknowledge a superiority which, as often as not, is non-existent?

> But nevertheless the imaginary authority of men, many times surges to such a height that it seems to them insupportable, to hear anything of a woman's contradiction, thinking that all whatsover they do is absolutely perfect and uncontrollable.

The stingy husband is undoubtedly a sad affliction, and particularly to be abhorred when he calmly pockets his wife's dowry and then forces her to sue for every necessary farthing and to render an account of even the most trifling expenditure.

[30] *Ibid*, p 158.

It is against all reason, that she, like a servant, should give an account to her husband, what, wherefore, or how that money is laid out; because the necessaries also for housekeeping are so many, that they are without end, name or number, and it is impossible that one should relate or ring them all into the ears of a Man.

The obvious solution must be that the wife become bursar because " when men pay out anything, it goes out by great sums . . . this cannot be done with every pittiful small thing that belongs to housekeeping. Insomuch that the Husband can then, with all facility, demand what money is needful for his occasion from his wife." Unfortunately, husbands feel that without the keys of the Money-chest they are " deprived of all their superiority, and like Men unmanned." A woman with a stingy husband must face the prospect that, by a truly fearful deterioration, he may become a " Peep in the Pot." For such prying penuriousness there is practically no remedy. Jealous prying, however, is even worse. Such a husband does

nothing but pout, mumble, bawl, scold, is cross-grained and troubled at everything, nay looks upon his wife and the rest of his Family like a Welsh goat, none of them knowing the least reason in the World for it. In the meanwhile, he useth all means privately to attrap his wife; for to see that which he never will see; and at which he is so divellishly possessed to have a wicked revenge; nay, which he also never can see though he had a whole box-full of spectacles upon his nose; because she never hath, or ever will give him the least reason for it. In that manner violating loves knot, and laying a foundation of implacable hatred.

The best remedy in this case is for the wife to be " a little light-hearted and merry-humoured." Thus she can derive a certain amusement from the contemplation of these absurdities, " but otherwise there is no greater Hell upon Earth."

The husbands so far enumerated have all the faults of rigidity. There is, however, another class—the royal and ancient order of " Whiffling Blades." These are the tipplers, the gamesters, the roysterers, the resourceful fabricators of alibis; but they would need to adduce some better evidence than " a multitude of lame excuses, before they can blind the eyes of a quick-sighted woman or pin it on her so far that she perceives not he seeks

o

his pleasure from her in whom his whole delight ought to be." Such men go about drinking, racketing and wasting their lives and their money. Their avocations afford them an excellent pretext for idleness, and it is enough to make any wife despair when she finds that whether her spouse is a physician, lawyer, exciseman, solicitor, merchant, or shopkeeper, his supposed duties are his best camouflage. Aphra Behn's description of this type of husband is really inimitable. She writes with the malicious humour of a woman who knows by heart all men's devices for playing truant. It is unbelievable that anyone but a woman could have written thus or given to her words so strong a sense of personal reinforcement. As a picture of Restoration London this part [31] of *The Confession* is very valuable. We bless the delinquents who lead us into the vivid, roaring life of coffee-houses, strong-water shops, fairs, horsemarkets, coursing, pigeon-racing, cock-fighting, dog-fighting, bull and bear-baiting; although we cannot but agree these husbands are

> so dull-brained and so excessive careless, that if they had not the good fortunes to get notable sharp-witted young women to their Wives; they themselves would soon have been out of breath, and might now perhaps be found in the Barbado's or Bermoodo's planting Tabacco. [32]

Aphra Behn's great panacea for all matrimonial ills consists in mutual forbearance:

> It is the principallest satisfaction, and greatest pleasure in marriage, when a woman winks or passes by the action of her husband; and the husband in like manner the actions of the wife; for if that were not so, how should they now and then in passing by, throw a love-kiss at one another. [33]

There are crosses and dissatisfactions in every marriage, but still " One pound of the hony of sweet love, can easily balance a hundred weight of that terrible and bitter Wormwood." [34] And for a woman there is a particular pleasure which makes everything worth while:

[31] *The Confession,* Fifth Pleasure.
[32] *Ibid,* Sixth Pleasure. p. 218.
[33] *Ibid,* Fifth Pleasure, p. 209.
[34] *Ibid,* Fifth Pleasure, p. 213.

The Family must be well taken care of; going to market with
the maid to buy that which is good, and let her dress it to your
mind; and every Market day precisely, with the Maid neatly
drest, and following you with a hand-basket, go to take a
view of Newgate, Cheapside, and the Poultry Markets; and
afterwards, when your got a little farther, then to have your
Baby carried by you, neatly and finically drest up; and in
hearing of it, whilst it is in the standing stool, calling in its
own language so prettily Daddy and Mammy. O that is such
an extraordinary pleasure, that where ever you go, what soever
you delight in, all your delight is to be at home again in your
shop, by your servants, and most especially (when you have it)
to be by your baby. 35

Domestic affairs, however, are not unalloyed bliss. One must
take into account that much-abused tribe—the "base-natured,
lasie, tatling, lavish and ill-tongued servants . . . It was a much
less trouble for Arion and Orfeus to charm all the senceless
creatures both of Sea and Land in those daies, than it is for
housekeepers to bring their servants to due obedience." Jane,
being dismissed for "hair-brained" behaviour,

runs to Goody Busie-body that hires out servants; where she
makes no small complaint of her Mistresses insulting spirit;
and asks whether she knows not of a hire for her by some
housekeeping Batchelor or widower; because she understands
the ordering of her work very well, is a special good Cook,
and loves Children &c: Then she would leave her Mistriss,
and tell her that her Aunt was very sick and lay dying, and
that she would go thither.

Then, there is the maid who cannot be restrained from pur-
loining food and drink, and the maid who refuses to postpone
her outing,

having gotten leave to go to church in the evening, tho she
knows there are friends invited to supper, the children must
be got to bed and all things set in good order . . . That it is,
that makes them look like a Dog in a Halter, when they cannot
get leave on Sundaies to go agadding; and it is a wonder
they do not bargain for it when they hire themselves. 36

35 *The Confession*, p. 151.
36 *The Confession* . . . 9th Pleasure.

Some indeed do bargain thus, and depart for Church even if the house were falling about the ears of the mistress, and this, not because of extreme devotion, but " really for no other end than to catch some Tailor, Baker, Shoomaker, Cooper, Carpenter, Mason or such like journey man." Marriage is their object, even though they may thereby exchange a plentiful livelihood for one that is poor and wretched. Observe the vivid realism not only of the foregoing, but particularly of this description of a soldier courting a servant-maid. The soldier entreats the maid to marry him, and she deliberates:

> In short, the Maid begun a little to listen to him (and so much the more because that very morning she had a falling out with her Mistress) and told him, she would take it into consideration. He answered her again, what a fidle stick, why should we spend time in thinking? We are equally matcht: a Souldier never thinks long upon any thing, but takes hold of all present opportunities, and it generally falls out well with him. But she drawing back a little, he saith, ah my dearest, you must take a quick resolution. *Behold there, yonder comes a Cloud driving towards the Moon: I'll give you so much time till that be past by;* quick, for otherwise I must go and seek my fortune by another. Because a soldier neither wooes nor threatens long.

Mrs. Behn does not understate the troubles which a wife may find in marriage, that state in which sometimes husband, children and servants are so many hornets about one's ears. Nevertheless, she is sure that it is worth all its pains if it is a marriage of true minds: " Certainly to be of one mind may very well be said to be happily married, and called a Heaven upon Earth." [37] She has some shrewd remarks to make as to the efforts of incompatible couples to be divorced: " Happy were those restless Souls, if they did like the wise and prudent Chyrurgians, who will not cut off any member, before they have made an operation of all imaginable means for cure and recovery thereof; And that they might the better excuse those of their adversary." [38]

It would be difficult to over-stress the importance of *The Ten Pleasures of Marriage and . . . the Confession of the New Married Couple* as an example of " plain, broad, humorous

[37] *The Confession . . .* p. 152.
[38] *Ibid,* p. 279.

English realism," [39] of that realism which, despite the indifference of aristocratic literary fashions, stoutly persisted in enduring from age to age. It is curious to note how aristocratic and popular genres, existing side by side and tending towards the same goal, refused for long to learn from each other and seemed each intent on working out its own destiny. The romantic genre had learned in a general way to tell a story, and when it considered reality at all, it sought it in the vivid pages of the Italian *novelle*. Apparently it did not realise or was indifferent to the possibilities of stories fashioned from everyday life. On other hand, the popular school kept a tight hold on real life, but somehow, probably because its fullness bewildered them, they could not select and weave material into a sustained narrative. Bunyan was a tidal wave by which one must not measure the average advance, and even Bunyan was sustained by allegory. How long a period was to elapse before Bunyan's realism, characterisation and narrative power were to be employed in depicting everyday life! In the days of Sydney the cleavage between aristocratic and popular prose fiction was complete. In Restoration times it was still evident, but the gap was lessening. Aphra Behn had a firm foot on either bank and, but for the need of enlisting the patronage of the leisured classes, we well know which foot would have followed the other. We have enumerated at the end of Chapter V the many ways in which she overtopped the fiction writers of her age. It remained only to prove her an English realist, and *The Ten Pleasures of Marriage, and . . . the Confession* proves that. It is the coping stone in her great achievement for English prose fiction. It is a characteristic of genius that its ideas find their full fruition in after-time, and it is illuminating to remember in this connection that Aphra Behn, poet, dramatist, novelist, satirist, translator, Aphra Behn of the prophetic inspirations, was a woman " unlearned in schools." [40]

[39] "But there was that other side of the English genius to which Mrs. Behn might have turned in her novels: the plain, broad, humorous, English realism which would so excellently have suited her temper." V. Sackville West, *Aphra Behn 1640-1689* (Representative Women Series, 1927), p. 76.
[40] *Works of Aphra Behn* (ed. Summers), vi, 'Poem to Mr. Creech . . . on his excellent Translation of Lucretius.'

CHAPTER VII.

FROM 1689 TO 1744.

"A cast-off Dame, who of Intrigues can judge,
Writes scandal in Romance—A Printer's Drudge!
Flushed with Success, for Stage-Renown she pants,
And melts, and swells, and pens luxurious rants."
(Savage, *The Authors of the Town*, 1725)

The example of Mrs. Behn led a number of women to embark on professional writing, but it is not to be supposed that these, her immediate successors, made any notable contribution to the novel. While Defoe and Swift were establishing realism, these women rallied to the tattered banner of high-flown sentimentality, and avoided realism as if it were the plague. Mrs. Manley and Mrs. Haywood as exponents of the key-novel and the *novella* succeeded in debauching these types of prose fiction to an almost incredible extent. Their artificial and poisonous concoctions were doomed to perish by their very excesses, but they could not, in any case, survive the robust, eager life of Defoe's writings. In the stark daylight of Defoe's realism the Ismenias and Licentias stood revealed as raddled wantons, and all the whining fops melted away. Roxana was an honest trull compared with the silken decadence of the boudoirs. Not only so, but there was the growth of a conventional reading-public who would no longer subscribe to a cynical representation of love. Let there be transgressions certainly, but never unaccompanied by repentance. Eros is dead; so is Silenus and all the satyrs and nymphs. Robinson Crusoe falls on his knees and thanks God with unfailing regularity, and Moll Flanders, although she wallows in evil for about seventy years, always condemns her lapses in the most high-souled manner. The ethical focus returns to fiction. This new spirit of moral earnestness did not become marked, however, until the first two decades of the eighteenth century had passed. It is seen in the works of Mrs. Barker, Mrs. Davys, Mrs. Aubin and the excruciating Mrs. Rowe. But before we can arrive at this God-fearing and piously sentimental ground we must pass through noxious swamps. Here be crocodiles, here be stenches! Let us clench our teeth, hold our noses and advance.

We must journey half the way with Mrs. Manley, that football of fortune. Fate kicked her down into the field at first. Thereafter she was the sport of many, and she gathered mud all the way. She was the daughter of Sir Roger Manley, who lost his fortune in the Stuart cause and did not regain it at the Restoration. He devoted himself to literary pursuits (he is involved in the mystery of *The Turkish Spy*) and paid little attention to his motherless children. At his death Mary Manley was left £200 and a share in the residue of his estate. It was fortunate for her that she also inherited a modicum of literary ability, because soon she was a pariah, living partly by her wits and partly by her pen. The man who brought her to these straits was her cousin, John Manley. She and her fortune were committed to his direction, according to her father's wish. John Manley decoyed her into a false marriage, his wife being then alive, and he used her money for his own purposes. When he deserted her, she was left, penniless and disgraced, to fend for herself, and thereafter it was a swift descent from bad to worse. She passed from one protector to another, endeavouring at the same time to earn some part of her living by her pen. In 1696, two years after she had been dropped by the notorious Duchess of Cleveland, and after she had passed the intervening time in obscurity, she published a volume entitled *Letters written by Mrs. Manley*. This was reprinted in 1725 as *A Stage Coach Journey to Exeter*, and is worthy of note as a contribution to the epistolary form. In 1696 also Mrs. Manley took to the writing of plays, two of which were produced within the year: *The Lost Lover; or, the Jealous Husband* at Drury Lane, and *The Royal Mischief* at Lincoln's Inn Fields. In 1706, *Almyra, or the Arabian Vow*, a play based on *The Arabian Nights*' was

produced at the Haymarket, but before then Mrs. Manley had
hit on a much more remunerative form of writing. From
gathering mud to throwing it is an easy transition. Mrs. Manley
collected filth with the relentless energy of a dredger, and aimed
it with the deadly precision of a machine gun. It was her revenge
on a condemnatory world. *The New Atalantis* was by no means
a literary innovation. Even the ponderous Heroic Romance had
often been made the vehicle for political and personal satire, as
Barclay's *Argenis* and Lady Mary Wroath's *Urania* testified.
With the decadence of the Heroic Romance it was increasingly
used as a means of satirising one's enemies, and in France this
practice had attained great popularity, Bussy de Rabutin's
Histoire Amoureuse des Gaules (1660) being the most outstanding of these works. Aphra Behn's *Love-Letters between a Nobleman and his Sister* (1683) are openly based on the *cause célèbre*
of Lord Grey of Werk.

The New Atalantis, published in several different parts, was
a heterogeneous mass of scandal aimed at well known people.
The first part, *The Secret History of Queen Zarah and the Zara-
sians* (1705), chiefly attacked the Duchess of Marlborough. It
was in two volumes. The second part, consisting also of two
volumes, was *The Secret Memoirs and Manners of Several
Persons of Quality, of both Sexes . . . From the New Atalantis,
an Island in the Mediterranean* (1709). This was followed by
a second edition including another part which also appeared
separately as *Memoirs of Europe Towards the Close of the Eighth
Century. Written by Eginardus, Secretary and Favorite to
Charlemagne* (1710); and finally there appeared *Court Intrigues,
in a Collection of Original Letters, from the Island of the New
Atalantis* (1711).

Mrs. Manley's writings were so libellous, and were so violently
anti-Whig that she was arrested in 1709, together with the
publishers and printers of *The New Atalantis*. She was admitted
to bail, and was the following year discharged without punish-
ment. In *Memoirs of Europe* she says in self-defence:

> Methinks 'tis hard, and I have often wondered at it why that
> Man shou'd be thought uncharitable, a Satyrist, or Libeller,
> who but repeats with his Pen what every Body fearlessly reports

with their Tongue : Is it because the Reproach is more indelible?
Let the Great take heed then how they give the Occasion; let
'em beware how they set to have Picture of their Vices made
immortal. Do you believe the Liberty suffered at Athens, in
their Dramatick Pieces, did not restrain several who were
viciously enclin'd, fearful of seeing themselves represented?
The Satyrist must be thought of use to his Country, tho' I
can't forgive him that betrays the Weakness of his Friend, or
any Secret that he happens to be let into, of what Nature soever :
or who, having been oblig'd, or receiv'd into Families, finds the
defenceless part, and exposes their Foibles to the world; Those
are meannesses below Contempt, scarce any can be guilty of
'em. I must always condemn the Person from whom Scandal
first arises; he that gives a Man or Woman to the ruin of
Tongues (perhaps yet young in Vice) and throws their Reputation to the Winds, to be torn and scattered by malignant Fame.
I wou'd have every one tender even to repeat any thing dis-
advantageous of another, 'till he were very well assured not
only of the Truth, but that the Mater of Fact were no longer
a Secret; Nay, and even then, I wou'd have him distinguish
between a Start, and a confirm'd Habit of Vice. We have all
our Frailities, the Suppression of 'em is doubtlessly meritorious ;
but the glorying in 'em, by an ostantatious long course of Evil,
and refuging under the splendor of a great name and Quality,
is something so abominable as must give Offence to every
honest Man.[1]

But Mrs. Manley was, in some cases, not merely repeating with
her pen what everybody fearlessly reported with their tongues.
Sunderland, at her trial, was so much at a loss to imagine the
sources of her information that he asked her to reveal them. She
refused, saying that perhaps she wrote under inspiration, but she
admitted, when cornered, that inspiration could come from evil
sources as well as from good. Mrs. Manley's pose of moral
indignation was really trying her readers too high. Her self-
defence would have them believe that her scavengings were merely
in the interests of public hygiene, but unfortunately the deliberate
prurience of her writings makes her real purpose only too evident.

We are concerned here only with estimating *The New Atalantis*
as a contribution towards prose fiction, therefore it is unnecessary
to identify the objects of Mrs. Manley's attacks, particularly since
this information is so easily available in the keys which are
appended to Mrs. Manley's volumes, and has been summarised by

[1] *Memoirs of Europe*, i., 254.

several writers.[2] *The New Atalantis* is, on the whole, an endlessly involved and an extremely dull book. The fact that the *double entendre* has died with the years, and has to be deliberately revived in our minds, before we can understand the references, makes the task of literary criticism all the easier. No longer vivified by the breath of scandal these volumes are now dead things. It must be very many years since decomposition first set in. By this time to make their acquaintance is like encountering a skeleton. The wind blows through the grinning jaws with meaningless sound, the empty eye-sockets leer, a bony digit is placed knowingly on what was once a nose. In vain: the foul insinuations, the sneers, the grudges as now as dead as those whose time they wasted. These scandals have found sanctuary in the tomb, and it is strange that in recording them Mrs. Manley should at one stroke have secured for herself notoriety and for her pen oblivion—both unending.

Who now reads *The New Atalantis* save those who endeavour to trace the growth of the novel? Had this work been distinguished by intelligent construction, a graceful style, or by wit, however mordant, these qualities would suffice to triumph in a great measure over the ephemeral nature of the subject. But actually *The New Atalantis* is devoid of such characteristics. The construction is execrable. It consists of endless conversations between vague individuals, or rather monologues so long and so involved that we forget the speaker, and are surprised when a question or a reply reminds us of their existence. There is either no effort or no ability to achieve verisimilitude.

For example, in *Memoirs of Europe* Horatio, immortal conqueror of Iberia, deprived of his military command, wanders through Europe, until near the river Neva he comes upon Solitude and Sincerity between whom an extraordinary dialogue ensues. "Well, my dear," says Solitude to Sincerity, "Did I not prophecy to thee aright? Did I not tell thee thou would'st return to me again, that the world was unworthy of thee?" After which domestic introduction Solitude in a prolonged harangue, exposes all the hypocrisy of the world. The words are those of a scolding woman, that is to say of Mrs. Manley. Sincerity

2 E.g. Lord Earnle, *Light Reading of our Ancestors* (1927), p. 175.

replies with an encomium on Horatio, and he departs sped by
the good wishes of this egregious pair. But he has not travelled
a league when night overtakes him, and he discovers in the midst
of that wild and desolate country " a sumptuous Tent (as it is
the Custom in that Country when Persons of Quality travel,
because the Cabarets are few and very ill provided), ostenta-
tiously enlightened with a vast number of white-Wax-
Flambeaux." He is invited to spend the night in this magnificent " Field Apartment," and is entertained by Merovius, Prior
of Orleans. This entertainment consists in a monologue of
incredible length with which Merovius inveighs against the
corruption of politics and social life, particularly in Sarmatia
(England). Intermingled (there is no other word for it) with
this diatribe is the story of Merovius' early passion for an idiot
girl, a very disgusting and irrelevant episode. The monologue proceeds with a rambling description of the marriage
of the Princess of Sarmatia (Mary) to the Prince of
Illyria (William of Orange), and introduces secret notes, papist
plots and counterplots, innumerable adulteries, all so confused,
so wandering, hidden beneath such a weight of conceits and
verbiage that it is extremely difficult to arrive at the author's
intention, even if it were worth while. In the main narrative
there is not one iota of humour and only an occasional touch of
wit. Were Mrs. Manley but content to be plainly abusive we
should at least have the satisfaction of knowing exactly what she
wished to say. But alas! some delusion of intellectuality
betrayed her into an elephantine style, heavily sentimental, dully
ironic, enlivened only by highly absurd bursts of ranting. As
thus:

> View here, my Lord, said I, addressing the High-Priest, view
> the Fair, but Murther'd Honoria! Honoria! The Vertuous
> as well as charming! View her as the Trophy of Prince
> Alexis's Victory and Inconstancy! Honoria dy'd by her
> Lover's Infidelity!
> A Lover! who by holy and interchangeable Vows was sworn
> to become her Husband; having subdu'd her Heart, he wou'd
> have basely profited himself of the conquest by triumphing over
> her vertue; but finding the Heroick Maid set the Value upon
> it that she ought, he abandon'd what he should have worshipped,
> and from that moment thought no longer of Her, or of his

Vows! Oh! Apostate to Love and Chastity! Thou did'st prepare thyself (after being engag'd by Oaths and solemn Imprecations to Honoria, in the sight of Juno the Awful Goddess, and Queen of Marriage-vows), thou did'st prepare, as all Sarmatia knows, to wed the Princess Emely! Oh! Unpresedented Perjury! Oh! inconsiderate Youth, to barter real Merit for glaring Titles. Oh! capricious God of Love, How wert thou so easily disgusted? . . . Behold her a Monument of Infidelity; it was the Arm of Treachery, and not her own that lifted the fatal Draught to her despairing Lip! It was Prince Alexis's Cruelty and Apostacy, that determin'd and gave her to swallow the stupifying Death! Revenge! Revenge! you immortal Powers! You that are ever excellent! Revenge upon his Name and Family, Honoria's Wrongs; take Possession of him all ye Furies! Seize him ye Infernal Powers! May his life be short and miserable, but may his hereafter Torments be never-ending.

Such rhetoric and indeed such punctuation is by no means rare in *The New Atalantis*, but even when the narrative takes a saner tone, it still suffers from the faults already indicated. There is a prurience which seizes upon and describes with voluptuousness every possible occasion of sensuality. Such writing is seducing without being seductive. Mrs. Manley's idea of setting the stage for an amorous interlude is sublime in its vulgarity:

The Duchess softly enter'd that little Chamber of Repose, the Weather being violently hot the Umbrelloes were let down from behind the Windows, the sashes open, and the Jessamine that covered 'em blew in with a gentle Fragrancy; Tuberoses set in pretty Gilt and China Posts, were placed advantageously upon Stands, the Curtains of the Bed drawn back to the Canopy, made of yellow Velvet embroider'd with white Bugles, the Panels of the Chamber Looking-glass, upon the Bed were strow'd with a lavish Profuseness, plenty of Orange and Lemon Flowers, and to compleat the Scene, the young Germanicus . . . in a lose Gown of Carnation Taffety, stained with Indian Figures, his beautiful long flowing Hair for then 'twas the custom to wear their own tied back with a Ribbon of the same Colour . . .

Equally unfortunate are the blowzy euphemisms with which she fondly hopes to raise her language to the true converse of the gods. " The honey-moon " is " The Hymenial Moon," and when, for example, she wishes to say that the rascally crew willingly drowned so that their master should be saved, she says:

" The ignoble Crew willingly devoted themselves to the Sea-green Deity, to secure the Life of their Master."

Mrs. Manley did much better when she was vindictive without circumlocutions. Then by her very maliciousness she succeeds in driving home her blade very neatly. She says:

> I wou'd positively have some Method found out to acquaint all Women with their Decay. They should be told when they begin to be no longer charming, for they will never know it else: Nothing is so ridiculous as their carrying things to Extremity: they would joyn the Spring to Autumn, May to December, the two Ends of Time, in a True-love's Knot. [3]

And again, speaking of a paragon named Porcia who is married to a morose husband:

> Propetious Heaven! unloos'd the rugged Chain: He dy'd, she was no longer marry'd, left very young, very handsome, very rich, but very wise. The three former Qualifications drew Crowds of Adorers, the latter as dexterously dispersed 'em.[4]

Sometimes Mrs. Manley achieves a pithy terseness:

> Surely you must have observed Julius Sergius: he began to sprout in your time; but, alas, his Growth is now past knowledge. [5]

And speaking of Maro (Addison), who has put himself under the protection of Julius Sergius: " Farewell, Maro, 'till you abandon your artificial Patron, Fame must abandon you!" But most frequently Mrs. Manley was not satisfied to attack one individual at a time. She had to a very marked degree the power of hitting in many directions at once. Possibly that multiple desire of wounding largely accounts for the teeming confusion of her narrative style. Here is a clear example of this savage irony, a double-edged and (were it possible) double-pointed dagger of which every stab goes home. She has been speaking of the abhorred Julius Sergius, and his indiscriminate patronage of writers good and bad. Sapho the younger is one of this number,

[3] *Memoirs of Europe*, i, 262.
[4] *Ibid*, 275.
[5] *Ibid*, 276.

a female writer who, we are told, is bad in every sense of the
word.   But as for Lais! :

> Nor has another of the Sex forebore to intrude herself, Con-
> stantinople abounds in Pretenders of both kinds, the result of
> that Silence, which has invaded those who are truly Master of
> the Muses; but this Thing without a name, is only known
> by the permission Julius Sergius gave her to invoke him as a
> Patron; if she had any other Art of pleasing him, he had best
> conceal it, lest he make himself the laugh of those numerous
> Coxcombs, by whom her Address and Adulations have been so
> often rejected : Much good may it do you Sergius, with Lais's
> Charms, the Leavings of the Multitude.

Finally there is the neat comment on the lady who married a
profligate.   He had already buried a Wife, to whom during her
life-time he had been consistently unfaithful.   Mrs. Manley
says of the second wife:

> She had the good fortune to fix, as well as to survive this
> wandering star, though it must be own'd, *that there are Follies
> like some Stains, that wear out of themselves among which,
> Love is generally reckon'd to be one.*

These triumphs of vindictiveness are, however, rare.   For the
most part Mrs. Manley seeks to maintain her readers' attention
simply by obscenity and slanderous *tours de force*.   We see her
launch herself on the thin ice of contemporary scandal, and for
the remainder of the time we watch in shocked fascination her
intricacies, her convolutions, her daring unabated even when the
ice is cracking under her.   She is a professional skater, trying by
reckless feats to gain the applause on which her bread depends.
Or perhaps it would be truer to say that she is the decayed
soubrette in a cheap music-hall, trying to achieve by lewdness
what she is unable to win by charm.   But, alas! charm is
unlimited because unpredictable.   Lewdness is an immense bore-
dom, and the more extreme the more boring, because there is
no hope of further variety.   Hence it is that in her efforts to
titillate Mrs. Manley is driven even into the ramifications of
unnatural vice.   Mrs. Manley's effort to exhaust exhaustion, to
saturate saturation point is her greatest mistake in the composition of *The New Atalantis*.   She cries " wolf, wolf! " and that

predatory animal appears slavering for his prey. We observe him complete his horrible meal, and depart, licking his chops. Before we have time to breathe, the cry goes up again, the lupine repast is again consumed, and another and another, until finally we are so bored with the performance that no variety of wolfish meals, eaten singly or *en masse*, could cause us a tremor of alarm or horror. That Mrs. Manley realised this difficulty is clearly shown in the following passage, with which she stigmatises a fellow-writer, without, however, recognising that her words are really a self-portrait:

> 'Tis a hard Task to be forced to be witty be one in never so opposite an Humour, but he has still Fire and Malice enough to do our Business. They call him in contempt a Bread-Writer, a sorry (half Sesterce) fellow; but his pen is generally acceptable, he pleases those whom he stings; a commodious useful Hireling, stops at nothing, goes through thick and thin; He cants admirably, and pretends to Vertue, but is as ingrateful and unfair as one could desire. He'll lay on any Colours, and is so great an Artist, he can metamorphose in a Twinkling, the brightest Hero into a dirty Scavenger.

And yet, although in the main *The New Atalantis* has all the faults we have described, it is for one reason significant in the development of prose fiction. It is to be observed that Mrs. Manley wove detachable stories into the framework of *The New Atalantis*. These are all modelled on the Italian *novelle*, but are heavily laden with romantic superstructure. These inset tales seem superior to the seven stories, most of which she later adapted from Painter's *Palace of Pleasure*, and published under the title of *The Power of Love* (1720). But it is difficult to decide whether they truly are superior, or whether they merely achieve a kind of humanity in contrast with the scurrilous and unreal background. In *Secret Memoirs and Manners of Several Persons of Quality*, the story of the woman nailed dead to the gibbet is, however, really well told. The narrator is a country woman, and it is interesting to note that the language put into her mouth is compatible with her station in life. Another tale worthy of mention is that of Charlot and the Duke.

The Duke, a widower and Charlot's guardian, designs her for marriage with his son, and does everything in his power to guard her innocence and to strengthen her mind against evil influences. She lives with the Duke's family about fifteen miles from the capital in a country-house to which the Duke sometimes comes " to taste a rest from Power, a calm of Greatness, a Suspense of Business, a respiration of Glory." One evening the company diverts itself with amateur theatricals; Charlot excels in the role of Diana, and the Duke, overcome by his delight in her performance, kisses her. This is the beginning of a passion which he is soon unable to curb. But the Duke is a statesman, and he is endeavouring to arrange for himself a marriage of international importance. He hopes to marry a Princess Dowager of a petty State, and therefore has no intention of making Charlot his wife. But he cannot renounce his passion for her. His struggle against the dishonour of his desires is very well described. He determines to make her his mistress, and immediately is confronted by the necessity of undermining that modesty in her which he has so laboured to strengthen. How scale the ramparts he has himself erected? By giving her access to erotic books he gradually saps her spiritual health. He absents himself that she may feel his loss, and then returns to overwhelm her with caresses. She falls into a state of spiritual enervation. Now the least germ of immorality will be sufficient to undo her. In order that vitiation without may second the inward vitiation he removes her to Court, and her moral principles begin to totter. But now another effect of her reading and observation is a hindrance to the Duke:

> Charlot by this time had informed herself, that there were such terrible things as Perfidy and Inconstancy in Mankind; that even the very Favours [men] received, often disgusted; and that to be entirely Happy, one ought never to think of the faithless Sex. This brought her back to those Precepts of Virtue that had embellished her Dawn of Life.

Still, it was useless for the wheel to come full circle, while the Duke was there awaiting her at every point of the circumference. He could never have defeated her moral objections, but it only remained now for him to assure her of his constancy. She yields at last. She is happy for a while, although her liaison makes it necessary for her to live completely in seclusion. Her only guest and her sole confidant is a young Countess, a lovely widow. " But Charlot could not escape her destiny." The Duke becomes weary of her and enamoured of her friend. His political marriage fails of achievement, and, forsaking his ward whom he has taken such pains to seduce, he immediately marries the Countess who has never shown him any particular favour. The story has a moral, because the erring Charlot " dy'd a true Landmark: to warn all believing Virgins from shipwrecking their honour upon (that dangerous Coast of Rocks) the Vows and pretended Passion of Mankind." Mrs. Manley adds a second moral which is a splendid example of practical cynicism: " That no woman ought to introduce another [woman] to the man by whom she is belov'd."

This story, which is after the style of the Italian *novella*, has obviously benefited by the *Princesse de Clèves* and the *Portuguese Letters*. The dissection of Charlot's mind, the struggle between inculcated principles and temptation, the description of her doubts, fears, hopes, desires, despairs; the tracing of every phase in the degeneration of innocent love into guilty passion—all this is very well done, and belongs to that trend in fiction which later found a notable exponent in Richardson. A more obvious result of the *Princesse de Clèves* is Mrs. Manley's story of how the Lady of St. Amant died for love. (This lady's husband dies, and she is deterred by scruples from marrying her lover.) As for the *Portuguese Letters*, we hear very occasionally in the diction of Mrs. Manley's tales an echo of those profound outpourings, in scenes, alas! most alien to such accents. Once, we even have the exact words of the nun of Beja, that prior to the coming of her lover she had only known people who were disagreeable to her.

There are many other inset stories in *The New Atalantis*, none better than that of Charlot, and many worse. Some are borrowings or inventions, some are simply a medium for scandal. In *The Power of Love* Mrs. Manley borrows very largely from Bandello.[6] She does not justify unprincipled love as Mrs. Behn

---

6 *The Fair Hypocrite* taken from Painter's *Duchess of Savoy* (45th novel). *The Physician's Stratagem* not identified in Painter, but obviously on the Italian pattern.

The Wife's Resentment from Painter's *Didaco and Violenta* (42nd

P

had done, and seldom loses an occasion of moralising. Like
Congreve, she verbally indicates her dissatisfaction with the
romantic tradition, and still, like Congreve, adheres to it. In *The
Husband's Resentment* (first example) Desideria says: " I must
own myself perfectly weary of Groves and Purling Streams! I
should never have liked the Life of a Shepherdess, tho' I had
found never so many Corydon's to have endear'd it to me." And
in the introduction to *The Happy Fugitives*, Mrs. Manley
remarks:

> When we reflect upon those examples left us by Antiquity,
> as well in their Real as Fabulous Histories, we may observe
> that Love was quite another thing in the Souls of their Heroins,
> than it is now in ours. What Ariadne, Medea or Helen, as of
> old, do now leave their Fathers, Husbands and Country, to
> pursue the Fortune of their Lovers who were not always over
> grateful for the Favour? Fashions are changed! alas the Time!
> We speak only of Interest, Portion, Joyntures, Settlements,
> Separate Maintenance now-a-days! with other worldly con-
> siderations; which clearly proves, that Cupid has either blunted
> his Darts, or makes them of quite another sort of Stuff. Or,
> perhaps, he rarely concerns himself in modern Wedlock where
> Hymen officiates in his Robes, rather dip'd in Gall than Saffron!
> This Degeneracy causes us to look upon former Precedents
> without Complacency, as if we were unbelievers. The Constancy
> and Fortitude of Lovers in ancient Times, instead, of raising
> our Admiration, are called Stale, Romantick Stories, and the
> Legends of the Nursery: so easy is it to despise what we
> never mean to imitate. All this I very well understood when
> I set myself to draw forth of Obscurity the true History of
> our Happy Fugitives. There appears to me something so
> Heroick, so praiseworthy in their Passion and Perseverance,
> that however diffident I may be of the Success, from the
> different Taste of the present Age I have resolved to pursue
> the Undertaking.

But not only was she resolved to present the power of love, but
resolved to present it in the romantic style. One instance will
suffice to show how artificially she embroidered the direct, vivid

novel). *The Husband's Resentment*: example i:—Painter's *Of a Lady
of Thurin* (43rd novel); example ii:—from Painter's *President of
Grenoble* (58th novel). *The Happy Fugitives* from Painter's *Alerane and
Adelasia. The Perjured Beauty*, based on the St. Gregory legend, which
gave Walpole the plot of his play *The Mysterious Mother*.
    (For these identifications see E. A. Baker, *History of the English
Novel*, iii).

tales in Painter. *The Happy Fugitives* describes the love of Alerane and Adelasia:

Painter's *Alerane and Adelasia*:

This good Prince had one daughter in whom nature had distributed her gifts in such wise, as she alone might have vaunted herself to attaine the perfection of them all, which ever had anything, worthy of admiration, were it in singularity of beauty, favour and courtesie, or in disposition and good bringing up. The name of this fayre Princess was Adelasia.

Alerane:

This yonge Prince, besides that he was one of the fayrest and comliest gentlemen of Almaigne, had therewithall, together with Knowledge of armes, a passing skill in good sciences, which mitigated in him the ferocitie both of his warlike Knowledge, and of the nature of his countrey. His name was Alerane.

Mrs. Manley's *The Happy Fugitives*:

The Princesse was the Favourite of Nature, who drew her extremely beautiful, with a Spirit full of Fire, a Greatness of Soul and Heart in which the God of Love took up his chiefest residence.

Alerane:

The young prince was distinguishingly handsome, called Hugo Alerane. He was formed to draw to him the Hearts of the Fair Sex, who doat on Beauty in their Lovers, much as their Lovers do in them; and are sooner surprised and caught by it, because it is more rarely found amongst them. The next Attractive in those Days of Chivalry, was Valour and Dexterity in Feats of Arms; in which Alerane outwent all his Contemporaries. He learnt these exercises with wondrous Ease, and performed them with infinite Applause! He was the Hero of the Age and the Pride of the Court! his Behaviour was Warlike in the Field; but in the Apartment, Civilised and Soft; so gentle and submissive to the Fair, that he subdued them all.

When Adelasia heard that Alerane had saved the Emperor's life:

She no sooner cast her eyes upon Alerane, but love which had prepared the ambushe so pierced her delicate breast as he took possession of her . . . Alerane by taking careful heed to the looks which the Princess continually did stealingly cast upon him . . . assured himself unfainedly to be beloved . . . . which caused him . . . to beare unto her like affection.

Alerane and Adelasia were both deeply in love:

A passion truly most intollerable for a yonge Princesse, as well because she never had experience of semblable sorow, as for her tender age, and yet more for a natural abashmente and shame, which with the vails of honor doth serve, or ought to serve for a bridle to every Ladie covetous of fame, or like to be the ornament or beauty of her race.

The fair Princess who was born under an amorous Constellation, found something so worthy her Heart in the Merit and Person of Alerane that she held herself excused for that sweet Violence by which she found it impossible to withhold hers from him. Love had, by Alerane's Beauty, prepared the Toils, and so entangled her Breast, that she knew not how to extricate herself . . . Alerane, who was under the Tuition of the same Deity, learn'd Penetration from him; he taught him to discover the Distemper of the Princess . . . . As Alerane's Looks were never from Adelasia he saw those Glances which by Stealth, she continually shot towards him . . . . Adelasia, floating on a tempestuous Sea of Passion, guided by a Master who is too often pleased with the Shipwreck of those whom he conducts; was withheld by Shame and Modesty, which like a Veil covers, or ought to cover, the Desires of those Virgins who would preserve their Fame; and are to be either The Ornament or Blemish of their Race.

The superiority of Painter's version is quite clear in regard to style, but it must be said that Mrs. Manley endeavoured to particularise the characters, not, it is true, enough to give them individuality, and yet sufficient to add to the probability of their actions. Sometimes she effects some minor change in the structure of the story.

Among Mrs. Manley's libellous works must be reckoned *Rivella*, her autobiography. The frontispiece has an extreme conventionality in marked contrast to the narrative which follows. We see stately houses well walled in from common life, trees growing in symmetrical rows and some courtly figures engaged in polite conversation. Unreal swans tower so high over the water as to seem poised on a mudbank, while over all a fantastic sun casts its mathematical beams. Here in Somerset-House Garden Sir Charles Lovemore (Lieutenant-General John Tidcomb) tells Mrs. Manley's story to the young Chevalier D'Aumont, and this recital curiously combines egregious vanity and unintentional pathos. Take Lovemore's dissertation on Mrs. Manley's writings:

> I have not known any of the Moderns in that point [amorous descriptions] come up to your famous Author of the *Atalantis*. She has carried the passion farther than could readily be conceived: Her Germanicus on the Embroider'd Bugle Bed, naked out of the Bath; Her Young and Innocent Charlot transported with the powerful Emotion of a just kindling Flame, sinking with delight and Shame upon the Bosom of her Lover in the Gallery of Books . . . . are such Representations of Nature, that must warm the coldest Reason . . . . After perusing her Inchanting Descriptions which of us have not gone in Search of Raptures, which she everywhere tells us, as happy Mortals, we are capable of tasting. But have we found them, Chevalier, answered his friend? For my Part, I believe they are to be met with solely in her own Imbraces.

The Chevalier is inclined to agree with Lovemore, but as he has never seen Rivella, he cautiously demands an inventory of her charms. What follows is a strange mixture of truth and self-deception on the part of Mrs. Manley: " Is not this being a little too particular, answered Sir Charles, touching the Form of a Lady who is no longer young, and was never a Beauty? Not in the least, briskly. reply'd the Chevalier, provided her Mind and Her Passions are not in Decay." That they are not we may judge from this encomium:

> Speak to me of her eyes, interrupted the Chevalier, you seem to have forgot that index of the Mind: is there to be found in them, store of those animating Fires with which her writings are fill'd. Do her eyes love as well as Her Pen? You reprove

me very justly, answer'd the Baronet, Rivella would have a great deal of Reason to complain of me, if I should silently pass over the best Feature of her Face. In a Word, you have your-self described them; Nothing can be more tender, ingenious, and brilliant with a Mixture so languishing and sweet, when Love is the Subject of the Discourse . . . .

But nothing will satisfy the exigent D'Aumont:

How are her Teeth and Lips, spoke the Chevalier? Forgive me, dear Lovemore, for breaking in so often upon your Dis-course; but kissing being the sweetest leading pleasure, 'tis impossible a Woman can charm without a good Mouth.

He is assured that Rivella's mouth is unexceptionable. So the catechism proceeds, and we look beyond the words at the woman who penned them, the woman thus described by Swift two years previously:

Poor Mrs. Manley . . . is very ill of a dropsy and sore legs; the printer tells me she is afraid she cannot live long. I am heartily sorry. She has very generous principles for one of her sort, and a great deal of good sense and invention; she is about forty, very homely and very fat. [7]

Here is Mrs. Manley's description of herself:

Her Person is neither tall not short; from her Youth she was inclined to Fat; when I have often heard her Flatterers liken her to a Grecian Venus. It is certain, considering that dis-advantage, she has the most easy Air that one can have; her Hair is of a pale Ash-colour, fine, and in a large quantity . . . But to do Rivella justice, till she grew fat, there was not I believe any defect to be found in her body: her Lips admirably colour'd; Her teeth small and even, a Breath always sweet. Her complexion fair and fresh; yet with all this you must be us'd to her before she can be thought thoroughly agreeable. Her Hands and Arms have been publickly celebrated: it is certain that I never saw any so well turned . . . her Feet small and pretty.

Small and pretty—those swollen, dropsical feet! Few things are sadder than a woman who knows, but will not own, that her day is done. So it is with this entire autobiography. It is the expression of a life, foolish, immoral, revengeful, brave.

[7] *Journal to Steila,* 28th Jan., 1712.

We watch her juggling with words, talking feverishly on, building
up an illusion of beauty, brilliancy and success, but we are no
more deceived than she. She has ten years to live, she is poor,
plain, middle-aged, alone, disreputable; but she is gallant. No
one in her lifetime denied her that. It is not, however, merely
for this reason that the history of Rivella has on us a peculiar
effect of pathos. If we knew nothing of her actual circumstances,
the effect would still be the same. It is only as to her writings
that she believes her boasts. For the rest, she knows the truth,
and we are conscious of the painful contrast between her words
and her underlying mood. There is the sadness of her backward glance at youth, and her knowledge that never now can
she extricate herself from the tangle of her life; there is her
regret for what she was, and our regret for what she is. She
has not even the happiness of being too stupid to see the ruin
of her life. After the introduction Lovemore becomes a kind
of doppelgänger, that better self that stands apart and watches
her downward way.

> There are so many Things Praise and yet Blame-worthy in
> Rivella's conduct that as her Friend, I know not well how with
> a good Grace, to repeat, or as yours to conceal, because you
> seem to expect from me an impartial History. Her Vertues are
> her own, her Vices occasion'd by her Misfortunes.

Her father dies; her villainous cousin " marries " her biga-
mously: the descent has begun. He goes on securely in respect
and honour, becomes a member of Parliament and Surveyor-
General, but " here begins Rivella's real Misfortunes: it would
be well for her, that I could say here she dy'd with Honour,
as did her Father . . . She told me all her Misfortunes with an
Air so perfectly ingenuous, that, if some Part of the World who
were not acquainted with her Vertue ridicul'd her Marriage, and
the Villainy of her kinsman; I who knew her sincerity could
not help believing all she said . . ." " But Time," says the
doppelgänger, " time which allays all our Passions, lessen'd the
Sorrow I felt for Rivella's Ruin . . . her Wit and Gaiety of
Temper return'd, but not her Innocence." She loses caste, she
is taken up and contemptibly dropped by the Duchess of Cleveland, against whose false accusations she successfully defends

herself. After two years in the country two of her plays are successfully produced. " Behold another wrong Step towards ruining Rivella's character with the World: the incense that was daily offer'd her upon this Occasion by the Men of Vogue and Wit . . . I had still so much concern for Rivella that I pitied her Conduct, which I saw must infallibly center in her Ruin: there was no Language approached her Ear but Flattery and Persuasion to Delight and Love."

Then follows her association with Sir Thomas Skipworth, recounted with unquotable indecency; and the complicated affair of Lord Montagu and the Monk family, which takes up so great a part of the narrative as to be out of all proportion. There is no doubt of the relish with which she narrates this scandalous intrigue. She becomes the mistress of Mr. Tilly and probably of many others. She says that on his wife's death she refused to marry him. Be that as it may, he marries someone else. " After that time, I know nothing memorable of Rivella, but that she seemed to bury all Thoughts of Gallantry in Cleander's Tomb." This is not true, but it was the better self who made her stand her ground when three persons were arrested in reference to the *Atalantis*: " She resolved to surrender herself into the Messenger's hands whom she heard had the Secretary of State's Warrent against her, so as to discharge those honest people from their Imprisonment." She goes to Newgate, is tried and the case falls through. But Rivella is unchangeable. In 1712 she is the mistress of John Barber, the printer, and this liaison she maintained until her death. In 1714, in her very autobiography, despite her professed repentance for the *Atalantis*, she deprives her enemies of every shred of character, until we see them as thoroughly disreputable as herself, and her excuse is that " she was become a misanthrope, a perfect Timon, or Man-Hater; all the World was out of Humour with her, and she with all the World."

" But has she still a Taste for Love, interrupted young Monsieur D'Aumont? Doubtless, answered Sir Charles, or whence is it that she daily writes of him with such Fire and Force?" She knows the pity of " appearing Fond at her Time of Day," and is full of raillery against those ladies "who sue when they are no longer sued unto." She knows what her attitude should be, " which is to say, knowing herself no longer young, she does not seem to expect the Praise and Flattery that attend the youthful . . . she converses now with our Sex in a Manner that is very delicate, sensible, and agreeable." Yes, she understands that, but it is too late to be born anew. The past is never past: it is graven into our bodies and minds, and lives in our reactions to habitual stimuli. So it is that to the bitter end this woman remains the same. She sits at her desk scribbling libels, ogling the world out of her weary eyes. She waves a podgy hand at " a Bed nicely sheeted and strow'd with Roses, Jessamines or Orange-Flowers, suited to the variety of the season." Orange-flowers! Alas, Rivella!

By far the most prolific writer among Aphra Behn's female followers was Eliza Haywood. The daughter of a London tradesman named Fowler, she married at an early age the husband who soon abandoned her, and she then turned to quill-driving to support herself and her two children. Whether her evil reputation was really deserved or was due merely to her key-novels is a point too difficult to determine. Swift considered her a " stupid, infamous, scribbling woman." [8] Walpole contemptuously refers to her as the counterpart of Mrs. Behn.[9] Pope lashes her with scorpions in the *Dunciad* [10] (1728). In a note he describes her as one of those " shameless scribblers who, in libellous memoirs and novels reveal the faults or misfortunes of both sexes, to the ruin of public fame or disturbance of private happiness." Mrs. Haywood's reply to this attack was the contribution of a few mild pages to *The Female Dunciad* (1729). Steele alone is credited with some good-natured remarks about Mrs. Haywood. It is possible that he was well-disposed towards her, since one remembers his patience with Mrs. Manley's alternate slanders and eulogies.

Eliza Haywood's imaginative writings include key-novels,

[8] *Swift's Works* (ed. Scott), xvii, 430.
[9] *Letters* (ed. Cunningham), i, 251.
[10] *The Dunciad*, Bk. 2, II. 157 seq.

sentimental *novelle,* cloak-and-sword intrigues, letters, pious effusions and two novels which make a really useful contribution to the school of domestic sentiment. In addition she was a translator, a successful playwright, and a " poetess " (in the weakest sense of the word). She was the first woman to bring out a periodical for women—*The Female Spectator* (1744-1746) and *The Parrot* (1746)—lumbering and humourless productions, but nevertheless the forerunners of the modern spate of women's periodicals. She wrote for about thirty years, and her fictional works were extremely popular.

Her stories are mainly of three kinds: (a) the sentimentalised *novella*; (b) the key-novel; (c) the novel of domestic sentiment and of manners.

It is unnecessary to give a detailed account of her contribution to the first two genres of fiction. These types of story-telling were decadent in themselves, and were chiefly of importance in feeding the growing demands of the novel-reading public. Mrs. Haywood wrote more than twenty sentimentalised *novelle* the first of which was *Love in Excess: or, the Fatal Enquiry* (1719-1720). This ran into six editions in four years. *The British Recluse: or, Secret History of Cleomira supposed Dead* (1722) represents the average level of Mrs. Haywood's sentimentalised *novelle*. It consists of two stories connected in the slenderest and most improbable way. Two beautiful young ladies, Cleomira and Belinda, bruised and spent by the storms of life, happen to take refuge in the same boarding-house, where they mingle their tears and confidences. Cleomira, whose retirement from all human intercourse has earned her the name of the British Recluse, tells her story first.

This exquisite damsel, of excellent lineage and fortune, lives a very retired life with her mother in the country. One evening she is permitted to attend a ball in town, where she meets Lysander, whose beauty ravishes her at once into the seventh heaven of love. She returns home, and although she sighs, pants, burns and languishes, she manages to do so unknown to her mother, who is also unaware that an illicit correspondence is being carried on through the agency of Lysander's man-servant. Then, one morning, Lysander rides by Cleomira's window, and she is overwhelmed anew with the beauty of this paragon:

> At length he came, and with a Mien and Air, so soft, so sweet, so graceful, that Painters might have copied an *Adonis* from him, fit indeed to charm the Queen of Beauty. He was dress'd in a strait Jockey-coat of Green Velvet richly embroider'd at the Seams with Silver; the Buttons were Brilliants, neatly set in Fashion of Roses; his Hair, which is as black as Jet, was ty'd with a green Ribband, but not so straitly but that a thousand little Ringlets stray'd o'er his lovely Cheeks and wanton'd in the Air; a crimson Feather in his Hat, set off to vast Advantage the dazzling Whiteness of his Skin. In fine, he was all over Charms!—all over glorious! and I believe it impossible for the most Insensible to have beheld him without adoring him!—What then became of me?—O God! how fruitless wou'd any Endeavours be to represent what 'twas I felt! Transported!—Ravish'd!—I wonder the Violent Emotions of my *Soul* did not bear my Body out of the Window! O wou'd it had been so.

Such emotions could not fail to be observed by Cleomira's mother who confines her to her room, but: " For many Days I did nothing but weep, and that in so violent a manner, that the servants, whom my Mother sent in to wait on me, apprehended I should fall into fits."

No wonder that for two months the mother of this sentimental heroine rarely allows her out of her sight, but Cleomira escapes from this surveillance by having some dishonest people called Marvir appointed her guardians. She goes to live with them in town, and Mrs. Marvir and her husband encourage the romance with Lysander, but they turn her away when the romance has dwindled to a mere seduction. Lysander turns away also to worship at another shrine, and Cleomira retires to the necessary seclusion of the country. While there she learns that her mother has died of grief at her unfilial behaviour. When she returns the Marvirs have swindled her out of the greater part of her fortune. She has no redress, as they threaten to expose her affair with Lysander if she should endeavour to call them to account. There is no end to Cleomira's misery; betrayed, deserted and fleeced, she now has to endure the news that Lysander—long since unfaithful to her—is about to marry a charming and virtuous friend of hers. This news throws her into strong convulsions. She debates whether she will go to the house of this lucky lady to persuade her to relinquish her claims, or whether it would be better to remind Lysander that she herself should have first option on his matrimonial schemes. However, we are not surprised that in the true romantic convention, she pours all the passions of her soul into a letter: " To the Inconstant, Ungenerous and Perfidious Lysander." He replies with some terse remarks on the transitory nature of passion, and marries his lily-bud. Cleomira, whose vitals are now gnawed by all the vultures of Hope, Despair, Love, Passion, Remorse, Jealousy and Horror, decides to drown her sorrows in some liquid poison. Before she quaffs it, she writes another letter " *To the Dear Ruiner of my Soul and Body.*" " A Draught of poison stands before me," she writes, " and the Moment I conclude this Letter, I take my Journey to that World, whence there is no return." Having begged him not to make her sufferings the subject of ridicule (which was trying him rather high) she signs herself " Only Yours, Cleomira." But she muddles even her suicide. She awakens after a long sleep to find she has taken merely an opiate. Lysander on reading her letter, had expressed relief that, as she was dead, it needed no answer; upon hearing which Cleomira decides that she will live to scorn him (" Love alone shall die! "). She has finished with the follies of life, and betakes herself to the boarding-house, there to brood over her misfortunes.

Belinda, whom Cleomira meets in the boarding-house, is the daughter of a country gentleman. She was wooed by Worthly, a suitor of solid virtues. She was willing to marry him since her father wished it, and since, although she does not love him, neither does she love anyone else. Her father dies, and just when she is about to marry Worthly, a new adorer makes his appearance—Sir Thomas Courtal. One glance at this hero and Belinda is enslaved. She experiences " A Mixture of Delight and Pain, a kind of racking Joy, and Pleasing Anguish." She has " drawn in an Infection at Eyes and Ears, which, mixing with my whole Mass of Blood was to poison all the Quiet of my future Days." Belinda and Courtal, having gone through the formality of wooing in letters, meet in a wood. Fortunately for Belinda, Worthly intervenes. A duel is fought, and Worthly is fatally wounded. Belinda, overwhelmed with misery, flees to town, where one evening at the play she sees again her Adonis, but this time accompanied by his wife and mistress; and she learns that his real name is Lord Bellamy. On hearing this, the British Recluse exclaims that her deceiver and that of Belinda are one and the same—the composite seducer Lysander-Courtal-Bellamy! With so much in common, it is only natural that a great friendship should spring up between these ladies, who resolve to spend their lives together in a house about seventy miles from London, " sometimes bewailing their several Misfortunes, sometimes exclaiming against the *Vices*, sometimes praising the *Beauties* of their common Betrayer."

Idalia: or, The Unfortunate Mistress (1723) is a curious discord, containing echoes of the *Portuguese Letters* and elements of the picaresque. As in *The British Recluse*, her efforts at revealing the heart of a woman in love result only in melodrama, although it must be said that *Idalia* has qualities which *The British Recluse* lacks. *Lasselia: or, The Self-Abandon'd* (1723) is the usual mess of pottage, this time served hot in an environment of court intrigue. Mrs. Haywood's tempestuous emotions rarely become real, rarely identify themselves with individualised men and women. This melodramatic fustian bears a superficial resemblance to Aphra Behn's worst novels, but without Aphra Behn's power and without her flashes of realism.

Of Mrs. Haywood's key-novels one can only say that they are as scurrilous and as prurient as those of Mrs. Manley, with similar flashes of mordant pithiness. The best known of these libellous works are *A Spy upon the Conjurer* (1725); *The Memoirs of a Certain Island Adjacent to the Kingdom of Utopia. Written by a Celebrated Author of that Country. Now Translated into English* (2 vols., 1725-1726); *Bath Intrigues* (1725); *The Secret History of the Present Intrigues of the Court of Caramania* (1727); *Eovaai* (1736); and *The Invisible Spy* (1754).

A Spy upon the Conjurer [11] is based, like Defoe's *Secret*

---

[11] For a detailed discussion of this work in relation to Defoe's *Secret Memoirs of Duncan Campbell* see G. F. Wicher, *Life and Romances of Mrs. Eliza Haywood* (Columbia Univ. Studies in English . . . ., New York, 1915).

Memoirs of Duncan Campbell (1732), on the occult powers of
a certain Scotsman. But whereas Defoe was interested in the
phenomenon of Campbell's prophetic powers, Mrs. Haywood
characteristically concentrated all her attention on the amorous
intrigues which were likely to be confided to the fortune-teller.
Her work consists of supposed confidences given to Duncan
Campbell by various ladies whose secrets Mrs. Haywood served
up with her usual garnishing of passion.

To give a detailed account of Mrs. Haywood's other secret
histories would serve no useful purpose. They would, in
Fuller's words, " stain through the cleanest language I can wrap
them in." Speaking of *The Invisible Spy* (1754) written under
the pseudonym *Exploralibus*, Mr. G. F. Wicher says "Love is
still the theme of most of the anecdotes, no longer the gross
passion that proves every woman at heart a rake, but rather
a romantic tenderness that inclines lovely woman to stoop to
folly." [12] This criticism is wide of the mark. *The Invisible
Spy* is an extremely distasteful book. Exploralibus, with a belt
of invisibility and a recording tablet, spies on the habits of society.
They are the habits of the farmyard, grossly described. There
is the merest pretence at unity of construction: the shadowy spy
is far too unsubstantial to link the episodes together. *Eovaai*
and *The Injured Husband: or, the Mistaken Resentment* have
sufficient unity of plot to render them worthy of more detailed
consideration. *Eovaai*, owing to its pseudo-oriental background,
will find mention later. *The Injured Husband* may usefully be
examined here since it possibly represents the fusion of the
histoire scandaleuse and the sentimentalised *novella*, a coating
of fiction rendering more lurid the less sensational colours of
truth.

The Injured Husband; or, The Mistaken Resentment appears
to be another secret history. In the preface, Mrs. Haywood
insists on defending herself against an alleged accusation that
the story is a veiled account of certain events which happened
in London a short time previously. She insists so much that
one suspects her of cleverly stressing the fundamental truth of
her narrative, although indeed the tale is so improbable in parts

12 G. F. Wicher, *Op. cit.*, p. 168.

that, if it was substantially true, it must have been intricately embroidered by Mrs. Haywood. The story concerns one Mme. de Tortille and a pander called Du Lache. Mrs. Haywood wards off any accusation of satirising an English lady of fashion by disclaiming any attack, and by putting on any possible accuser the onus of finding a shameful similarity between the iniquitous De Tortillé and an English lady. Mrs. Haywood still further safeguards herself by alleging that any man who sees this similarity must, like the infamous Du Lache, be deep in the shameful secrets of this lady whom he endeavours to defend. Naturally guilt would prevent such a lady from self-defence, and fear of implication would muzzle any would-be defender, while all the time Eliza Haywood smugly enjoys this stalemate, and profits by it to write what was probably as scandalous a piece of libel as has ever soiled paper.

There is in this novel the same moral looseness which characterised the writings of Mrs. Manley and Mrs. Haywood: there is the same sentimentalised picture of innocent beauty, the same luscious descriptions of scenes which the author professes to abhor, but which she prolongs and enlivens in a way which makes her purpose only too clear. There is also the same attitude towards men as something ranging between suave lechers and charming, well-intentioned, but too amorous beaux, not weighed down by a " soul much more refin'd than Man is ordinarily possess'd of."

The middle-aged Baron de Tortille becomes enamoured of Mlle. La Motte, an exquisite demi-mondaine, whose extravagant and ill-regulated life makes her grasp at the chance of marriage. She continues her old way of life, unknown to her besotted husband, who believes her to be an angel. But her many lovers are never valued once she has ensnared them, and she always wishes to conquer someone who seems beyond her reach. Such a one was Beauclair, whose engagement to marry the lovely and innocent Mlle. Montamour would seem to ensure him against the wiles of the Baroness de Tortille. But this accomplished adventuress, by means of baseless slander spread about by her paid tools, manages to destroy Monsieur Beauclair's faith in Mlle. Montamour. He writes bitterly to Mlle. Montamour cancelling their engagement which he fears may prevent her from her pleasures, and then with masculine logic proceeds to take his own at the house of the Baroness. But it is Lethe he seeks more than love, and, from time to time, an inner conviction forcing him to reject belief in Mlle. Montamour's baseness, throws him into mental conflict, and makes it necessary for the Baroness to entangle him further in her web of passion and deceit. She herself, having achieved her aim, begins to tire also and derives her chief pleasure not from Beauclair, who, after all, is not different from the throng of other lovers whom she entertains, but from a vindictive joy in the humiliation of Mlle. Montamour. However, it is Beauclair who seizes his chance of discontinuing the *affaire*. To her greater humiliation, an indiscreet letter of hers falls into the hands of her other lovers, who realising that she has been playing one off against the other, desert her *en masse*. "Wanting the Means of Vengeance on those who had occasioned it, her unavailing Rage recoil'd upon itself: She tore her Hair and Face, and bit her very Flesh in the Extremity of her Passion." Her despair is all the greater since, the town ringing with her scandalous name, her husband comes to call her to account. Then with Du Lache, her erstwhile pander, she decides to murder him and gain possession of all his property, with freedom to live as she wishes. Unfortunately for her, however, her bad luck persists, and the Baron escapes the daggers of her bravos, who, captured, admit their guilt and state her complicity. Meanwhile, Mlle. de Montamour, ravaged with grief at the treatment she has received from her lover, enters a convent for the same reason as she would take a sedative. Beauclair discovers where she is. He is now convinced of her innocence, and cannot live without her. In his efforts to secure an interview with her he is as inventive of disguises as a small boy on a wet half-holiday: "Sometimes he was thinking to disguise himself as a Cripple . . . another stratagem was to dress himself as a Woman . . . but this his Stature forbid." Finally he decides to dress as a labourer. Thus disguised, he manages to catch a glimpse of his lady in the garden where she tunes her "Guitter" and sings love ditties for which she would be expelled from any convent on the face of the earth. To cut a long story short, they are married on the day on which she was to have been professed, and the wicked Baroness swallows poison.

Mrs. Haywood sinned against the improved artistic and moral standards of a later age, but she was well in touch with the fictional demands of her own period. She had, to a very considerable extent, the power of adapting herself to varying aspects of fiction, and it is to this opportunism that her only notable achievements are due. We have seen that she adhered to the established genres of the sentimentalised *novella* and the *histoire scandaleuse*. She responded also to tendencies which constituted the growing point of fiction. She contributed, as we shall see later, to the epistolary and oriental genres, but her most important contributions to the novel were more vitally adapted to the revolution which was taking place in fiction, both morally and artistically. Mrs. Haywood is the chameleon of English novelists. In scurrility, in eroticism she had yielded an inch to no one—not even to Mrs. Manley. Now, when she was forced to realise a new attitude in the reading public, she could strike her breast and cast her eyes heavenward with the best of them. It does not appear that her reformation was more than skin deep, because even in her period of moral earnestness, an occasional anonymous or pseudonymous work seemed to be the offspring of the old Haywood spirit. After all, what could be more natural than that Eliza, exhausted from playing the impeccable lady, should find private relaxation in blowing on her tea?

But she had become determined to be polite and impeccable, since she was determined not to starve. One imagines Mrs. Haywood gritting her teeth at the contradictions of her lifetime. In her young days bawdy writers were sure of bread; now they were sure only of stones. For her own part, she had been stoned quite long enough. From 1728 until 1736 she had written almost nothing. From 1736 until 1742 she had written nothing at all. If she were ever again to please the public she knew that she must give them what they wanted. Well, so she would! She would roar them as t'were any sucking dove; she would roar them as t'were any nightingale. Mrs. Haywood's first cooings were entitled *A Present for a Serving Maid* (1741). This emanated from a mind filled with Pamela. It is a worthless

Ω

production, full of prudent sermonising, but not unamusing if the reader cocks an ironic eye at the former Eliza Haywood. For example, it is not easy to remain serious when we hear the author of *A Spy Upon The Conjurer* warning young women against the wickedness of consulting fortune-tellers. In 1749-50 appeared *Epistles for the Ladies,* and in 1755 *The Wife, by Mira,* followed in 1756 by *The Husband.* These were in the vein of Mrs. Rowe's heavy moralising, and would have argued a transformed Mrs. Haywood had she not shown the cloven hoof by her *Invisible Spy,* published pseudonymously in 1754. Despite such incidental lapses, she continued to follow the new moral conventions, and to attempt literary experiments. The influence of *The Spectator* is seen in her efforts to produce an imitation written especially for women.

But if Mrs. Haywood had only trained her pen to moralise politely, she would have found that, to a writer, oblivion is even more fatal than being publicly stoned. Fortunately she was able to adapt herself to the new fashion in story-telling, and this adaptation was indeed a surprising achievement. Towards the end of Mrs. Haywood's life a great change was evident in the conception of the novel, and it argues much elasticity of mind and unsuspected literary resource that she was able, even at the age of fifty-eight, to share in this new orientation, and actually to achieve her best works at a time when, if one were to dance at all, one must dance to the piping of Richardson, Fielding, and Smollett, with Dr. Johnson as master of ceremonies. The day of stock vices and virtues was over. God's cheerful fallible men and women, with all their good intentions, failings, foibles and mannerisms now began to live within the covers of the English novel.

Mrs. Haywood had no intention of being a wallflower. To interest the public it was necessary to abandon the old romantic extravagances and to depict real emotions, motives and characters. This she strove to do in *The Fortunate Foundling* (1744). At this time the Foundling Hospital in Lamb's Conduit had aroused much interest, and had given what might be called a foundling motif to some contemporary writings. Mrs. Haywood's preference for tracing the fortunes not of one foundling but of two, shows us at once her greatest weakness as a novelist. She had long accustomed herself to the writing of short tales, and whenever she had attempted a longer narrative she had found herself unable to construct a unified plot. Then, as in *The Memoirs of a Certain Island*, she had endeavoured to string a number of disconnected anecdotes and stories on one loose thread; or, as in *The British Recluse*, she had artificially united a double-barrelled story. Now, although she had seen how it might be done in *Pamela* and in *Joseph Andrews*, she did not find it easy to learn the technique, so she fell back on the expedient of having two foundlings, so as to bring her novel to the length now required by the reading public. The result was much what might be expected.

Mrs. Haywood sets her story in the last quarter of the seventeenth century. In 1688 the foundlings are taken under the protection of a benevolent gentleman named Dorilaus. Louisa is simply another Marianne or Pamela; her virtue is equally impregnable and equally assaulted. Her trials begin when her guardian begins to pay her unwelcome attentions; they continue through her brief career as a milliner, and culminate when she becomes the companion of the indiscreet Melanthe. Louisa is a magnet for wicked men, and yet out of this evil came good, because finally the persecutions of a shocking rake win her the intervention of an honourable lover, who begs her to marry him. She refuses because of her inferior position, takes refuge in a convent, refuses to become a nun, and flees to Paris. There Dorilaus claims her as his own daughter, and, secure in her new status, she marries her lover.

The adventures of Horatio, Louisa's brother, are chiefly of a military nature. He leaves Westminster school to serve under Marlborough in Flanders. He is captured by the French, and later released to enter the service of the Chevalier. He falls in love with the beautiful Charlotte de Palfoy, and, so that he may speedily become rich enough to marry her, decides to serve under the King of Sweden. He wins a colonel's commission and some booty, but is taken prisoner by the Russians and cast into a dungeon at St. Petersburg. Finally he succeeds in making his way to Paris. He too is claimed by Dorilaus, and he marries Charlotte.

The Fortunate Foundlings shows Mrs. Haywood at the parting of the ways. The synopsis makes the faulty construction abundantly evident. Mrs. Haywood may possibly have wished to contrast the sort of adventures likely to beset a young woman and a young man, but this does not excuse her from the necessity of correlation. Her attempts at unification are too slight. There is, nevertheless, a very considerable improvement in her handling of sensational incident. It is true that she still seems unable to resist introducing erotic scenes and spicy gossip, but she does not often yield to this temptation. She was beginning to learn that incident must be subordinated to plot.

The Fortunate Foundlings had been in the tradition of Marivaux and Richardson. *The History of Miss Betsy Thoughtless* (1751) and *Jemmy and Jenny Jessamy* (1753) belong also to the school of domestic sentiment, with an added flavour of the picaresque. *Betsy Thoughtless* is by far the best of all Eliza Haywood's novels. It achieves a greater unity of action, although there is an excess of incident. Mrs. Haywood's concentration on events puts one in mind of Defoe, although, of course, she was incapable of his realism. Neither had she the power of painting a convincing background, nor of suggesting atmosphere. It is said that *Miss Betsy Thoughtless* gave Fanny Burney the idea of *Evelina*. A comparison of these two plots shows clearly the great fault in Mrs. Haywood's construction. Fanny Burney knew how to prune away the superfluous, and to interweave her strands of narrative into a homogeneous whole. Mrs. Haywood, even in this, her best novel, strings loosely together a number of detachable events. Betsy's adventures are so numerous and so diverse that they create a picaresque effect, and this characteristic is particularly to be observed in Betsy's bogus marriage to Sir Frederick Fineer and its sequel. Mrs. Haywood's emphasis on the external is due to the fact that she was not capable of treating her material subjectively. Richardson and Fielding had depicted real emotions, motives and characters, but this was beyond the scope of Mrs. Haywood, as indeed it was beyond most writers at that time. Her characterisation is thin, and because she was unable to make action grow naturally from the inter-effects of personality, she was apt to stress mannerisms. This fault was also evident in Fanny Burney's novels, which achieved a far greater artistry in technique, but without penetrating the secret of real characterisation.

Miss Betsy Thoughtless is a skittish young lady with a genius for involving herself in incriminating situations. At school she aids the flirtations of a precocious school-fellow. Later, her parents being dead, she goes to live with one of her guardians appropriately named Mr. Goodman. This worthy gentleman, however, has a vicious wife, Lady Mellasin, who has bequeathed to her daughter Flora all the worst traits in her character. Betsy's morals are not undermined by this pernicious feminine influence —in fact, for a long time, she does not doubt the probity of Lady Mellasin and Flora. But her commonsense is atrophied. She skims over the surface of life, not suspecting the treacherous currents. She does not suspect the guilty, and because she herself is innocent, it does not occur to her that she can fall under suspicion. But she does, and she has many adventures which she incurs by a magnificent indifference to appearances.

She begins her career as a ravisher of hearts at the ripe age of fourteen. Her first admirers are an honest youth called Saving, and Gayland, the profligate. Saving's father sends him to Holland, and all his letters to Betsy are intercepted. As she does not love Saving, his removal from her life does not affect her. She is caught up in a whirl of gaiety; fêted and flattered to such an extent that her reputation begins to be doubtful, although her innocence is really beyond question. She is invited to Oxford by her brother, and it is arranged that she shall be accompanied on her visit by Flora, that pert minx. The scene is set for a strenuous contest between these little scalp-hunters. At Oxford all is triumph until Betsy is insulted by a gallant who thinks she speaks his language. But Betsy is like a child who knows many words, but no meanings. There is a duel. The social temperature drops to zero, and the young ladies return to London. Betsy's ostracism in Oxford is soon forgotten in the adulation now showered on her by a multiplicity of suitors. There is the forthright sea-captain, the bogus Sir Frederick

Fineer and many others, but Mr. Trueworth is the sincerest
lover, and unknown even to herself, Miss Betsy cares for him.
She is so sure of him, however, that she takes a giddy pleasure
in showing her power over him. He is not deterred by her
apparent heartlessness, but one by one a succession of incidents,
injurious to Betsy's good name, commences to undermine his
faith in her. Lady Mellasin proves herself an evil woman, and
her unfortunate husband dies shortly after her banishment from
his house. Flora, by no means an innocent girl, falls in love
with Trueworth, and by anonymous letters casts a cloud of
scandal over Betsy, until at last Trueworth abandons his courtship, and marries Harriet Lovitt. Betsy now realises that she
loves Trueworth and her passion is increased by the knowledge
that not only Harriet but also Harriet's sister find in Trueworth
their ideal lover. Harriet's sister dies of her unrequited passion,
and although Betsy is made of sterner stuff, she bids adieu to
her old carefree, flippant life. She marries the first person to
hand, who happens to be an avaricious, heartless, miserly youth
called Munden. He not merely kills her pet squirrel, but refuses
her pin money and finally is unfaithful to her—a variety of
faults which secures him Betsy's contempt. Nevertheless, she
bears with him until his death which, by a great stroke of fortune,
soon intervenes. "Nothing like death for cutting the Gordian
knot," Mrs. Haywood seems to say, as with another timely
stroke of her pen she kills Trueworth's wife. The lovers are
happy at last in a marriage founded on respect and past sufferings; in a world where pet squirrels flourish undisturbed, and
pin money flows like water.

In *Miss Betsy Thoughtless* Mrs. Haywood goes with the anti-
romantic tide:

"The deity of soft desires [said Mr. Trueworth] flies the confused glare of pomp and publick shews; it is in the shady
bowers, or in the banks of a sweet purling stream, he spreads
his downy wings and wafts ten thousand nameless pleasures
on the fond, the innocent and the happy pair."
He was going on, but she interrupted with a loud laugh: "Hold,
hold!" cried she, "was there ever such romantick description?
I wonder how such silly ideas come into your head? Shady
bowers! and purling streams! Heavens, how insipid! Well,"
continued she, "you may be the Strephon of the Woods, if you

think fit, but I shall never envy the happiness of the Chloe that accompanies you in these fine recesses. What, to be cooped up like a tame dove, only to coo, and bill, and breed? O, it would be a delicious life indeed." [13]

Despite its shallowness, *Miss Betty Thoughtless* is a good story. There is no excess of moralising, and our interest is easily won and retained by the energy and vivacity of the narrative. The novel was extremely popular with the English reading public, and was translated into French. This made it possible for Mrs. Haywood to snap her fingers at critics who were less kind. For example, when the *Monthly Review* complained that *Miss Betsy Thoughtless* lacked " those entertaining introductory chapters and digressive essays, which distinguish the works of Fielding, Smollett, or the author of *Pompey the Little*," Mrs. Haywood riposted in *Jemmy and Jenny Jessamy*, volume iii, chapter xviii, which, she said, " contains none of those beautiful digressions, those remarks or reflections which a certain would-be critick pretends, are so distinguished in the writings of his two favourite authors; yet it is to be hoped, will afford sufficient to please all those who are willing to be pleased."

In *Jemmy and Jenny Jessamy* Mrs. Haywood did not maintain the standard she had reached in *Miss Betsy Thoughtless*. *Jemmy and Jenny Jessamy* consists of many little stories quite insufficiently connected by the slender motif of the mutual love of hero and heroine. Jemmy and Jenny are two pleasant young people whose parents have always intended them to marry. They are quite willing to fall in with this arrangement, but wish to see a little of the world first. They are an affectionate, but very unromantic couple.

Neither of them felt those impatiences, those anxieties, those distracting fears, those causeless jealousies, or any of those thousand restless sensations that usually perplex a mind devoted to an amorous flame : they were happy when they met, but not uneasy when they parted. He was not in the least alarmed on finding she was frequently visited by some of the finest gentlemen in town; nor was she at all disconcerted when she was told that he was well received by ladies of the most distinguished characters . . . yet that they did love each other is most certain, as will hereafter be demonstrated by proofs much more unquestionable *than all those extravagances : those raging*
13 *Miss Betsy Thoughtless*, Ch. viii.

flights, commonly looked upon as infallible tokens of the passion :
but which, how fierce soever the fires they spring from may
burn for a while, we see frequently extinguish of themselves,
and leave nothing but the smoke behind. [14]

Many instances of married infelicity and infidelity impress
Jenny and Jemmy with the seriousness of the step they contemplate, and since each instance is followed by lengthy moralising, the book has some characteristics of the tract. The wise
Jenny gleans a lesson from everything that happens, and indeed
Mrs. Haywood makes the story subservient to this purpose.
Jenny's moral soliloquies, although well reasoned, are far too
sagacious for the fallible reader, and retard the story very seriously. Her views always express themselves according to a rigid
formula. They fall into three parts, each introduced respectively
by the phrases " said she", " continued she " and " went she
still on." After a few such soliloquies, this Procrustean bed
begins to creak loudly. There are at least ten stories of conjugal
suffering, and one notable attempt by the villain Bellpine to
alienate the lovers, who are, however, united in the end. Bellpine is quite a convincing villain. His deviousness in achieving
his aim is well worked out. His final bid for Jenny's hand is,
nevertheless, not in keeping with his former subtlety. Mrs.
Haywood foresees this objection, and explains that the deceiver
is deceived by his own vanity. It is noteworthy that Mrs.
Haywood, despite her moral earnestness, considered gallantry in
the hero quite compatible with his sincere love for the heroine.
Jemmy Jessamy is a Tom Jones rather than a Sir Charles
Grandison.

Mrs. Haywood often indulges in romantic circumlocution,
e.g., the wedding cake is " the oblation to Ceres." Sometimes
a mist of romanticism obscures the sense altogether. What could
Jemmy have meant by this postscript to a perfectly intelligible
letter: " P.S. If I have any friends among the intellectual world,
I would petition them to haunt your nightly dreams with the
shadow of me till propitious fortune throws the substance at your
feet "? What a colourful thing life must have been when Lord

14 *Ibid,* Chap. iv.

Huntly, falsely accused of bigamous inclinations, thus expresses himself:

> "Madam, I am pierced in too tender a part to stand upon punctilios;—both my love and honour are wounded—gashed—mangled in a most cruel and infamous degree; and it is only from your ladyship's justice and humanity that I can hope a cure."!

But Mrs. Haywood can turn a phrase with deft realism too, she speaks, for instance, of "the tumultuous din, the smoak, the stench, the rugged stones of London." And she can hit the truth sometimes with instinctive aim: "Oh, why will men endeavour to persuade us we are goddesses, only to create themselves the pains of convincing us afterwards that we are but mortals." She gives in a sentence the key to women's preoccupation with novels when she defines marriage: "Marriage . . . is the great action of our lives . . . the hinge on which our happiness or misery, while we have breath, depends."

Jenny is really a very sensible little creature—not so far from Jane Austen's idea of sense. But it is unfair to annihilate Mrs. Haywood by the mention of Jane Austen's name. Jenny's adventures in Bath have only to be mentioned in the same breath as those of Catherine Morland to reveal Mrs. Haywood's sins and omissions as a novelist. Jenny's exploits might just as well have taken place in Yorkshire. There is no background of assemblies and pump-room, no effort made to represent the fashion, the formality amid which Catherine Moreland later found such uncertain pleasure.

Mrs. Haywood, in her lifetime, attempted many kinds of fiction, and is the link between the older school and the new. In this period of transition we find some curious examples of outworn types of story-telling, as for example the two novels of Mrs. Arabella Plantin which appeared in 1727. These were *Love Led Astray: or, The Mutual Inconstancy;* and *The Ingrateful: or, The Just Revenge.* In the introduction to *Love Led Astray* Mrs. Plantin makes a great show of opposing tales of "obscure retreats" to those of "the shining courts." She says:

> I know that the name of a prince embellishes a story, and seems to interest a reader in it, tho' that pompous title is not always attended with all the gallantry which is often found in a private person; therefore I leave the Historians the choice of their illustrious name. I intend to confine myself to the passion of love, and as I am persuaded that a shepherd may in this point exceed the greatest king, I shall not go beyond the bounds of a forest to convince my readers of this truth.

What follows is an absurd travesty of the pastoral tradition. The shepherd Polemas who has no equal among the swains; the charming Cyparissa and the exquisite Lydippa form a triangle; cupids flutter incessantly in the background; even the sheep have an air of genteel simplicity, and go about wearing numberless knots of amaranth-coloured ribbon. There is a Country Ball for the feast of Pan, and the Nymphs go masked. They consult the oracle Apollo, although up to that moment no country has been designated as the background. *Love Led Astray* is a windy suspiration of forced breath. It is impossible to read it without one's lungs being tickled o' the sere. As for *The Ingrateful*, it is, if possible, even more deplorable. It begins: " In Arcadia there lived a Gentleman." But alas! too soon it transpires that he is really no gentleman at all, but a shocking deceiver. He befools the beautiful and wealthy Melissa to pay his debts before he marries her. Then he takes ship for Cyprus, and determines to marry a widow whose riches are beyond the dreams of avarice. When Melissa hears that the marriage day is appointed she sails for Cyprus, disguised as a man, and assassinates her recreant lover. This poignant and dramatic event is describes as follows:

> She was shewed into a Room, and Lysander soon sent to her. She approached him with a Letter in one Hand, and in the other a Dagger concealed, with which she stabbed him in the Breast, and had no sooner drew it from the Wound, but she struck it into her own Bosom. The cries which were occasion'd by the Wound, called in the Company, among whom was the designed Bride. Lysander had just Time enough to own his own Guilt and clear Melissa, she being Dead the moment she pierced her Heart.

Mrs. Haywood's moral didacticism at the end of her life, as opposed to her earlier licentious writings, merely reflected the

changed outlook which made itself felt in the second decade of
the eighteenth century. Puritanism, though it had been out
of power and therefore out of fashion, had not lessened its
hold on the bourgeois section. Indeed the growing wealth of
the middle class and its increased interest in refinements of life
rapidly provided a reading public which, though it accepted the
flashy at first, soon insisted on a supply which would suit its
particular demands. There was for a while a transitional period,
during which many writers tried to serve the old gods and the
new by lurid pictures of vice which they were careful to condemn
sanctimoniously, but an increasing spirit of conventional morality
finally ousted the cult of indecency.

The popularity of such works as *Friendship in Death* (1728)
by Mrs. Elizabeth Rowe (1674-1737) shows how the tide had
turned. This effusion reached its third edition in 1733, its fifth
in 1738, and continued to be printed until 1816. It consisted
of letters supposedly from the dead to the living, and the purpose was strongly evangelical. *Letters Moral and Entertaining*
(1729-1733) gave much pious teaching with a sugar-coating of
little stories, occasionally enlivened by dialogue. These letters
were, to all intents and purposes, religious tracts. Some of these
stories are reminiscent of the *novella* technique, some are pastoral
in type. Mr. Baker remarks on Mrs. Rowe's " idyllic painting
of scenery in a manner afterwards followed by John Buncle."
Mrs. Rowe's unctuous moralising had that point of view later
immortalised in the shrewd and shallow Pamela. Nevertheless
her works in prose and verse earned her the respectful admiration of such men as Dr. Watts, Klopstock, Wieland, Pope, Prior
and Dr. Johnson. These excellent men were willing to accord
to piety an admiration which expressed itself as literary criticism.
Pious mediocrity did not set their teeth on edge, and was
indeed regarded as peculiarly womanly. When later Hannah
More became the apotheosis of the Rowe tradition, she found
her pedestal awaiting her.

Mrs. Jane Barker belonged also to this female school of moral
didacticism. In 1715, appeared *Exilius: or, the Banished
Roman*. This was written not to win literary fame, but " for
the instruction of some young ladies of quality." Mrs. Barker

considered that "a learned lady was as ridiculous as a spinning Hercules." Judged by this standard she is far from ridiculous; by any other she stands condemned. *Exilius* is a deplorable medley of hair-raising adventures in which female paragons incredibly become entangled. These heroines are all righteous, matter-of-fact prigs. They manage their lives by a sort of moral etiquette which is applied like a yard-stick to everything from the interpretation of oracles to the regulation of suitors. And all the while they cant. These female Stigginses reappear in *A Patchwork Screen for the Ladies, or Love and Virtue Recommended* (1723) and *The Lining of the Patchwork Screen* (1726). Both works are collections of instructive novels. Mrs. Barker claimed that the stories in *A Patchwork Screen* were "related after a Manner intirely New," but the method of narration is not in the least original. Like Mrs. Rowe, but to a lesser extent, Mrs. Barker was a popular writer. Her heroines exactly suited the current taste—from which it is clear that in creating Pamela, Richardson conformed to the prevailing conception of what a heroine ought to be.

Another novel which in its priggish outlook suggests Richardson, and which has the definite didacticism of Mrs. Rowe, was published in 1724 by Mrs. Mary Davys. [15] Amoranda, the heroine of *The Reformed Coquet*, is a wealthy and giddy young beauty who seems in danger of losing her head through the adulation of the fops who surround her. Her guardian chooses as her future husband a young nobleman, who loves Amoranda as much as he deplores her foolishness. He disguises himself as a friend of her guardian, and goes to live in her house in the rôle of an elderly adviser. He soon disperses her worthless suitors, saves her from compromising situations, and then reveals himself as her ideal lover. "This," says Miss Charlotte

---

[15] Mrs. Mary Davys, an Irishwoman, was the wife of Rev. Peter Davys, or Davis, master of the free school at St. Patrick's, Dublin, after whose death she lived for some time at York. She knew Dean Swift. She afterwards kept a coffee-house in Cambridge where she died. In addition to the novels mentioned in these pages she also wrote *The Lady's Tale* (written in 1700): *The Cousins; Familiar Letters betwixt a Gentleman and a Lady;* and *The Accomplish'd Rake, or the Modern Fine Gentleman. Being the genuine Memoirs of a certain Person of Distinction* (1756).

Morgan, "is one of the earliest appearances in fiction of the perfect prig of which Sir Charles Grandison is the consummate example."[16]

A fresher breeze blows through the works of Penelope Aubin. She was didactic, but she had the idea of enlivening her stories with unusual backgrounds. Obviously she was much influenced by Defoe and by records of travel. As a result, her narratives bring a new note of adventure into the novel. She was not an advocate of genteel morality. A staunch Catholic, it was her object to win her readers towards the Catholic point of view. She uses her stories to show that the vicissitudes and miseries of this world matter little if one's gaze is fixed on eternity: "The virtuous shall look dangers in the face unmoved, and putting their whole trust in the Divine Providence, shall be delivered, even by miraculous means; or dying with comfort be freed from the miseries of this life, and go to taste an eternal repose."[17] So that her characters may be sufficiently tried Mrs. Aubin subjects them to the most extraordinary occurrences, of which one gains a sufficient idea from the long titles of her stories. For example: *The Life of Madam de Beaumont, a French Lady; who lived in a Cave in Wales about fourteen years undiscovered, being forced to flye France for her religion, and of the cruel usage she had there. Also her Lord's Adventures in Muscovy where he was a prisoner some years, with an Account of his returning to France, and her being discovered by a Welsh Gentleman who fetches her Lord to Wales, and of many strange accidents which befel them, and their daughter Belinda, who was stolen away from them and of their Return to France in the year 1718.*

In 1721, when this tale was published, there also appeared: *The Strange Adventures of the Count de Vinevil and his Family. Being an account of what happened to them whilst they resided at Constantinople. And of Mlle. Ardelisia, his daughter's being*

---

[16] Charlotte E. Morgan, *The Rise of the Novel of Manners* (Columbia Univ. Press, 1911), p. 70.
[17] Preface to 'Adventures of the Lady Lucy' in *A Collection of Entertaining Histories and Novels designed to promote the cause of Virtue and Honour, Principally founded on facts and instructive incidents,* (3 vols., 1739).

shipwrecked on the uninhabited Island Delos in the Return to France, with Violetta, a Venetian Lady, the Captain of the Ship, a Priest, and five Sailors. The Manner of their living. Their . . . Strange Deliverance . . . This echo of *Robinson Crusoe* was followed a year later (1722) by another tale of shipwreck: *The Noble Slaves: or, The Lives and Adventures of Two Lords and Two Ladies upon a desolate Island.* Mrs. Aubin made a determined attempt to imitate Defoe's realism, and in her best story, *The Life and Adventures of the Lady Lucy* (1726), she creates the impression of having been an eye-witness to certain happenings in the Williamite wars in Ireland, such as the sack of a castle after the battle of the Boyne.

As a translator Mrs. Aubin's choice lay with the wonderful. In 1726, before writing *Adventures of the Lady Lucy* she had rendered into English Pétis de la Croix's *History of Genghizcan The Great, First Emperor of the Antient Moguls and Tartars.* She also translated *The Illustrious French Lovers; being the True Histories of the Amours of Several French Persons of Quality* (1729). That interest in the Oriental which led to the translation of *The History of Genghizcan* is very evident in her last original work, a picaresque novel. *The Life and Adventures of the Young Count Albertus, The Son of Count Lewis Augustus, by the Lady Lucy* (1728). The young Count, overwhelmed by his wife's death, tries by foreign travel to divert his mind from his grief. He encounters many people who narrate their life-stories. Some of these inset stories are good, particularly the story of the old miser in Madrid, which is told with dramatic realism. Eventually the young Count becomes a Benedictine and goes as a missionary to China, where martyrdom awaits him.

Mrs. Aubin is worthy of remembrance despite her obvious didacticism, in that she endeavoured to weave together romance and realism, and was, in however slight a degree, one of the early contributors to Oriental fiction. She is notable also in her adherence to the popular theme of the virtuous maiden pursued by the charming rake. Finally, she was one of the very few women who essayed the picaresque.

We have seen that Mrs. Manley and Mrs. Haywood sometimes showed a picaresque touch. This was evident also in

Letters written by Mrs. Manley, 1696 (republished as *A Stage-Coach Journey to Exeter,* 1725), and in Mrs. Haywood's *Bath Intrigues,* 1725. Mrs. Davy's *Merry Wanderer* also shows the picaresque influence. It has, by way of introduction to a story of intrigue, a picaresque description of various incidents in a journey, the unusual people encountered at an inn, and the miserly hospitality of a friend's house. Mrs. Elizabeth Boyd united the picaresque and the tale of gallantry in a sorry concoction called *The Female Page* (1737). Its contents are indicated by its sub-title: *A Genuine and Entertaining History, Relating to some Persons of Distinction. Intermix'd with A Great Variety of affecting Intrigues in Love and Gallantry. Also the remarkable Letters that passed between the several Persons concerned.* Mrs. Boyd in her preface alternates between suggesting and denying that her novel actually records the doings of certain well-known people. She does not use the device of the key. The Female Page is a young woman who, besottedly in love with Duke Bellfont, dons male attire so that she may be near him in the guise of a page. It is unnecessary to describe all the voluptuous situations to which this masquerade and its discovery give rise. The story is written in a species of melodramatic blank verse, and is the dying gasp of the tradition of gallantry.

But the picaresque trend, so far from being extinct, was given a new lease of life by Fielding. *Joseph Andrews* (1742) and *Tom Jones* (1749) gave a great fillip to stories dealing with a varied succession of adventures—a vogue which Fielding's sister endeavoured to follow in the *Adventures of David Simple* (1744). Sarah Fielding's use of the picaresque medium was by no means a proof of sisterly admiration. On the contrary, she was one of Richardson's female adorers. Sarah Fielding sheltering under the wing of Richardson, and even acquiescing in his condemnation of that "low fellow," Henry Fielding, presents a curious anomaly. It seems fairly clear that she really considered Richardson a better writer than her brother, and yet her writings in part reflect some of Fielding's literary characteristics. She was dependent upon Fielding, with whom she lived. After his death she retired to Bath where she died in 1738.

David Simple, Sarah Fielding's best known work of fiction, is, strictly speaking, not a novel. It repays study as a peculiar mixture of influences, none of which appears to have been strong enough to triumph over the others. There is, therefore, no homogeneity, and the elements of Addison, Fielding and Richardson are separately recognisable from beginning to end. The book consists in the first part of a number of Addisonian essays, and in the second of a number of stories all loosely linked together by the ramblings of that cypher, David Simple. Its purpose is moral didacticism, and it achieves this sometimes by direct sermonising, sometimes by satiric reflections on human life. It can most nearly be classified as picaresque, although of all the picaresque characteristics, it contains only the motif of wandering. Sarah Fielding had the gifts of an essayist, insight into character and an ironic view of life. She evidently wished to exert these in depicting various aspects of human society. It was thus, no doubt, that she stumbled into using the very genre most unsuited for her purpose. The picaresque novel, since it depicted the adventures of a light-hearted filibuster, dealt with externals, stressed incident and obtained its effects by giving a strong sense of varied and vivid reality. The picaro knew life from the drawingroom to the stews, and laughed to find the same failings and foibles in every grade of society. Even if it were his nature to reflect, he did not need to point the ironic lesson. The picaro's objective account of his experiences contains an implicit satire on life. It is evident that Sarah Fielding could not succeed in the picaresque medium. In the first place, as a decorous woman she had no intention of describing the exploits of a rakish adventurer, nor would her limited experience have allowed her to do so. Therefore, while choosing the picaresque genre for the sake of its variety, she at once determined to omit the picaro. Small wonder that the result is like a beefsteak pie without the 'steak. Furthermore, Sarah Fielding's attitude was subjective, her technique was direct and all her lessons fully explained in words. In the picaresque medium the satire was oblique and cumulative. Again, in the picaresque there was universality of outlook; *David Simple* consists more of a number of bird's-eye views.

Strong interest in the hero could alone have integrated the scenes and incidents in this book, but who could be interested in that cardboard figure, David Simple? David is a bloodless, moralising sentimentalist. He wanders through the cities of London and Westminster in search of a true friend. " This was the phantom, the idol of his soul's admiration. In the worship of which he at length grew such an enthusiast, that he was at this point only as mad as Quixote himself could be with knight errantry." [18] David's sensibility is sorely tried in his wanderings, even to a great prodigality of tears and guineas which he expends on the unfortunates whom he continually encounters. His guilelessness is complete, and his ignorance of everyday facts so great that only a hair's-breadth saves him from being a bumpkin—and sometimes not even that. Since Sarah Fielding wished to pillory hypocrisy and selfishness, she could not allow the spotless David to take them in his stride as would the picaro. His blind innocence makes it necessary to explain everything to him constantly, and so as to provide an opportunity for social satire, he is made to ask innumerable obvious questions: " David begged an explanation of what she meant by a toad-eater "; " David begged her to let him know what she meant by *fine ladies* "; " Pray, Madam, what is the meaning of making a butt of anyone? " This transparency of purpose is very trying to the reader, but not more so than the awkward efforts of dialogue which Sarah boldly sets down as in a play.

Nevertheless, the incidents in themselves are recounted in a clear and telling style, and with the shrewd irony of one who views life detachedly. When David had been defrauded, and cast penniless on the world by his brother, Sarah Fielding ends the chapter thus: " And there, for some time, I will leave him to his own private sufferings, *lest it should be thought I am so ignorant of the world, as not to know the proper time for forsaking people.*" [19]

The most interesting and praiseworthy aspect of Sarah Fielding's work is her effort to achieve reality in characterisation. In view of the period at which she wrote, the following passage is very clear-sighted:

[18] *David Simple* (ed. 1825) ch. 2, p. 28 f.
[19] *Op. cit.*, ch. 1, p. 18.

R

> I hope [she says] to be excused by those gentlemen who are quite sure they have found one woman who is a perfect *angel*, and that all the rest are perfect *devils*, for drawing the character of a woman who was neither—for Miss Nancy Johnson was very good-humoured, had a great deal of softness, and had no alloy to these good qualities, but a great share of vanity, with some small spices of envy, which must always accompany it. And I make no manner of doubt, but if she had not met with this temptation she would have made a very affectionate wife to the man who loved her. [20]

Sarah Fielding was very much concerned with the interaction of human characteristics and motives. That she worked from within is very evident throughout the book, and one could quote many examples of this aim—in particular, perhaps, the story of Camilla and her stepmother. To Sarah behaviour is only a superficial stratum which more often conceals than exhibits the real man. We see, for example, that Mr. Orgueil's good-nature is a mere cloak for his extreme self-love. He is:

> One of a set of men in the world, who pass through life with very good reputations, whose actions are in the general, justly to be applauded, and yet upon a near examination their principles are all bad, and their hearts hardened to all tender sensations . . . The greatest sufferings which can happen to his fellow-creatures, have no sort of effect on him, and yet he very often relieves them; that is, he goes just as far in serving others, as will give him new opportunities of flattering himself: for his whole soul is filled with pride, he has made a god of himself, and the attributes he thinks necessary to the dignity of such a being, he endeavours to have . . . When he knows any man do a dishonourable action, then he enjoys the height of pleasure in the comparison he makes between his own mind, and that of such a mean creature. He mentally worships himself with joy and rapture: and I verily believe, if he lived in a world, where to be vicious was esteemed praise-worthy, the same pride which now makes him take a delight in doing what is right . . . would then lead him to abandon himself to all manner of vice; for if by taking pains to bridle his passions, he could gain no superiority over his companions, all his love of rectitude, as he calls it, would fall to the ground. So that his goodness, like cold fruits, is produced by the dung and nastiness which surrounded it . . . He makes no allowance for the smallest frailties, and the moment a person exceeds, in the least degree, the bounds his wisdom has set, he abandons them,

20 *Op. cit.,* ch 3, p. 46.

as he thinks they have no reasonable claim to any thing farther from him. If he were walking with a friend on the side of a precipice, and that friend was to go a step nearer than he advised him, and by accident should fall down, although he broke his bones, and lay in the utmost misery, he would coolly leave him, without the least thought of anything for his relief : saying, *if men would be so mad, they must take the consequence of their own folly*, Nay, I question, whether he would not have a secret satisfaction in thinking, that from his wisdom, he could walk safely through the most dangerous places, while others fell into them. [21]

On the other hand, there is Mr. Spatter who imputes the worst motives to everyone, and appears to be most vindictive. But his ill-nature " dwells no where but in his tongue," and he has a soft and generous heart. David, not knowing that Spatter's spleen is a sort of defence-mechanism, earnestly remonstrates with him, saying that the most he himself could do if he found a man capable of hurting him (unprovoked) was to avoid him :

" Indeed, Sir," says Spatter, " I am not of your mind; for I think there is nothing so pleasant as revenge : I would pursue a man, who had injured me, to the very brink of life. I know it would be impossible for me ever to forgive him, and I would have him live, only that I might have the pleasure of seeing him miserable."

David was amazed at this, and said, " pray, Sir, consider, as you are a Christian, you cannot act in that manner."

Spatter replied, " he was sorry it was against the rules of Christianity, but he could not help his temper . . ." [22]

Spatter appears briefly, but he is the most interesting, because he is the only live person in the book. Sarah Fielding's comprehension of character was sound, her aim was worthy of success, but nevertheless, she failed to create real people. She had not the ability to make her human beings objective. They are specimens pinned down, and examined in the study. Even when we are supposedly watching them in the Stock Exchange, at the play, in the stage-coach, they are not alive; and we are always conscious that what we see and hear has been filtered through the philosophic irony of Sarah Fielding's mind. Her

[21] *Op. cit.,* ch. VII, p. 103 f.
[22] *Op. cit.,* ch. X. p. 138 f.

minute dissections seem to leave the component parts in their disintegrated state.   We are shown an aggregate of traits, but (with one minor exception) never a personality.   The characters in the main stories are all the more unconvincing because, instead of being presented in action, the events in which they move are retailed to us at second, and even at third-hand.

Still, there are glimpses of reality.   For example, Cynthia expresses independent views on education and marriage.   She thus describes her up-bringing:

> If I was pleased with any book above the most silly story or romance, it was taken from me.   For Miss must not inquire too far into things, it would turn her brain; she had better mind her needle-work, and such things as were useful for women; reading and poring on books, would never get me a husband. Thus was I condemned to spend my youth, the time when our imagination is at the highest, and we are capable of most pleasure, without being indulged in any one thing I liked; and obliged to employ myself, in what was fancied by my mistaken parents to be for my improvement, although in reality it was nothing more than what any person, a degree above a natural fool might learn as well in a very small time, as in a thousand ages.   And what yet aggravated my misfortunes was, my having a brother who hated reading to such a degree, he had a perfect aversion to the very sight of a book; and he must be cajoled or whipped into learning, while it was denied me, who had the utmost eagerness for it. [23]

Such a young woman would hardly be likely to submit meekly to arbitrary match-making.   One may imagine then, the scene when a country gentleman, with her father's consent, proposes marriage.   He delicately expresses his offer as follows:

> Madam . . . I like your person, hear you have had a sober education, think it time to have an heir to my estate, and am willing, if you consent to it, to make you my wife; nowithstanding your father tells me, he cannot give you above two hundred pounds. [24]

He adds that, not being a nonsensical bore, he will not whine of love; he expects her to comply with his humours, rear his children, keep his house, and particularly provide for his love of good eating and drinking.   Cynthia curtsies, and replies that

[23]   *Op. cit.,* chapter XI, p. 148 f.
[24]   *Ibid,* chapter XI, p. 160.

she has no ambition to be his upper servant, but would be interested to know if, in return for all the offices allotted to her, he would, in addition to her food and lodging, think of giving her some small wages, " that I might now and then recreate myself with my fellow-servants."[25] The suitor departs, breathing fire, and Cynthia comments:

> I could not help reflecting on the folly of those women who *prostitute* themselves (*for I shall always call it prostitution, for a woman who has sense, and has been tolerably educated, to marry a clown and a fool*) and to give up that enjoyment which every one who has taste enough to know how to employ their time, can procure for themselves, though they should be obliged to live ever so retired, only to know they have married a man who has an estate."[26]

David Simple fails because its form stresses a variety of external events while its purpose stresses a variety of character analyses, but still it merits recognition since her inward approach to character hit accidentally on what was to prove the growing point of the modern novel.   In its own day this work was adjudged a success, so much so, in fact, that it was ascribed to Fielding. In a preface to the second edition he denies authorship, so that he may " do justice to the real and sole author."   He praises his sister's book warmly and even says that it contains some touches that " might have done honour to the pencil of the immortal Shakespeare himself."   Richardson wrote after Fielding's death: " What a knowledge of the human heart! Well might a critical judge of writing say, as he did to me, that your late brother's knowledge of it was not (fine writer as he was) comparable to yours.   His was but as the knowledge of the outside of a clock-work machine, while yours was that of all the finer springs and movements of the inside."[27]

Lack of money, and also, no doubt, genuine (though unconfessed) ambition drove Sarah Fielding into print again and again.   She translated two books of Xenophon, the *Memorabilia* and the *Apologia*. With Jane Collier she wrote *The Cry* (1754). In 1757 appeared *The Lives of Cleopatra and Octavia*. This was reminiscent of Fielding's *Journey from this World to the Next,*

25 *Ibid,* p. 160 f.
26 *Ibid,* Ch. XI, p. 161.
27 *Richardson's Correspondence,* i, 104. The critical judge was Johnson.

but was too obviously didactic.   Cleopatra and Octavia meet in the underworld, and tell their stories in rather a classical manner. *The History of the Countess of Dellwyn*[28] (1759) has a poorly connected plot, and is too heavily laden with moralising.   Still, it has touches of Henry Fielding's attitude and style.   The story concerns a young woman who, dazzled by riches, marries a wealthy old lord.   Ease and splendour soften her moral fibres, she yields to the temptations of a rake, is divorced by her husband, endeavours to marry again, but fails, and is abandoned to repentance and grief.   Sarah Fielding's last novel *The History of Ophelia* is an echo of *Pamela*.   A young lord carries off a lovely and innocent girl.   She escapes his wicked intentions.   He repents, and they are happily united.

It may be said that the women novelists who are the subject of this chapter achieved nothing much.   In one sense it is true.   The majority of their works were mediocre.   Nevertheless, these women made a very useful contribution to the novel by their experiments with the various trends, and by their very fertility as novelists.   The novel, after Aphra Behn's death, was in a transitional stage, feeling its way between, on the one hand, the romantic tradition and, on the other, the conception of realism in fiction which Defoe and Swift were building up.   It was necessary during this critical period of evolution that the public appetite for fiction should be kept whetted, and that there should be sufficient novels to engross their interest, and to keep them from reverting to their former love of the drama.   All that could be expected at this time was the ability to experiment.   Even Defoe was only hammering out his own technique.   Towards the end of this period the rise of the great novelists gave more difficult standards to imitate, and however weak were the women's first attempts, they rose to the challenge and, as we shall find, eventually issued challenges of their own.   The women here mentioned were, for the most part, merely hacks.   They achieved results by trial and error, not by some intuitive spring towards the truth, but they prepared the way for the greatness to come.   We shall see in the next chapter how much women contributed towards the growth of the epistolary form, so that, by the time Richardson used it, it was ready at his elbow..

[28] Mr. E. A. Baker considers this the best of Sarah Fielding's novels.

CHAPTER VIII

THE EPISTOLARY FORM PRIOR TO 1740.

When, in 1740, *Pamela* took England by storm, it seemed at first as if Richardson, by a miracle, had created an entirely new method in fiction. What he really did was, by a stroke of genius, to crystallise certain tendencies which until then had been fluid. These tendencies had for a long time been increasingly evident, awaiting the mind which would gather them together, and evolve from them a work of art. To the evolution of *Pamela* went two tendencies of thought and one tendency of form. It is with the tendency of form that we are here concerned.

Richardson's choice of the epistolary form was not an accident. In fact, he had chosen the form before he realised that he was about to write a novel. That Richardson became a novelist was apparently fortuitous, but that he became an epistolary novelist was inevitable. It was inevitable because of his own particular bent, because of his subject, and because of a certain literary tradition.

His immediate object was to write, at the instance of two London booksellers, a small volume of *Familiar Letters* which were to unite elegance of style with the didactic purpose of showing " how to think and act justly and prudently, in the common Concerns of Human Life." He intended two or three of these letters " to instruct handsome girls, obliged to go out to service, as we phrase it, how to avoid the snares that might be laid against their virtue." With the idea of reinforcing his moral strictures he decided to recount the story of a servant-girl which he had heard some years before. This was the story of *Pamela*, which at once swept him away from his original purpose.

Richardson could have told his story directly, adopting the omniscient standpoint, as, for example, did Fielding, or he could have put the whole story into the mouth of the principal character as did Defoe, Swift, Marivaux, Goldsmith, Prévost, Thackeray and Charlotte Brontë. This latter way shares with the epistolary method the impossibility of giving a convincing portrait of the hero physically or mentally, without self-consciousness. The autobiographical narrative, has, moreover, a peculiar disadvantage in that the flow of events in the life of the narrator is arrested while he recounts the past, and that the vividness one would expect from a personal relation is often lessened by the deflection of interest from the living narrator to the happenings he describes. This method, nevertheless, gives a wider point of view, and a more impersonal attitude than that possible in letters.   The narrator may express his own thoughts, as it were, in soliloquy, without the embarrassment of confiding them to some particular individual.   For Richardson, however, the epistolary form was the ideal medium.   It exactly suited what he wished to express. All his life he had used letters to express his personality, and in his novels it was still his own personality which he was embodying in objective forms.   Richardson was, in every sense, a most extraordinary man. As women ordinarily turned to letter-writing to give vent to their love of intimate outpourings and familiar gossip, and for the expression of views so often denied them in daily intercourse, so Richardson, that retiring and sedentary man, that unobtrusive egoist, had been a voluminous correspondent all his life long.   Once the story of *Pamela* began to take shape in his mind, the peculiar suitability of the epistolary form must at once have become evident to him.   It was the ideal medium for what he wanted to express.   His mind was a hothouse within which a strange luxuriance of emotions fed on a sickly-sweet corruption, and grew out of all proportion in the vitiated air.   It was an essential of his being, and consequently it was the habit of a life-time, to observe minutely, to dissect every mood, impulse, reaction and motive, to magnify the emotions, and to luxuriate in sensibility.   His method of describing external events was microscopic also.   No detail was too minute for his observation, and he achieved his effects by tirelessly building up complete impressions from trifles light as air. Minuteness of external description could have been achieved without the epistolary form, certainly; but for the press and hurry of emotions, for the fluctuations of mood and sentiment, letters were a very apt medium. They constituted an eternal *now*; they gave a particular urgency to the events they described. They gave to Richardson's novels the tempo of a heart beat. No more effective form could have been found for the tale of sensibility, because whereas human fears, hopes, excitements often appear baseless in retrospect, and not worth recounting, they appear of great import if recorded while the mind is still agitated.

The epistolary method had also very serious disadvantages, but it was not likely that Richardson would recognise them. It postulated always a confidant, and it offered no clue to the inner mind, except through revelations made to another. This led to such incredible confidences as those of Lovelace to Bellford; and even when the noblest sentiments were expressed, it gave a most distasteful self-consciousness to the utterances of the heroine or hero. Even if Pamela and Sir Charles Grandison had not been prigs, they would have been forced so to appear since it falls to their own tongues to express their own moral earnestness. But it was not for nothing that Richardson was called in his schooldays "Serious and Gravity," or that, when barely eleven years old, he addressed a letter full of Biblical reproof to a widowed lady of fifty. Richardson's purpose was didactic, and since he was not himself revolted by the pietistic mouthings of his principal characters, it was not likely that he would realise the disadvantage of a method which afforded no escape from explicit self-revelation.

Since the epistolary form satisfied Richardson's purpose of telling a story in such a manner as to emphasise sensibility and moralising, and since letter writing was, in any case, his peculiar bent, it remains to show in how far there was a precedent for the epistolary novel, and to consider the contribution which letters, in one way or another, made towards the development of the novel.

When Richardson began his career as a novelist, letters, dialogues and character sketches had long been established in popularity, and were rapidly converging towards the enrichment of prose fiction. At that time letter-writing was a distinct accomplishment, and such people as Madame de Sévigné, Dorothy Osborne and Sir William Temple, Swift, Horace Walpole and Lady Mary Wortley-Montagu had made classic contributions to this literary genre. In the *Spectator*, the character-sketches had gradually lost their sharpness of outline, and ceased to be self-contained, becoming instead a continuous delineation of certain individuals who were no longer stock-types, but real human beings. These activities, however, were merely the culmination of similar literary efforts which had already been made for over one hundred years. Even in the days of the Pastoral and of the Heroic Romance letters were frequently interpolated in the narrative to afford variety or to concentrate interest on some crucial point of sentiment. It also became the custom to write collections of imaginary letters. These were used to essay character-sketches, to reflect a mood, describe an incident, or to suit various occasions or recipients. An early example was *A Poste with a Packet of Mad Letters* (1603)[1] by Nicholas Breton. In these there is as great variety as could well be imagined, ranging from various kinds of proposals, letters of advice, entreaty, expostulation, challenge to a duel, and a " disswasive from marriage." In vol. 2, no. 153, Breton curiously anticipated Richardson. Most of Breton's letters have answers and in some cases there are two and even three letters and answers exchanged on the same subject.

In considering whether or not Richardson's use of letters was anticipated it is necessary not merely to ask whether some previous writers endeavoured to tell a story in letters but also to determine whether, before Richardson's time, anyone attempted in letters to delineate character or to describe scenes. Early in the seventeenth century many collections of character-sketches appeared in the form of essays, notably *Character of Virtues and Vices* (1608) by Hall; Sir Thomas Overbury's *Characters* (1614); Nicholas Breton's *Characters upon Essaies Moral and Divine* (dedicated to Bacon) 1615; and again in 1616

[1] 1603 is the earliest dated edition, but possibly this was not the first edition.

Breton's *The Good and the Badde;* and John Earle's *Micro-cosmographie* (1628).

In the works already mentioned the epistolary genre had its nucleus. During the following century its growth was definitely aided by certain works which we are about to consider, and it will be observed that women ably assisted its development.

In 1664 the Duchess of Newcastle made a most notable contribution to the kind of writing which aimed at character-sketches, and she even went further than the mere portrayal of character.

> Among the mass of her writings [says Jusserand] ideas are scattered here and there which are destined to live, and through which she anticipated men of true and real genius. To give only one example, she, too, may be credited with having anticipated Richardson in her "Sociable Letters" *in which she tries to imitate real life, to describe scenes, very nearly to write an actual novel*: "The truth is," she writes, "they are rather scenes than letters, for I have endeavoured under cover of letters to express the humors of mankind, and the actions of man's life by the correspondence of two ladies, living at some short distance from each other, which make it not only their chief delight and pastime, but their tye in friendship, to discourse by letters as they would do if they were personally together." Many collections of imaginary letters had, as we have seen, been published before, but never had the use to which they could be put been better foreseen by any predecessor of Richardson.[2]

Margaret Newcastle wrote letters as she wrote everything else, with complete spontaneity and forthrightness. "In your last letter," she says, "you desired me to write some letters of complement as also some panegyricks, but I must entreat you to excuse me for my style in writing is too plain and simple for such courtly works; besides, give me leave to inform you, that I am a servant of truth and not of flattery . . . my mistress Truth, hath no need of such adornings, neither doth she give many words and seldom any praise . . . yet, howsoever, I being bred in her service from my youth, will never quit her till death takes me away." This was the clear and vigorous sort of language through which reality might well shine.

2 J. J. Jusserand, *The English Novel in the time of Shakespeare* (1890), p. 378.

An excellent example of characterisation ironically incised against a contrasted background is to be found in the Duchess's description of the lady who has newly embraced Puritanism:

> Yesterday Mrs. P.I. was to visit me, who prayed me to present her humble service to you, but since you saw her she is become an altered woman, as being a sanctified soul, a spiritual sister, she hath left curling her hair, black patches are become an abomination to her, laced shoes and galoshes are steps to pride, to go bare-necked she accounts worse than adultery; fans, ribbons, pendants, necklaces, and the like, are the temptations of Satan, and the signs of damnation; and she is not only transformed in her dress, but her garb and speech, and all her discourse, insomuch as you would not know her if you saw her, unless you were informed who she was; she speaks of nothing but of Heaven and purification, and after some discourse, she asked me what posture I thought was the best to be used in prayer? I said I thought no posture was more becoming, nor did fit devotion better, than kneeling . . . for the scripture says from earth we came, and to earth we shall return; then she spoke of prayers, for she is all for extemporary prayers, I told her, that the more words we used in prayer, the worse they were accepted, for I thought a silent adoration was better accepted of God than a self-conceited babbling . . . with that she lifted up her eyes, and departed from me, believing I was one of the wicked and reprobate, not capable of a saving grace, so as I believe she will not come near me again, lest her purity should be defiled in my company, I believe the next news we shall hear of her will be that she is become a preaching sister.

Then there is her notable description of Sir N.G. who, in an effort to preserve his health, travels endlessly from place to place:

> He stayes not anywhere for he is like a shadow, or a ghost, when you think it is so near as to speak to it, it straight appears afar off, or Vanishes away; and he is not onely in this City, but in every town, for he rides from town to town, as birds flie from to tree, and his onely business is for divertisement for health, so that his Life is as if it rid Post; but let him ride from Death as far as he can, and do what he can to shun it, yet Death will meet him at his journeys end, and there arrest him and imprison his body in a grave, for Time hath laid an action of battery against him, and hath now three score and fifteen years summoned him to appear, but as yet he keeps out of sight, and will as long as he can, as we may perceive by his riding, and short stay in every place he comes to.

That there were Pamelas and Mr. B.'s within the knowledge of the Duchess is well seen in the following passage:

> I am sorry Sir F.C. hath undervalued himself so much below his birth and wealth, as to marry his kitchen-maid, but it was a sign he had an hungry, or that he lived a solitary life, seeing no better company, or conversed not with women of quality; or else he had been too privately kind, and was loth to have it too publickly known; or he hath tried her virtue, and so married her for chastity . . . or else he married her for beauty, or wit, or both . . . But perchance Sir F.O. married his kitchen-maid in hopes she would make a nimble, and obedient which he might fear, one of equal birth might not be . . . Yet I write not this as believeing he may not be happy in his choice, for 'tis likely the match may be more happy than honourable, and if he thinks it no disgrace, or cares not for disgrace, all is well for it only concerns himself, as having no parents living to grieve or anger, nor no former children to suffer by.

Of her many descriptions of living scenes, one must suffice— her account of a winter city:

> If you were here in this city, now all the ground of the streets is covered with snow, you would see the young men and their mistresses ride in sleds by torch-light, the women and the men dressed antickly, as also their horses that draw their sleds; and then every sled having a fair lady, at least to her lover's thinking, sitting at one end of the sled, dressed with feathers and rich clothes, and her courting servant like a coachman, or rather a carter, bravely accoutred, driving the horses with a whip, which draw the sled upon the snow with a galloping pace, whilst footmen run with torches to light them. But many of these lovers, not using to drive horses so often as to court mistresses, for want of skill overturn the sled, and so tumble down their mistresses in the snow, whereupon they being in a frightened hast, take them up from that cold bed, and then the mistress appears like a pale ghost, or dead body in a winding sheet, being all covered with white snow; and the sled, when the mistress is seated again, instead of a triumphant chair, seems like a virgin's funeral herse, carried, and buried by torch-light; and her feathers seem like a silver crown, that usually is laid thereon, also the sled is drawn then in a slow, funeral pace, for fear of a second fall. By this custom and practice you may know, we have here recreations for every season of the year, and as the old saying is, that pride in winter is never cold, so it may be said, that love in winter is never cold; indeed, I have heard say, that love is hot, and to my apprehension it must be a very hot

amorous love that is not cold this weather. But leaving the hot lovers in the cold snow, I rest by the fire-side, Madam.

Your very faithful friend and servant.

Nor was the Duchess at a loss when words were needed to express what was in her heart. There are her letters to that fourth sister who was married to Sir Edmund Pye:

Dear Sister Pye,—Distance of place, nor length of time cannot lessen my natural, or rather supernatural affection to you; for certainly my love for you is more than a sister's love, nay, such a love, as when I lived with you, it could not choose but be somewhat troublesome, by reason my love was accompanied with such fears, as it would neither let you rest, pray, nor eat in quiet. For though it was a watchful love, yet it was a fearful love, for I remember I have oftentimes waked you out of your sleep, when you did sleep quietly, with soft breathing, fearing you had been dead; but oftener have I laid my face over your mouth, to feel if you breathed, insomuch as I have kept my self waking, to watch your sleeps, and as troublesome as I was to you concerning your feeding, as I was in your sleeping, for I was afraid that that which was to nourish you, should kill you. And I remember, I was so doubtful of every meat you did eat, as you were used to tell me, I was Sancapancha's doctor; neither could I let you pray in quiet, for I have often knocked at your closet door, when I thought you were longer at your prayers than usual, or at least, I did think the time longer; so as I could not forbear to ask you how you did, and whether you were well, and many the like impertinences which my extraordinary love troubled you with; and of which you are now quit, living so far asunder . . .

And again:

In your last letter you chid me for loving too earnestly, saying extreme love did consume my body and torment my mind, and that whosoever love to a high degree are fools; if so, Madam, I am as much a fool as ever Nature made, for where I set my love, it is fixed like eternity, and is as full as infinite. My love is not fixed suddenly, for it takes experience and consideration to help to place it, both which have been my guides and directors to love you, which makes me love you much, and shall make me love you long, if souls die not.

Lyly had used letters in his *Ephues* (1579-1580) to indicate the mood of a character or to advance the plot. With the publication of the *Portuguese Letters* (1669) a new estimate of letters as an artistic medium dawned upon Europe. The earliest English version was that of Sir Roger L'Estrange, *Five Love Letters from a Nun to a Cavalier* (Dec. 28, 1677). For long these letters were supposed to be authentic. Now modern critics are inclined to ascribe them to Guilleraques, who claimed merely to have translated them. Be that as it may; we are concerned solely with the impetus which the *Portuguese Letters* gave to the growth of the epistolary form. The story is simple: During the reign of Louis XIV, France gave some desultory aid to Portugal against Spain. French volunteers went under arms to the Peninsula, and amongst their number was Noel Bouton, afterwards Marquis of Chamilly and St. Leger. In the course of the intermittent campaign he became friendly with a young officer who belonged to an old and influential family of Beja in the province of Alemtejo. This officer had a sister who was a nun in the convent of Beja, and on one fatal day he went to visit her accompanied by his friend Chamilly. Mariana Alcoforado was entrusted to the convent when she was a child. She was professed at the age of sixteen. She was twenty-five when she saw and loved Chamilly—a young man of little intelligence and. no scruples. Although Mariana is careful not to blame him for more than his share, his character is clearly to be read between the lines. He stands revealed a slight philanderer, a poor fool playing with a diamond as if it were a worthless piece of glass. One can almost compassionate the stupidity of this courtly dolt who meant to kindle a little blaze, only to find himself involved in a volcanic eruption. Well might she say " You are more to be pitied than I." Chamilly returned hastily to France, where he rose later to the highest dignity. St. Simon tells us he was the best man in the world, the bravest and the most honourable, but he adds that no one after seeing him or hearing him speak could understand how he had inspired such an unmeasured love. Mariana lived to be eighty three years. " For thirty years she did rigid penance and suffered great infirmities with much conformity, desiring to have more to suffer." So runs a statement supposed to have been signed by the scrivener of the convent.

Indeed, it is not easy to describe the *Portuguese Letters*. They are the outpourings of a mind bent upon self-torture, preying

forever upon every detail of her fatal mistake and of her present
position. She knows now too well her lover's unworthiness,
and yet she cannot escape from the maze in which she is lost.
She alternates between remorse, remonstrance, hopeless love,
terrible longing, and a consciousness that she has within her
something beyond man's contempt. She does not allow emotion
to dull her moral sense. Truth is in her hand a merciless blade
which she plunges into her bosom, with which she cuts out her
heart and dissects it under our eyes. There is no self-pity.
There is in the letters every possible fluctuation of mind and
feeling:

> I conjure you to tell me why you set your heart on fascinating
> me as you did, when you knew very well that you were going
> to desert me? And why have you been so pitiless in making
> me wretched? Why did you not leave me in peace in this
> cloister? Had I done you any injury? But forgive me, I
> impute nothing to you. I am in no state to think of revenge,
> and I only accuse the harshness of my fate. In separating us
> it seems to have done all the harm we could have feared. But
> our hearts can not be separated; love, which is more powerful
> than destiny, has united them for our whole life. If you take
> any interest in mine, write to me often . . . Above all, come
> to see me. Farewell, I cannot leave this paper; it will fall into
> your hands; would that I might have the same happiness. Alas!
> how insane I am! I see that this is not possible. Farewell! I
> can write no more. Farewell, love me always, and make me
> suffer still more misery.

And then:

> I realise that I deceived myself when I thought that you would
> act in better faith than is usual, because the excess of my love
> seemed to lift me above any kind of suspicion and to deserve
> more fidelity than is ordinarily to be met with. But the desire
> you have to betray me overmasters the justice you owe to all I
> have done for you. . . . . Ought I not to have foreseen that
> my happiness would come to an end, rather than my love? . . .
> You are more to be pitied than I. It is better to suffer all that
> I suffer, than to enjoy the languid pleasures that the women of
> France may give you. I do not envy your indifference and I
> pity you . . .
>   At least, remember me. I could content myself with your
> remembrance, but I dare not be sure of it. I did not limit my
> hopes to your remembrance when I saw you every day . . .

How much suffering you would have spared me if your conduct had been as indifferent the first few days I saw you as it has seemed to me lately, but who would not have been deceived . . . by such devotion, and who would not have thought it sincere? How hard it is to bring oneself to suspect the sincerity of those one loves! I see plainly that the least excuse is enough for you; and without your taking the trouble to make any, my love serves you so faithfully that I can only consent to find you guilty in order to enjoy the keen pleasure of justifying you myself . . . You were not blinded like me, why then did you let me fall into the state I am in? What did you want of all my ardent demonstrations which could only be importunate to you? You knew very well that you would not remain in Portugal; and why did you choose me here to make me so unhappy? You could certainly have found in this country some more beautiful woman, with whom you might have had as much pleasure since you were only in search of that; who would have loved you faithfully as long as you were in sight; whom time would have consoled for your absence, and whom you might have left without perfidy and cruelty. Such conduct is much more that of a tyrant bent upon persecuting than of a lover whose only thought is to please. Alas! why are you so pitiless with a heart that is all your own? . . . What have I done to be so unhappy, and why have you poisoned my life? . . . What should I do alas! without all this hatred and all this love which fill my heart?

But, though torn yet by her emotions, she is increasingly conscious of deep remorse:

I lived for a long time in an abandonment and idolatry which fill me with horror now, and my remorse pursues me without pity . . . I know very well that I am still somewhat too concerned with my reproaches and your infidelity; but remember that I have promised myself a more peaceful state and that I will attain to it, or else that I shall take some extreme measure against myself, which you will hear without great distress. But I ask nothing more from you. How foolish I am to repeat the same things so often! I must leave you and think no more about you; perhaps even I shall not write to you again. Am I obliged to give you an exact account of all my varied emotions?

Gosse has said:

The extraordinary and at times the unique merit of the Portuguese nun, as a letter writer, lies in the fact that, in the full tempest and turmoil of her passion, she never yields to the temptation of giving herself up to rhetoric, or rather that whenever she does make a momentary concession to this habit of her age, she doubles upon herself immediately and is the first to deprecate such false flowers of speech.[3]

Coming in the age of French rhetorical extravagances, and English stilted circumlocutions, the *Portuguese Letters* were at once accepted as models of passionate sincerity. L'Estrange's translation continued to be reprinted for fifty years, and innumerable imitations poured from the printing presses. Most of these were of no intrinsic value, but they were of importance in that they showed an effort to express emotions and ideas in a vivid and spontaneous manner.

Something of the strength, sincerity and despair of the *Portuguese Letters* are echoed in Aphra Behn's *Love-Letters to a Gentleman.* These documents, eight in number, were originally published in the 1696 edition of the collected *Histories and Novels,* and in subsequent editions form part of the introductory *Life and Memoirs.* They are supposed to be authentic, and have, indeed, all the signs of authenticity. To whom were they addressed? One cannot say with any definiteness. During Aphra Behn's lifetime it was usual to ascribe to her a vast number of lovers, and after ages accepted the legend enthusiastically, and even added to the multiplicity. Nevertheless, only one man is definitely known to have been her lover: John Hoyle, a lawyer of Grey's Inn and the Inner Temple. In Tom Brown's *Letters of Love and Gallantry* there is a letter from Aphra Behn to Hoyle, remonstrating with him on his depraved way of life, and asking him in the name of "Our past endearments" to clear himself, if possible, of the allegations made against him. This is not the letter of a woman in love, but of a kindly friend, so that if Hoyle was the object of Mrs. Behn's *Love Letters to a Gentleman,* these must have been written at an earlier stage, before Hoyle stood branded as " an athiest, a sodomite professed, a corrupter of youth and a blasphemer of Christ." One thing at least is certain, that Aphra loved in vain, and that she suffered all the miseries of uncertainty, hope and longing. These letters do not attempt to tell a connected story, but they do record

[3] Sir E. Gosse, 'A Nun's Love Letters,' *Fortnightly Review,* 43 (1888), p. 514.

vividly and poignantly the emotions which agitate this woman's heart. They bear in every line the impress of the writer and of the mood, and even of the atmosphere in which they were written. They alternately plead and remonstrate. Some are written in a breathless hurry; some with all the weariness of a heavy heart:

> Though it be very late, I cannot go to Bed, but I must tell you I have been very good ever since I saw thee, and have been a writing, and have seen no Face of Man, or other Body, save my own People. I am mightily pleased with your kindness to me tonight, and 'twas I hope and believe very innocent and undisturbing on both Sides . . . If thou hast Love (as I shall never doubt, if thou art always as to-night) shew that Love I beseech thee; there being nothing so grateful to God, and Mankind, as Plain-dealing. Tis too late to conjure thee further: I will be purchased with Softness, and dear Words, and kind Expressions, Sweet Eyes and a Low voice.

Clearly, at this stage, Aphra's lover had sufficient interest in her company to make him appear all she believed. She expresses her sense of security in intimate little references to their friends and to places they have visited together:

> I stay'd after thee to-night, till I had read a whole Act of my new Play, and then he led me over all the Way, saying, Gad, you were the Man: and beginning some rallying Love-Discourse after Supper, which he fancy'd was not so well received as it ought, he said you were not handsome, and called Philly to own it; but he did not, but was of my side, and said you were handsome; so he went on a While, and all ended that concerned you. And this, upon my Word, is all.

But she cannot long deceive herself as to his attitude. Very well, then! If need be she will tear up her passion by the roots, while it is still possible: " I grow desperate fond of you and would be used well; if not, I will march off. But I will believe you mean to keep your Word, as I will for ever do mine." She tells him truly that her nature is proud and cannot bear his slights. But she does bear them, because she cannot help herself:

> For God's sake, make no more Niceties and Scruples than need, in your way of living with me: that is, do not make me believe this distance is to ease you, when indeed 'tis meant to ease us

> both of love . . . How could anything but the Man that hates
> me, entertain me so unkindly? Witness your excellent Opinion
> of me, of loving others; witness your passing by the End of the
> Street where I live and squandering away your time at any
> Coffee-house, rather than allow me what you know in your soul
> is the greatest Blessing of my Life. Your dear, dull, melan-
> choly Company. I call it dull, because you can never be gay or
> merry where Astrea is.

And then, the end. He is not only unfaithful but he has the
cruelty to tell her so, possibly with the desire to break with her
completely:

> You left me to torments. You went to love, alone, and left me
> to love and rage, fevers and calentures, even madness itself.
> Indeed, indeed, my soul, I know not to what degree I love you:
> let it suffice I do most passionately, and can have no thought of
> any other man whilst I have life. No! Reproach me, defame
> me, lampoon me, curse me and kill me when I do. Farewell, I
> love you more and more every moment of my life. Know it
> and goodnight.
>
> Astrea.

Very different in type are Mrs. Behn's *Love-Letters between
a Nobleman and his Sister* (1683). These libellous effusions are
based on a notorious scandal which had attracted great attention
in England a short time previously. Lord Grey of Werk eloped
with his sister-in-law, Lady Henrietta Berkeley. He was brought
to trial on a charge of conspiracy on 23rd November, 1682. He
appeared in court accompanied by his mistress and many of the
powerful Whig lords. He was found guilty. Mrs. Behn's
" fictitious gallimawfry "[4] is chiefly in verse. The key is
given in the preface. Lord Grey is Philander, Silvia is Lady
Henrietta, and the Duke of Monmouth is Cesario. The *Letters*
are merely romantic fustian, bristling with rhodomontade.
Nevertheless, the story is carried on partly in the letters, but
principally by the postscripts, which are in prose. There are
some prose letters also, which are important to the narrative.

Two notable letters in prose are from Cesario to the Count
of ——, and from Melinda (Silvia's maid) to Philander. Melinda
(who is in the lover's pay) describes very well how the wife

---

4 So Horace Walpole calls it in his *Royal and Ancient Authors*, iv, 4.

discovers her sister writing a love letter to the husband. The wife suspects nothing, and jokingly insists on seeing it. Silvia passes it off by pretending that it is from the maid to her lover, Alexis, under the names of Silvia and Philander.

To-day many ominous things have happened. Madam the Countess had like to have taken a letter writ to your Lordship to-day; for the Duchess of —— coming to pay her a visit, came on a sudden with her into my Lady's Apartment, and surprised her writing in her Dressing Room, hardly giving her time to slip the paper into her Comb-box. The first ceremonies being over, as Madam the Duchess does not use much, she began to commend my Lady's Dressing-Plate, and taking up the Box, and looking into it, saw the Letter, and laughing, cry'd, oh, have I found you making Love! At which my Lady, with an infinite Confusion, would have retrieved it, but the Dutchess, still keeping her hold, cry'd—Nay, I'm resolved I'll see in what manner you write to a Lover, and whether your Heart is tender or cruel; at which she began to read aloud. My Lady blushed, and changed Colour a hundred times in a Minute; I almost died with fear; Madam the Countess in infinite Amazement; my Lady interrupting every word read by the Dutchess by Intreaties and Prayers, which served to heighten her Curiosity, being airy and young, regarded not the indecency to which she preferred her Curiosity; who laughing cry'd, she was resolved to read it out, and find the Constitution of her Heart; when my Lady, whose Wit never fail'd her, cry'd, I beg you, Madam, let us have so much Complaisance for Melinda to ask her Consent in this Affair, and then I shall be pleased that you should see what Love I can make upon occasion. I took the Hint, and cry'd with a real Confusion—I implore you, Madam, not to discover my weakness to Madame the Dutchess, I would not for the World be thought to love so passionately as your Ladyship, in favour of Alexis, has caused me to profess, under the name of Silvia and Philander. This gave my Lady Encouragement, who began to say a thousand pretty things of Alexis, Dorillus' son, and my Lover, as your Lordship knows, and who is indeed no inconsiderable Fortune, for a Maid, only by your Lordship's Bounty enriched. After this my Lady took the Letter, and all being resolved it should be read, she did it herself, and turned it so prettily into burlesque Love, by her way of reading it, that Madam the Dutchess laughed extreamly.

There is no need to describe the rest of the story. The wife becomes suspicious and sets spies to observe the lovers. She appeals in vain to Sylvia, who after struggling with herself, yields to Philander. Finally all is discovered and they elope.

In 1686 appeared an anonymous love-story in Letters, *Love's Posy*.[5] This is "A collection of seven and Twenty Love Letters, both in verse and prose; That lately pass'd betwixt a Gentleman and a very young Lady in France."

In *Letters written by Mrs. Manley* (1696) all the letters are from Mrs. Manley to John Hoyle. They recount continuously all the main events of a stage-coach journey to Exeter. The narrative is quite free from the romantic tradition. There is much humour and realism, and considerable power of presenting character by a few deft touches. There is not much story, but continuity is established by the fact that the same characters speak from day to day, and that the travellers develop acquaintance with each other under our eyes.

Mrs. Manley's references to the inns imply some customs which would be peculiar if true. She says "They unmercifully set us to Dinner at Ten-a-Clock upon a great Leg of Mutton. 'Tis the Custom of these Dining Stages to prepare one Day Beef, and another our present fare! 'tis ready against the coach comes." On the whole, however, she does not take any trouble with background. "I need say nothing to you of Salisbury Cathedral: If in a Foreign Country, as the Lady in her Letters of Spain, I could entertain you with a noble description: but you have either seen, or may see it; and so I'll spare my Architecture."[6]

5 B. M., no. 10910. a. a. 22. Printed for J. Hindmarsh. 12⁰.

6 Mrs. Manley had in mind Mme. La Mothe's: *The Ingenious and Diverting Letters of the Lady—Travels into Spain describing the Devotions, Mummeries, Humours, Customs, Laws, Militia, Trade, Diet and Recreations of that People, Intermixt with Great Variety of Modern Adventures and surprising Accidents."* The 2nd ed. of this translation was in 1692. Detailed treatment of Mme. La Mothe's book does not lie within our scope, since she belongs to French literature. There is no doubt whatever that she was a very important contributor to the development of the epistolary novel. The letters give a detailed description of all the towns on the route, the inns at which she stayed, the people she encountered on the way. Often there are inset stories (of the *novella* type) which are recounted to the lady by those whose plight seems to need self-explanation. Especially well told is the second story, the story of the Hermit, and the story of the haunted castle at Nios. The fault in Mme. La Mothe's *Travels into Spain* is that nothing really happens to the lady herself, and that her journey is not much more than a convenient thread with which she strings her stories and anecdotes together. Her

Mrs. Manley atones for her scanty backgrounds by her racy descriptions of the people she meets on her journey. There is the landlord who is "a perfect Beaux," the "Mrs. Mayoress" who "now she is acquainted, has all the low, disagreeable Familiarity of People of her Rank," and the two unfortunates who are so deplorably plebeian that they never before travelled by stage-coach. These last Mrs. Manley savagely describes as follows:

> The two other Fellow-Travellers were never so promoted before, and are much troubl'd their Journey is to last no longer, and wish the four Days four Months. I hope every Jolt will squash their Guts, and give 'em enough on't: But they are proof against any such Disasters, and hugely delighted with what they are pleased to call Riding in State. After this ridiculous Account, you need not doubt but I am thoroughly mortified.

Then there is her excellent description of the foppish young lordling, his egregious vanity, his cocksure advances, all of which she ignores. Finally, determined to win her attention, he insists on giving an account of one of his love affairs. Mrs. Manley very cleverly characterises him by the words she puts into his mouth. His story, and his manner of telling it give us a complete picture of this self-opinionated young jackanapes. Mrs. Manley is a keen observer and her humour has sometimes a vitriolic touch, that same touch which afterwards burned its way through the pages of *The New Atalantis*. She thus presents some new arrivals at an inn:

> . . . Presently saw alight a tall blustering, big bon'd raw Thing, like an over-grown School-Boy, but conceited above anything. He had an Appurtenance call'd a Wife, whom he suffer'd to get out as well as she cou'd; as long as he had layn with her, he did not think her worth the civility of his Hand. She seemed a Giant of a Woman, but very fine, with a right Citt Air. He blustered presently for the best lodging.

There are also present in the party several young females, quite lacking in attractions and in poise. To one of these "awkward things" the beau transfers his attentions—"a Gold-

descriptions of scenery are a mere tabulation of facts; she mentions objects of interest with the assiduity of a Baedeker. In fact, this work is a kind of Heptameron-cum-guide book. *Travels into Spain* was extremely popular in England, the translation reaching its tenth edition in 1735.

smith's Daughter with a tolerable face." Mrs. Manley strikes up an intimacy with a Mrs. Stanhope, who confides in her some of her adventures. At Bridport, where the party spends the night, a friend of the beau's arrives, and greatly adds to the general interest. By the time Mrs. Manley arrives at Exeter, the beau has returned to his allegiance, and sends her three foppish letters. But she remains unmoved. " I can now with cold indifference shake Hands with all Things beyond this Solitude. . . . I repeat with Stoical Pride—keep me, ye Bounteous Gods, my Caves and Woods in Peace: let Tares and Acorns be my Food."

These letters of Mrs. Manley, afterwards published as *The Stage Coach Journey to Exeter* (1725), are not only vividly alive and completely real in the experiences they recount, but the bustle and hurry of the journey are well suggested in remarks which are, as it were, asides: " Tis now past 11, and they'll call us by two. Good Night; I am going to try if I can drown in Sleep that which most sensibly affects me—the cruel Separation we have so lately suffered." And: " The Trouts are just brought upon the Table, which are the only good thing here; they look inviting, and won't stay for cooling Compliments." And even: " I forgot to leave Orders with the Jew about the Chocolate: Pray, take care that it be sent me and excuse this trouble."

In 1696, the same year as *Letters of Mrs. Manley,* appeared Antony Hamilton's *Zénéyde.* This was an unfinished tale in letter form, but it cannot be said to add much, if anything, to the epistolary method, since it consists of one single letter. It is by the interchange of letters, or by a succession of letters from one person that an epistolary story should develop. A story told in a single letter differs from an autobiographical narrative only in the superscription. Nevertheless, that Antony Hamilton should decide to embody his story in a letter was evidence of the growing preoccupation with letters as a narrative form. It is strange that the French did not fully develop this genre of writing, although they far surpassed the English as letter-writers, and were enraptured by Richardson's novels when they appeared.

In 1702 appeared a work which still further anticipated

Richardson: *The Lover's Secretary*, or, *The Adventures of Lindamira*, by Tom Brown.   In twenty-four letters[7] Brown told an amusing and well-connected story, with much realism in characterisation and background.   Lindamira, a young lady of quality, gay but good, writes to her friend Indamora, who lives in the country, confiding in her all her love-affairs.   Lindamira steers a safe course through the beaux and fops.   She enjoys *billets doux* as she enjoys visiting the playhouse, and she has a sound respect for her mother's advice.   The last letter shows her at the end of her adventures and her trials, happily married to the faithful Cleomidon.

Early in the eighteenth century there appeared in the *Tatler* and *Spectator* short stories, romantic or domestic, either in one letter or in a series of letters.   The story of Amanda (*Spectator*, No. 375, May 10, 1712) has been suggested as the original of Richardson's *Pamela*, although indeed, as we have seen, for example, in the Duchess of Newcastle's Letters, and shall see in Mrs. Rowe's *Letters Moral and Entertaining* the story of *Pamela* was a commonplace, and it was Richardson's treatment which made it a masterpiece.

Perhaps another proof of the great popularity of letters, even in the beginning of the eighteenth century was the modernised version of Lyly's *Euphues* which appeared in 1718, under the title of *The False Friend and the Inconstant Mistress*: *an instructive Novel . . . displaying the artifices of the female sex in their Amours*.   This book made its appearance not very long before *Pamela*, and it is cogent to observe that whereas in the text of the original *Euphues*, the interpolated letters appeared merely incidental, in the abbreviated version, these letters, all of which were retained, appeared very conspicuous in relation to the shrunken context.   Jusserand observed that the table of contents in this modernised *Euphues* was quite Richardsonian. " Here we find enumerated the many wise recommendations by which Lyly so long anticipated Richardson and Rousseau."[8]

Mrs. Haywood was in the main stream of this epistolary tendency.   Her *Letters from a Lady of Quality to a Chevalier*

[7] 228 duodecimo pages.

[8] J. J. Jusserand. *The English Novel in the Time of Shakespeare* (1890), p. 141.

(1724) were merely a loose translation of Edmé Boursault's *Lettres Nouvelles . . . avec Treize Lettres Amoureuses d'une Dame à un Cavalier.* [9] They tell a hackneyed story in the flamboyant style of gallantry, but as they did not originate with Mrs. Haywood, they cannot be considered here. Far superior, in any case, is Mrs. Haywood's own work: *Love-Letters on all occasions lately passed between Persons of Distinction* (1730). In letters XIII to XXXVI there is the story of Theano and Elismonda. The tale develops through the interchange of letters between the pair. In the first letter Theano, who has obtained "the last favour," reproaches Elismonda with her indifferent looks on the following day. Elismonda in reply states that her apparent coldness was due to her subsequent shame. To which explanation she adds this astounding remark: "The Manner of my yielding admits of no Excuse, and leaves not the least Room to hope I can maintain any place in a Heart filled only with the most noble and refined Ideas." Theano magnanimously forgives her for yielding to him, and has the noble and refined idea of visiting her that same evening. All goes well for a time, but soon the inevitable serpent raises a hissing head in this Eden. Armida, the friend with whom Elismonda lives, becomes jealous of her happiness and refuses to allow Theano's visits. "In spite of the Secret which a reasonable Person would imagine must put her infinitely more in my power, than I can possibly be in hers, [she] has given me some Hints, that if I continue any Correspondence with you, she will expose me to the utmost censures of the ill-judging World." Elismonda fears that, through seeing her seldom, Theano may grow indifferent to her. Theano replies reassuringly. Even the most venomous serpents cannot always remain poised to strike. Armida, "the curst enemy," will be away from home tomorrow, so Elismonda can meet Theano. But she fails to keep this appointment, because when the time came for the false Armida to set out on her expedition, she "fell into a Spleen, fancy'd herself sick, undrest and went to Bed." Elismonda fears Theano must have been very disappointed, but her apologies soon turn to furious recriminations when she hears that

2nd ed. Paris, 1699.

Theano also failed to keep the appointment. She now sees her sin, and leaves her avengement to Heaven. Theano, however, has a perfectly good excuse, and Elismonda decides that, after all, she is not a sinner, but a great romantic. Other obstacles now present themselves, and Elismonda fluctuates between ecstasy and despair, until at last the pair are reunited.

Despite the high-flown language, the story is vividly told. We feel impatience at the delays and the hindrances which beset the lovers, and this suspense is well maintained. The events are easily credible; in fact, they are commonplace, but their effect is out of all proportion to their importance. This is quite in keeping with the psychology of lovers. Mrs. Haywood knows the Richardsonian trick of taking emotions and happenings at their very moment: " I saw you but last Night . . . yet do I find already that I have utter'd but half the meanings of my soul . . . another soft Adieu, but 't'will not be allowed; the Coach is ready, my Friends wait for me . . . and I but take this moment to remind you of your Vows." When Theano is called out of town we see how every stage of the journey increases Elismonda's fears, suspicions and anxieties. So it is with his return. He writes from every post-town, and as his haste swallows the miles which separate them, there is a convincing crescendo of excitement and emotion.[10]

It remains to consider the letters of Mrs. Elizabeth Rowe in relation to the development of the epistolary form of novel-writing. *Friendship in Death, in twenty letters from the Dead*

10 G. F. Wicher thinks otherwise. Speaking of the letters of Theano and Elismonda he says, "in the course of the whole correspondence nothing more momentous happens than the lover's leaving town. Indeed, so imperceptible is the narrative element in Mrs. Haywood's epistolary sequences that they can claim no share with the anonymous love story in letters entitled *Love's Posy* (1686), *Letters written by Mrs. Manley* (1696) and *Adventures of Lindamira* (1702) . . . . [in] the honour of having anticipated Richardson's method of telling a story in epistolary form." But does anything momentous happen in *Letters written by Mrs. Manley*? On the contrary, there is a far slighter and looser plot in Mrs. Manley's *Letters,* if indeed the motif of journeying can be called a plot at all. Wicher also stresses the fact that Mrs. Haywood never followed up the attempt she had made at epistolary narrative in *Elismonda and Theano*. What of it? Mrs. Manley never followed up her *Letters,* and Wicher does not consider that this lessened her claim as an anticipator of Richardson's use of the epistolary form. See G. F. Wicher : *Life and Romances of Mrs. Haywood* (Columbia Univ. Press, 1915) p. 11, footnote 18.

to the Living (1728) is nothing to our purpose. These are single letters on dreary subjects. They do not tell a story. Their didactic and pietistic intention is stated in the preface: " The Drift of these Letters is, to impress the Notion of the Soul's Immortality; without which, all Virtue and Religion, with their temporal and eternal good consequences, must fall to the Ground." *Letters Moral and Entertaining* (1729-1733) are equally bombastic and sententious. They are of import only in their bearing on the epistolary novel. These effusions are merely dressed-up tracts, and their morality is entirely prudential and self-conscious. It is, in fact, the morality of Richardson's novels. Some of these letters are mere sermonising; some contain stories. Sometimes there is a sequence of letters on the same subject; sometimes a single letter is complete in itself. There are a number of single letters containing stories, as, for example, those describing an unhappy amour, a murder, and the love of Bellamour for Almeda. In some cases letters in the first part have a sequel in the second part of the volume. Mrs. Rowe is occasionally willing to enliven her preaching with the art of the *novella,* and again her tracts sometimes take a pastoral turn, as in the three letters at the beginning of part two, *To Lady Sophia, from Rosalinda, relating the true occasion of her flying from France, and leaving her father's house in the disguise of a country girl* (with a sequel in the next part of the book).

Rosalinda, a staunch Protestant like her mother, flees the persecutions of her Papist father, who not only restricts her religious exercises but has, with the utmost villainy, arranged a splendid marriage for her with a French Catholic, Count Altomont. Aided by her mother, she runs away, and takes service in a Protestant household so purely religious that not only does the mistress give plentiful alms to the poor, but her children " to mimick their mother gave away all the little treasure they had in their pockets to the beggars' children, and then fell a-crying because she would not suffer them to pull off their own shoes and stockings, to give to some that were barebooted." The master is so honest that he pays his servants every day. He is a farmer, but it would be mere vulgarity to assume that there were any pigs to be fed, cows to be milked, or potatoes to be dug on his land. "A more agreeable situation cannot be imagined, nor a greater variety of Sylvan Scenes. The wide landscape round is all my Master's property; his snowy Flocks are ranging on the Hills, his grazing Herds lowing through the plains, the Mountains are crowned with the great Creator's Bounty and the Valleys made vocal with his Praises." Rosalinda's unctuous humility rivals even that of Pamela. Pamela revelled in the proud dignity of being a servant; Rosalinda goes one better by glorying in "my splendid distinction of being a head servant." It was indeed a splendid distinction. No field work, no dairy work, even no house work sullies the lily-white fingers of this remarkable domestic, who spends her time rapt in high-souled ecstasies. "But I am not always in the sublime. I sometimes descend to gather Cowslips and Daisies or pursue some gaudy Butterfly with my pretty Companions." How heartily we believe her when she says "I am as fine as any Shepherdess in an Opera!" We need scarcely record that, before long, a gentle youth sighs for her, and to him we consign her with a breath of relief.

Looking backwards at the writers who experimented with letters as a means of sketching character or telling a story, we observe with particular interest the women's contribution. We have seen that in her use of letters the Duchess of Newcastle anticipated Richardson. We have seen that Aphra Behn's *Love Letters to a Gentleman* gave sincere and vivid expression to varying emotions and moods. In *Love-Letters between a Nobleman and his Sister* she made a further advance in the use of the epistolary form. This is most evident in the scene where Silvia's maid, Melinda, pretends that she herself is the writer of Silvia's love-letter to Philander. As the quoted extract shows, this episode is described in the liveliest and most spontaneous manner. The dramatic quality, the interplay of wits, the suggestion of background and the urgency of the events narrated certainly anticipate Richardson's manner, and though the greater part of the book is in verse, the story does advance through the prose letters and postscripts. It is far from Richardson's use of letters, but it certainly points that way.

In the anonymous *Love's Posy* the story is carried on from

letter to letter, but again the interpolation of verse constitutes an essential difference from Richardson's form.   Nevertheless, *Love's Posy*,[11] like *Love Letters between a Nobleman and his sister*, does lead towards the Richardsonian technique.

In *Letters Written by Mrs. Manley* the use of verse is eliminated and the epistolary form approximates to Richardson's use of it.   In her use of letters, in her detailed realism, in the vivid delineation of scenes, Mrs. Manley definitely anticipated Richardson.   Her use of the road and its incidents suggests somewhat the attitude of Fielding.

There is no doubt that in *Love-Letters on all occasions* (1730), and particularly in the story of Theano and Elismonda, Mrs. Haywood also shadowed forth Richardson's epistolary method of presenting the fluctuations of emotion and sentiment.

Mrs. Rowe's significance as a forerunner of Richardson cannot be overlooked.   Intrinsically her stories deserve no commendation: her characterisation is of the most stereotyped; her backgrounds even when detailed are wooden; her moral standards are distasteful; her works are all devoid of the faintest ray of humour.   In *Urania* there was a certain incongruity when the heroine entered a cave and found a love sonnet, but what are we to say to a hero who enters a house and finds a harpsichord, hymns and anthems, two atlases and a pair of globes?   Despite all this, and not for the reasons that her own generation eulogised her, she is worth mentioning because she really did tell stories, not only in single letters, but in sequences of letters.   And it was not only thus that she anticipated Richardson.   She anticipated also his canting and self-interested morality and that sensibility which, whether gallant or righteous, had been steadily growing for a long time, and which the *Portuese Letters* and later the powerful influence of Marivaux brought into prominence before Richardson took up his pen.   These are the two tendencies of thought and the single tendency of form which went towards the evolution of *Pamela*.   It is clear that women-writers of fiction played their part in preparing the raw materials which Richardson excellently fashioned—so excellently, indeed, that his work was hailed as the first modern novel.

11 Mentioned here with the female contributors because there is the possibility that the writer was a woman.

INDEX

The references are to pages; (n) signifies a footnote.

Addison, 37.
Artistic creativeness 13 f.
Mrs. Penelope Aubin, 215, *253 ff.*
Jane Austen (1775-1817) 31, 38, 41 ff, 179, 249.

Robert Bage, 20 (*n*), 41.
E. A. Baker, 53, 79, 188, 225 f (*n*).
Bandello, 145, 58, 225.
John Barclay, 63.
Mrs. Jane Barker, 215, 251 f.
Aphra Behn (1640-1689) 18, 25 f, 29, *148 ff,* 237, 274 ff, 285.
E. Bernbaum, 174 ff, 186.
Biography, 70 f.
Roger Boyle, 147.
Elizabeth Boyd, 36, 255.
Nicholas Breton, 21, 66 f, 69, 202, 266.
Charlotte Brontë (1816-1855), 31, 44, 179.
Emily Brontë (1818-1848), 14, 31, 39, 44.
Tom Brown, 281.
John Bunyan, 147, 213.
Fanny Burney (1752-1840), 37 f, 41, 44, 46.

Duncan Campbell, 28.
Lady Elizabeth Carew, 68.
Mrs. Susannah Centlivre (1667?-1723), 18, 22 (*n*).
Chapbooks, 51.
Character studies, 201, *266 f.*
Theophilus Cibber, 27.
Classic art, 47.
Classification of women-writers, 20.
Jane Collier, 261.
Condemnation of women-writers, 19 ff.
Congreve, 25, 146.

Mrs. Mary Davys (F1 1756), 35 f, 215, 252, 255.
Defoe, 28, 33 f, 188, 214, 237, 253, 262.
Dekker, 190, 202.
Deloney, 51, 202.
Drama, 18 f, 25, 28, 140 ff, 147.
John Dryden, 25.
Isaac Disraeli, 83, 92.
Domestic sentiment, 44, 244 ff.

Double standard of criticism, 23.

Education, 13, 16, 68, 82 f, 86, 101, 108, 213.
George Eliot (1819-1880), 17, 40, 44, 46.
Elizabethan Times, 68, 145; Genres, 47.
English background in fiction, 134ff, 152 ff, 203 ff, 229, 224 ff, 256 ff.
Epistolary works, 266 ff.
John Evelyn, 81.

Fables, 136.
Fabliaux, 144.
Lady Fanshawe (1625-1680), 31 f, 107 ff, 120 f.
Mme. de la Fayette (1632-1693), 151, 225.
Henry Fielding, 15 f, 29, 242, 255.
Sarah Fielding, 255 ff.
Marie de France (F1 1175), 12, 21.

Charles Gildon, 31, 173, 169 (*n*), 187.
Francis Godwin, 124.
Sir Edmund Gosse, 29 f, 51, 152 (*n*), 174 ff.
Gothic novel, 44.
Count de Grammont, 80 f.
Green, 51, 179, 202.
Grobianism, 203.
Guild tales, 17 f.

Anthony Hamilton, 147, 280.
John Harvey, 197.
Mrs. Eliza Haywood (1693?-1756), 27, 214, 233 ff, 254 f, 282 ff.
Heine, 47.
Mary Herbert (died 1621), 18 (*n*), 20 f.
Heroic Romance, 51, 141, 146, 158.
Mrs. Lucy Hutchinson (c. 1620), 31 f, 93-107.

Imaginary journeys, 124 ff.

Dr. Johnson, 242, 251, 267.
Ben Jonson, 21, 143.
J. J. Jusserand, 138, 142, 281.

Julia Kavanagh, 183.
Key-novels, 216 ff, 237 ff.

Catherine Killigrew, 28 (n).

Charles Lamb, 84.
Langbaine, 21, 31 (n).
Langlande, 51.
Mrs. Mary Latter (1725-1777), 35 f.
Charlotte Lennox (1720-1804), 45.
Letters, 265 f.
Edmund Lodge, 92.
T. Longueville, 85.
John Lyly, 51, 68, 270, 281.

Mrs. Mary Manley (1672?-1724), 18, 26 f, 34 f, 63, 214 ff, 254 f, 278 ff, 283 (n).
Marivaux, 244, 286.
Clémont Marot, 193.
Harriet Martineau (1802-1876), 39.
Milesian tales, 49.
Molière, 143, 147.
Anne Clifford, Duchess of Montgomery: vide Countess of Pembroke.
Hannah More (1745-1833), 37, 251.
Mme. La Mothe, 278 (n).

Novella, 21, 51, 202.
Margaret of Navarre (1495-1540), 21, 145.
Allardyce Nicol, 25, 149.
Novel of Manners, 44.
Duchess of Newcastle (1624?-1674) 20, 22, 29, 31 f, 81 ff, 122-138, 267 ff, 281, 285.

Oriental tales, 254.
Ostracism of women-writers, effects of, 26 ff, 194 ff.

Pastoral Romance, 17 f, 47-69.
Painter, 51, 227.
Pepys, 33, 81, 92, 143.
Countess of Pembroke, vide Anne Clifford; vide Mary Herbert.
Philosophic Novel, 44.
Catherine Philips, 29 f.
Picaresque trend, 17 f, 237, 244, 253 ff.
Mrs. Pix (1666-1720?), 18, 148, 194 f.
Arabella Plantin, 249 ff.
Pope, 150, 233, 251.
Portuguese Letters, 46, 225 ff, 270 ff, 286.

Pre-Restoration women-writers, 17, 47-69.
Pseudo-scientific tale, 44.
Puritanism, 251.

Mrs. Ann Radcliffe (1764-1822), 44, 179.
Realism, 44, 151, 177 ff, 188 ff, 213 f, 262.
Restoration period, 18, 27, 139-213.
Richardson, 46, 53, 138, 242, 244, 252, 255, 262 ff, 281 ff, 283.
Mdlle. de la Roche Guilhem, 64, 285 ff.
Romanticism, 48.
Romance of Chivalry, 49, 145.
Mrs. Elizabeth Rowe (1674-1737).

V. Sackville-West, 172 ff, 188.
Antoine de la Salle, 190, 201.
Satire, 188-213.
Sir Walter Scott, 26, 42.
Sentimentalised novelettes, 159-172, 219-230, 234-240, 250, 255.
Shakespeare, 18, 53, 143.
Mary Shelley (1797-1851), 44.
Frances Sheridan (1724-1766), 37f.
Single standard of popular taste, 25.
Smollett, 242.
Spectator, 201, 242, 266, 287.
Spenser, 21.
Southerne, 166 (n), 187.
Rev. Dr. M. Summers, 174 ff.
Sir Philip Sydney, 12, 21, 29, 49, 53, 59.
Swifte, 128, 188, 214, 233, 262.

Tatler, 281.
Technique, 17.
Mrs. Catherine Trotter (1679-1749) 18, 148.

A. P. Upham, 94 ff.

Sir Horace Walpole, 92 f, 233.
Anne Weamys, 18, 64 ff, 72.
Webster, 53.
Jane Weston, 28.
Whincop, 21, 31.
Anne, Countess of Winchelsea, 29 (n).
Virginia Woolf, 39 (n).
Lady Mary Wroath (born c. 1586) 12, 47, 53-64, 72.